THE UNFINISHED BOMBING

Preserving Memory: The Struggle To Create America's Holocaust Museum

Sacred Ground: Americans and Their Battlefields

Symbolic Defense: The Cultural Significance of the Strategic Defense Initiative

History Wars: The Enola Gay And Other Battles For The American Past
(co-edited with Tom Engelhardt)

American Sacred Space (co-edited with David Chidester)

A Shuddering Dawn: Religious Studies and the Nuclear Age
(co-edited with Ira Chernus)

THE UNFINISHED BOMBING

Oklahoma City

in American Memory

EDWARD T. LINENTHAL

OXFORD
UNIVERSITY PRESS

OXFORD
UNIVERSITY PRESS

Oxford   New York

Auckland   Bangkok   Buenos Aires   Cape Town
Chennai   Dar es Salaam   Delhi   Hong Kong   Istanbul   Karachi
Kolkata   Kuala Lumpur   Madrid   Melbourne   Mexico City   Mumbai   Nairobi
São Paulo   Shanghai   Taipei   Tokyo   Toronto

First published by Oxford University Press, Inc., 2001
First issued as an Oxford University Press paperback, 2003
198 Madison Avenue, New York, New York 10016

Library of Congress Cataloging-in-Publication Data
Linenthal, Edward Tabor, 1947–
The unfinished bombing : Oklahoma City in American memory / Edward T. Linenthal.
p. cm.
Includes bibliographical references and index.
ISBN 0-19-513672-1 (cloth) ISBN 0-19-516107-6 (pbk.)
1. Oklahoma City Federal Building Bombing, Oklahoma City, Okla., 1995—Psychological aspects.
2. Memorials—Oklahoma—Oklahoma City—Psychological aspects.
3. Oklahoma City National Memorial (Okla.)
4. National characteristics, American.
I. Title.
HV6432.L54 2001
976.6'38—dc21   2001039090

Book design & composition by Mark McGarry, Texas Type & Book Works
Set in Minion

1 3 5 7 8 6 4 2
Printed in the United States of America
on acid-free paper

To the memory of my father
Dr. Arthur J. Linenthal

and to the memories of
Walter H. Capps
Lisa Capps
Robert S. Michaelsen
Ninian Smart

Contents

Acknowledgments

Preparing acknowledgments is a form of memorialization. As I recall names I am drawn to faces, to conversations, to stories, to places. I am immensely grateful for the generosity of so many for enriching this book in so many ways and thankful for new and enduring friendships.

In 1996 I had an exploratory conversation regarding the possibility of my writing about the memorialization of the bombing with Robert Johnson, then chairman of the Oklahoma City National Memorial Foundation, and for several years chairman of the Oklahoma City National Memorial Board of Trustees. We eventually agreed that the Foundation would help me with various logistical matters and allow me unlimited access to its archives. Bob Johnson has been a supportive presence throughout my time in Oklahoma City, and I offer him my deepest thanks for his trust and enthusiasm for this project.

In the spring of 1997, Toby Thompson, whose brother was killed in the bombing, and who was active in the Foundation's work, invited me to visit Oklahoma City, a trip that remains vivid in my mind. We went directly from Will Rogers Airport to the bombing site, where I saw popular memorial expression on the fence that protected the site of the former Alfred P. Murrah Federal Building, and appreciated for the first time the immense destructive power of this event. I met with a number of family members of those killed, survivors, and other members of the community. Our conversations were intense, direct, and it quickly became apparent to me that there were important stories to be told about the cultural afterlife of the bombing. For four years, I traveled often to Oklahoma City, both to work in the Foundation's magnificent archive, and to meet—often more than once—with many people, some of whom readers will meet in the book. I thank Toby Thompson for a most important phone call, and so much else.

My early visits were mostly spent in the archives, where the Foundation's curator of collections Jane Thomas, guided me through, for example, the massive collections of documents, artifacts, and design competition boards. She also identified and often called people she thought it important for me to meet. Without her energetic and enduring help this book would not have been possible. It was often very difficult working with certain materials in a setting where the human cost of the bombing was everywhere. Jane, Carol Brown, Charles Spain, Arlean Todd—who kept us well stocked with chocolate chip cookies—June Ranney and Brad Robison made each day in the archive a special one. I will treasure those times forever.

Kari Watkins was the first employee hired by the Memorial Foundation in March 1996 as Communications Director. She now serves as the Foundation's Executive Director. From the beginning of my work in Oklahoma City, Kari has made me feel welcome, talked with me about all sorts of important issues that I was thinking about, and I will never forget the incredible energy and intense commitment she brought to the Foundation's work. And I thank as well Hardy Watkins, who gave me a lengthy tour of the Memorial Center well before it was finished, and wrote the text of the Memorial Center's exhibition.

I also thank Karen Luke, who served as the initial vice-chairperson of the Memorial Task Force (the forerunner of the Foundation), and eventually served as chairperson of the Foundation from the summer of 1998 until January 2001. Karen was enthusiastic about the project from the beginning, and offered important suggestions about people I needed to interview.

Many of my research trips were filled with lengthy interviews, sometimes four or five a day, and for almost two years Beth Tolbert, who was active in her own right in the work of the Foundation, graciously offered to construct a schedule of interviews for me. For this and so much else, I am grateful to her.

Of course, I could not have even begun this project without significant financial support, and I thank President and Executive Director Anita May of the Oklahoma Humanities Council for offering me a grant to begin my work. Besides the financial support, I have appreciated her enthusiasm for the project, and I hope she finds the book worthy of the Council's investment. I also thank the Faculty Development Program at the University of Wisconsin, Oshkosh. This program has consistently supported my research efforts, and I remain ever grateful for this. I also thank the National Endowment for the Humanities for supporting this project with a summer research stipend. This was my second such award from NEH, and I am thankful for their continued support.

During the 1998-1999 academic year, I had the pleasure of being a research fellow at the Institute for Research in the Humanities at the University of Wisconsin-Madison. I thank the Institute's director, Paul Boyer, for years of friendship and support for various projects. I was not in residence during this year, but enjoyed the company of the other fellows when I attended various programs.

I could write a good deal about many of the names that follow. Some have become cherished friends. All have contributed to the book. I offer thanks to: Dr. Jihad Ahmad, Judy Albert, Cindy Alexander, Dr. Don Alexander, Dr. James Allen, Dr. Thomas Altepeter, Fred Anderson, Traci Ashworth, John Avera, Phil Bacharach, The Very Reverend George H. Back, Mark Bays, Reverend Lee Benson, Jason Bingenheimer, Ray Blakeney, Sharon Blume, Thomas Boldt, Mary Bomar, Eve De Bona, Dr. Edward Brandt, Jr., Dr. Hans Brisch, Dennis Bueschel of California Task Force 5, Sam Butcher, Hans and Torrey Butzer, Dr. Stephen Carella, Michal Carr, Ernestine Clark, Milford Clay, John and Sandy Cole, Reverend Donna Compton, Lisa Conard, Fran Cory, Jannie Coverdale, Oklahoma State Representative Kevin Cox, Melissa Cryer, James Danky, Thomas Demuth, Rowland Denman, Sydney Dobson—who was the Foundation's Executive Director when I began this project and helped in many ways—Dianne Dooley, Oklahoma State Senator Brooks Douglass, Mary Early, Oklahoma Attorney General Drew Edmondson and Linda Edmondson, Dr. Thomas Elliff, Jerry Ennis, Dr. Brian Espe, Maj. Gen. Don Ferrell, USAF (ret.), Sally Ferrell, Deb Ferrell-Lynn, Chris Fields, Pam Fleischaker, Mark Foust, Mary Frates, Dr. Gene Garrison, Woody Gibson of Virginia Task Force 2, Jeannine and J. L. Gist, Dr. Kay Goebel, Kathi Goebel, Carolyn Goldstein, Jimmy Goodman, Brenda Peck Green, Dr. Robin Gurwitch, Larrene Hagaman, Patti Hall, Carol Hamilton, Debra Hampton,

Oklahoma City Assistant Fire Chief Jon Hansen, Michael Hanson of the Emergency Service Unit of the New York City Police Department, Reverend Nick Harris, Michael Harrison, Lawrence Hart, Dr. Paul Heath, Donna Hendrickson, Dot Hill, John and Debra Hnath and Mickey, Dr. David Hockensmith, Jr., Dr. Ibrahim Hooper, Jerry Howard, George Humphreys, Reverend Goree James, Sr., LeAnn Jenkins, Oklahoma City Councilwoman Willa Johnson, Doris and Bobby Jones, Jackie Jones, Stephen Jones, Ben Kates, Jr., Governor Frank Keating and Cathy Keating, Marsha and Tom Kight, Aren Almon-Kok and Stan Kok, Daniel Kurtenbach, Rabbi Harold Kushner, Linda Lambert, Diane Leonard, James Loftis, Dr. Elinor Lottinville, Reverend Mary McAnally, Pat McCrary, Dan Mahoney, Peg Malloy, Reverend Tish Malloy, Oklahoma City Fire Department Chief Gary Marrs, Debi Martin, Dr. Gary Massad, Sunni Mercer, Dr. Robin Meyers, Oklahoma State Senator Angela Monson, Faith Moore, Lisa Moreno-Hix, Calvin and Ginny Moser, Leslie Nance, Pam Neville, Dr. Rita Newton, Polly Nichols, Chuck Nicole of California Task Force 5, Mayor Ronald Norick, Timothy O'Connor, Jacquelyn Oliveira, Penny Owen, Rabbi David Packman, Russell Perry, Wendy Peskin, Amy and Randy Petty, Chaplains Jack O'Brian Poe and Phyllis Poe, Charles Porter IV, Sister Helen Prejean, C. S. J., Betty Price, Dennis Purifoy, Gen. Dennis Reimer, Roxanne Rhoades, Joanne Riley, Edie Rodman, Florence Rogers, Father Joseph Ross, Dr. John Rusco, Charles Van Rysselberge, Priscilla Salyers, Bill Scroggins, Cheryl Scroggins, Janet Shamiri, Beth Shortt, Dr. David Smith, Alyson Stanfield, Barbara Stanfield, Donald Stastny, Debbie Stewart, Garner Stoll, Phyllis Stough, Edye Smith Stowe, Umaru Sule, Lecia Swain-Ross, Sara Sweet, Dr. John Tassey, Deresa Teller and Bella, John Temple, Jo Thomas, Phillip Thompson, James Tolbert, Thomas Toperzer, Dr. Linda Ware Toure, Kathleen and Michael Treanor, Susan Urbach, Tony Vann, Cheryl Vaught, Dr. Robert Vincent, Kenny Walker, Bud Welch, William Welge, Pam West, Pam and Melinda Whicher, Rafael White, Dr. Geoff White, Debby Williams, Chaplain Joe Williams, Laverna Williams, Richard and Lynne Williams, Chaplain Ted Wilson, Reverend Robert Wise, and Kathy Wyche.

I also wish to thank a number of Oklahoma artists who responded to an inquiry I made about artistic responses to the bombing: Ronald Anderson, Billy Atkinson, Carol Bormann, Mark Bruner, Jan Burer, Greg Burns, Una

Jean Carter, Rosalind Cook, Marilyn Coulson, Janey Crain, Gloria De Duncan, Cliff Doyeto, Elizabeth Eickman, Carolyn Faseler, Elaine Gammill, Judy Gard, Tom Gaut, Leonard Good, Martha Green, Mary Beth Haas, Connie Herlihy, Sally Holmes, Nancy Hunter, Dolly Lee, Dena Madule, Randy Marks, Sunni Mercer, Jill Moore, Corinne McCloskey, Tuan Nguyen, Tom Pershall, Inez Running-rabbitt, Mitsuno Ishii Reedy, Diane Salamon, Rita Sandlin, Frank Simons, Monte Toon, Melanie Twelves, Dixie Van Ess, Susan Van Zandt, Carol Whitney, Shirley Wilson, and Gaylord Younghein.

I had the good fortune to meet Oklahoma City photographer David Allen, who has an extraordinary photographic history of the site and of special events and individuals. David began his work on April 19, 1995, and has been compiling a photographic history ever since. Six of his photographs appear in the Memorial Center. It is a collection worthy of a book of its own. Allen's photographs have appeared in several exhibitions: "The Oklahoma City Bombing Remembered," at the International Photography Hall of Fame, April 6-10, 1998, and "Images of My Home: 1995-2000," at the North Gallery of the Oklahoma State Capital, April 5-May 3, 2000. I thank David for his kindness, and for his magnificent photographs.

I owe a great deal to Dr. Bob Blackburn, the executive director of the Oklahoma Historical Society. Bob is without question a state treasure, carrying with great modesty a rich history of his beloved state, and sensitive insights about that history. In addition to helping me with this project, Bob asked me to attend and briefly speak about memorial processes at several meetings of the Tulsa Race Riot Memorial Commission, which he chaired. He was also instrumental in involving me in the exploration of the many controversies surrounding the battle of the Washita at a National Park Service symposium in Cheyenne, Oklahoma. I have appreciated Bob's friendship and look forward to the dedication of the magnificent new Oklahoma Historical Society building in the near future.

I asked various people in Oklahoma City, including some family members and survivors, to read certain sections of the book, and in some cases, the entire manuscript. Not everyone agreed with my interpretations, of course, but I appreciated careful readings and helpful conversations. For this I thank: Dr. Carol Brown, Ernestine Clark, Chris Fields, Jeannine Gist, Dr. Kay Goebel, Dr. Robin Gurwitch, Robert Johnson, Doris Jones, Aren Almon-

Kok and Stan Kok, Peg Malloy, Beth Shortt, Jane Thomas, Toby Thompson, Jim and Beth Tolbert, Kathleen Treanor, Dr. Robert Vincent, Kari Watkins, Pam Whicher, and Richard and Lynne Williams.

In February 2000, I had the pleasure of serving as the Feaver-MacMinn Visiting Scholar at the University of Oklahoma. For five days, I worked with a group of undergraduates in a seminar, "Memory and Memorials in American Culture: Violence and the American Landscape." I am indebted to Sue Schofield, coordinator of the Graduate Advising Programs in the College of Liberal Studies for the invitation. We visited the Murrah site, Jane Thomas introduced students to the archive, and on an unforgettable Saturday morning, we sat fixated for well over four hours as memorial designers Hans and Torrey Butzer, Jeannine Gist, whose daughter was murdered in the bombing, and Richard Williams, who survived the blast, spoke about their experiences. The fact that one of the students in the seminar had lost her father in the bombing made our work even more intense. My thanks to all these people for a memorable time together.

Numerous colleagues also helped me understand issues that were new to me and some read and commented on part or all of the manuscript. I especially thank Allan Young, Professor of Anthropology in the Departments of Social Studies of Medicine, Anthropology and Psychiatry at McGill University, and also two old friends who always help me understand my own writing better, David Chidester and Tony Sherrill. David Blight, while working on his own important book on Civil War memory, found time to read the entire manuscript. And I thank other colleagues for their assistance: Michael Berenbaum, Gordon Baldwin, Lonnie Bunch, Paul Cassell, Eric Dean, John Dower, Tom Engelhardt, Kai Erickson, Patrick Hagopian, Peter Homans, James and Lois Horton, Arthur Kleinman, Lawrence Langer, Thomas Laqueur, Sanford Levinson, Robert Orsi, Leonard Primiano, Robert Rundstrom, Jeffrey Shandler, Stephen Sloan, Stuart Taylor, Jeffrey Toobin, Lawrence Tribe, and as always, I thank the esteemed Board of Directors.

I have been blessed with excellent editors for each project, and I thank Peter Ginna for his sharp eye and his enthusiasm for this book. I have now worked on a number of projects with literary agent Mildred Marmur, and thank her yet again for her friendship and support.

At the University of Wisconsin, Oshkosh I thank Dean Michael Zimmerman for careful reading and enduring friendship, Cindy Schultz for making day-to-day life in the office a joy, Heather McFadden, an excellent student and most reliable research assistant, Marguerite Helmers for helpful suggestions on the using the Web and for sending me interesting articles, William Urbrock for his always sharp editorial skills, a member of my "Memory of Catastrophe" seminar, Sarah Sauer, for catching all sorts of typographic errors that eluded the rest of us, and Mike Donker, Ellen Lloyd, Laurie Von Endt, and Jane Wypiszynski for just being there.

My family in Boston and Oshkosh has lived through many projects that required long absences and preoccupation. That probably won't change, but I'm glad they are there.

Just as this book came to completion, my father died in mid-April 2001. The last time I saw him, just a few weeks before his death, I told him that the book would be out in the fall, and he crossed his fingers. He did not live to see this published, but as with all my writing, he remains a part of it. To him, and to other friends who made Santa Barbara a cherished home, this book is dedicated.

The Alfred P. Murrah Federal Building, opened in April 1977.
(Oklahoma City National Memorial Foundation)

Introduction: April 19, 1995

Several months after her father, Secret Service agent Alan Whicher, was murdered in the Oklahoma City bombing, Melinda Whicher wrote a poem as part of a high school English paper. The poem ends:

> *And I discover a dark and lonely place*
> *Where no person should have to go*
> *And I claw my way out as best I can.*

This poem has haunted me since I began working in Oklahoma City in the spring of 1997. The powerful images of dark and lonely places and people clawing their way out of them capture well the mood of this book. When I first thought of writing about the bombing, it was in the familiar terms of a biography of memorial processes. Having written about changing interpretations of American battlefields, the making of the United States Holocaust Memorial Museum, and the controversy over the ill-fated *Enola Gay* exhibition at the National Air and Space Museum, I envisioned a book in which I would tell the story of the creation of the Oklahoma City Murrah Federal Building Memorial Task Force—now the Oklahoma City National Memorial Foundation—and how it navigated the shoals of contending memorial visions in order to create a public memorial. That fascinating story is a part of this book.[1]

After a few days in Oklahoma City, however, I knew the book needed to be about much more. The story I wanted to tell was not just about memorialization, but about the rich afterlife of the bombing—its enduring and profound impact on individuals, on the city, and on the wider culture. The bombing not only imprinted itself on the minds and bodies of those immediately affected but it also became a powerful symbolic presence in the American cultural landscape.

There are many reasons why the bombing in Oklahoma City resonated so powerfully. Even though airline terrorist attacks claimed more victims—270 in the downing of Pan Am 103 on December 21, 1988, for example—they are viewed as distant events, the horrible scenes of recovery only fleeting media images. Acts of air terrorism are recognized nightmares of international travel.

The bombing in Oklahoma City killed 168 people, more people than any other single act of domestic terrorism in American history. Consequently, Oklahoma City could claim the dubious distinction of being "first and worst" in the hierarchy of American terrorist attacks. It took place in what was envisioned as America's "heartland," shattering the assumption that Middle America was immune to acts of mass terrorism as well the assumption that the nation still had "zones of safety," such as day care centers. It murdered not only government employees and other adults but also babies and young children, many of them in the America's Kids Day Care Center, located in the Murrah Building. "The death of such precious beings," wrote Harrison Rainie in *U.S. News and World Report*, "violates the order and meaning of life."[2]

From the Oklahoma City bombing emerged a photograph that symbolized a particular horror, the murder of children: the image of Oklahoma City fireman Chris Fields holding the shattered body of one-year-old Baylee Almon in his arms. Children are, of course, murdered in acts of airline terrorism, but the public does not live for days with the images of broken bodies being carried out of a day care center or follow for weeks the televised grief of parents.

The bombing immediately became a social spectacle of suffering as the media saturated a worldwide audience with the drama of rescue and recovery operations from April 19 until May 4, 1995. People followed the search for survivors, the grim recovery of bodies, the anguish of grieving family members, the public memorial ceremonies, and in some cases even the televised funerals of those killed. Intense and enduring media coverage made it possible for millions to imagine themselves part of a worldwide bereaved community, participating in the pathos of the event and connecting with families of those murdered through a variety of fund-raising efforts, tens of thousands of letters, early memorial suggestions, music, poems, memorial services, visual arts creations, and travel to the site.

The bombing also occurred at a time when, in the words of Rochelle Gurstein the "party of exposure" had triumphed over the "party of reticence" in the culture. The reticent sensibility, she wrote, finds genuine intimacy in the "mutual baring of one's innermost self to another person and to no one else; this is quite unlike the modern therapeutic mode of effusive openness and confession to anyone who will listen, and it could be maintained and flourish only in the most guarded relationship." In a time when the boundaries between the public and the private vanished, when people's "insides" were deemed public property, there were also no boundaries to membership in the imagined bereaved community.[3]

All too often, there were also no boundaries separating appropriate expressions of human concern from shockingly inappropriate intrusions into the intimate world of people dealing with the mysteries of violent death. Oklahoma City became a kind of experiential tourist destination. There was widespread fascination with the experiences of those granted most favored cultural status as "victims" and "survivors," exposed to worlds of danger that most people did not know. There was an intense desire to "bump up" against those worlds by touching—from a safe distance—the traumatic experiences of those immersed in the world of the bombing.

This event also called into question cherished assumptions of American national identity. Were we truly an innocent nation in a wicked world, victimized yet again by foreign evil or by domestic terrorists who were "in" but not "of" the nation? Or was the bombing merely the lastest symptom of a diseased nation, disfigured throughout its history by populist violence?

The bombing quickly became an ideological commodity as debates raged

[handwritten margin note: Yet, post 9/11, ♦ how much is this still remembered?]

about its political and social consequences: the dangers of the militias, the culpability of talk radio, the need for new antiterrorism legislation, and the wisdom of curbing the sacred liberties of free speech. The bombing moved from "event" to "story," as family members of those killed and survivors lived out several stories: a progressive narrative, a redemptive narrative, a toxic narrative, and a traumatic narrative. These private, intimate narratives became public stories through which the event was interpreted.

And the bombing occurred at a time when memorialization had become a significant form of cultural expression. Much more than a gesture of remembrance, memorialization was a way to stake one's claim to visible presence in the culture. At sites all over America, memorialization became a strategy of excavation and preservation of long hidden ethnic American voices and grievances[It was a strategy of revision] as new memorials or new text on existing memorials sought to offer new perspectives on what was being commemorated ("faithful slaves" memorials, for example). Memorialization of certain events—such as the Holocaust—supposedly illustrated how civic memory was eager to extract cautionary lessons from the past as a guide to proper civic behavior. Unlike so many others, it was often said, Americans exhibited a unique integrity of memory. (The integrity of memory often foundered in this country, as it did in other countries, when it came to engaging stories more threatening to cherished convictions of national identity, such as slavery.)

Contemporary American memorial culture was also characterized by the democratization of memorials and memorial processes, the compression of time between event and memorial planning, and the rise of activist memorial environments. People democratized memorials, for example, by transforming them through spontaneous acts of memorialization, such as the increasingly popular act of leaving items at the Vietnam Veteran's Memorial or at the fence around the perimeter of the area where the Murrah Building once stood. In Oklahoma City, the memorial process involved hundreds of people, and it was consciously designed to be therapeutic: to help the community engage the traumatic impact of the bombing.

Nor was there any pause between the bombing and widespread public interest in memorialization. Until recently, intense periods of memorialization did not usually occur until the generation marked by a powerful event (e.g., the Civil War) saw their numbers dwindle and feared that their sacrifices and the lessons supposedly learned from the event would not be actively recalled by subsequent generations. Consequently, decades often passed before large-scale memorial activity began.

Immediately after the Oklahoma City bombing, however, unsolicited memorial ideas, revealing a remarkable American memorial vocabulary, poured into the mayor's and governor's offices in Oklahoma City. A formal memorial task force began its work only two months after the bombing, and the physical memorial was dedicated only five years after the bombing.

The intense desire to erect a public memorial in Oklahoma City revealed a dramatic transformation in the way the culture treated sites of mass murder. Americans, noted cultural geographer Kenneth Foote, have dealt with these places in very different ways. Some sites have been obliterated, as if destroying all vestiges of the murder could wipe away the horror of what happened on the site. John Wayne Gacy's home in a Chicago suburb was demolished, and family members of those murdered burned paintings he had created. The Milwaukee apartment building in which Jeffrey Dahmer had lived was also torn down. Other sites, such as the Chicago apartment building in which Richard Speck killed eight student nurses or a boat shed in Houston where over twenty-seven boys were murdered in 1973 were, in Foote's term, "rectified," returned to previous uses.

Only a small number of sites, he observed, were "sanctified," remembered through some kind of memorial. Among them is the site of James Huberty's murderous 1984 rampage in a McDonald's restaurant in San Ysidro, California. The restaurant was torn down and replaced by a makeshift memorial and a memorial garden. Finally, Southwestern College's education center was built on the site. A modest memorial remembered the 1991 murders in a cafeteria in Killeen, Texas, which was reopened. "American society," Foote wrote, "has no ritual of purification to cleanse people and places of the guilt and shame that arise from events such as mass murder." The higher the death toll, he observed, "the more likely becomes its obliteration." This, of course, did not hold true in Oklahoma City.[4]

A few thought a memorial would prolong painful memories and encouraged the city to return to business as usual. But most people feared obliteration—the act of intentional forgetfulness. Family members and survivors often told me of their fears that the dead would soon be forgotten, reduced to anonymous statistics in a culture of violence.

The incredible afterlife of the Oklahoma City bombing—in public debate, in the active grief of family members and survivors, in popular and official memorial expression—resulted from the violence that took place on April 19, a day that had once marked part of the creation story of the United States but has recently come to signify more ominous events.

I recall attending Patriot's Day events at Concord Bridge some years ago, how the vibrant colors of proud Minuteman reenactors and the dignified silence at the bridge seemed an appropriate New England way to honor the celebrated clash there in 1775. I wonder if recent events have transformed forever the meaning of April 19. What clashing, uncomfortable memories would be evoked were I to return to Concord, since April 19 is now, as one reporter observed, "the day America holds its breath."[5]

On April 19, 1993, the FBI carried out its controversial attack on the Branch Davidian compound in Waco, Texas, bringing to a violent conclusion a fifty-one-day siege resulting in the deaths of eighty Branch Davidians— including twenty-one children—and four federal agents. On April 19, 1995, the same day as the Oklahoma City bombing, Richard Snell, a member of the Order (a terrorist offshoot of the white supremacist organization Aryan Nations) was executed for two racially motivated murders. Snell would become a martyr for the racist right. Shortly before his execution, he reportedly watched televised news of the Oklahoma City bombing and said, "Look over your shoulder. Justice is coming."[6]

Some members of militia culture also believe that federal agents began their siege in Ruby Ridge, Idaho, on April 19, 1992, leading to the celebrated deaths of the wife and son of white supremacist and fugitive Randy Weaver. Consequently, April 19 is a "day of infamy" for the militia culture. For them, Patriot's Day had a bitter ring to it, as it signified the murderous hand of the federal government. There seems little question that Timothy McVeigh and Terry Nichols, the Oklahoma City bombers, picked April 19 purposefully, in part as an act of revenge for the events in Waco. April 19 would never be simply Patriots Day again, in Concord or anywhere else. It would, rather, continue to be a day marked by violent death and fear of violent memorialization of these deaths through continued terrorist attacks.[7]

The ominous associations with April 19 were not on the minds of people ✳
in Oklahoma City that cool sunny morning in 1995. When asked by the
Oklahoma City National Memorial Foundation how they would like to
begin telling the story in the Memorial Center museum, family members
and survivors often wished to emphasize what an ordinary day it was.
Indeed, these last moments of ordinary time were disconnected from what
came after 9:02 A.M., spoken of as if they belonged to a distant time in
another world, frozen moments to be portrayed in a museum.

In that morning's ordinary time, over one thousand people attended the
Mayor's Prayer Breakfast, and the Oklahoma Restaurant Association was in
the second day of its trade show. The city was preparing to host its annual
Art Fair, which attracted thousands of people, and bids were due soon for
the remodeling of the Alfred P. Murrah Federal Building. Of no significance
yet that morning was the Ryder truck caught on film by a security camera at
the high-rise Regency Tower apartment building one block from the Murrah
Building.

Oklahoma City's *Final Report* offers concise, dispassionate detail of 9:02
A.M.:

> The explosion came from the detonation of a 4,800 pound ammonium
> nitrate fuel oil bomb carried in a truck that was parked at the north entrance
> of the Alfred P. Murrah Federal Building. The force of the explosion
> destroyed the Murrah Building, collapsing most of the north front into a pile
> of rubble. The explosion severely damaged the surrounding buildings, with
> the Water Resources Board Building, the Athenian Building, the YMCA
> Building, the Journal Record Building, the Regency Tower Apartments, and
> the nearby churches sustaining the worst of the damage. Windows were shat-
> tered in a ten block radius. The force and heat of the blast set fire to cars
> parked on the street and in the lot across from the building. The dust from
> the collapsing building and the smoke from the burning cars billowed into a
> tall, almost mushroom-shaped cloud that turned from white to black and
> quickly towered over the city. Debris rained down. Pieces of paper, blasted
> free from desks and file cabinets ... were blown into the air and swirled about
> like snow in a blizzard. ... There was a 30-foot-wide, 8-foot-deep crater on
> NW 5th Street where the bomb had detonated. ... Dust and smoke filled the

remains of the Murrah Building. . . . The structure groaned and creaked as pieces of debris and chunks of concrete were still falling from the edges of the shattered floors. . . . Thousands of strands of twisted rebar, plumbing pipes, air ducts, telephone lines, and electric and computer wires hung throughout the shattered structure, creating mazes. Some of the electric wires were still live. A piercing elevator alarm rang through the building. [8]

Firemen were on the scene within minutes and witnessed bloodied people emerging from the buildings. Many survivors turned around and rushed back into the building with rescue teams to bring out the wounded. The blast, heard and felt as far away as Norman, Oklahoma, turned a large area of downtown Oklahoma City into a scene that reminded many people of images from Beirut or other cities laid waste by terrorist acts. Few thought of a bomb. It was a gas explosion, a sonic boom, an airplane crash.

Ernestine Clark, who worked in a city library only a few blocks from the Murrah Building, recalled looking "to see if the silver nose of a plane engine

In the lower left, the badly damaged YMCA, and evident directly across from the Murrah Building are the ruins of the Water Resources building and the Athenian building, and the larger Journal Record Building. On the far right a partial view of the Regency Towers apartment building. (City of Oklahoma City)

is coming through the window, like in those terrible farces about airplanes and airports," but she saw "only the window blinds banging wildly, still sending glass all over." People walked on streets newly paved with shattered glass. Several months later, after breaking a glass at her home, Clark wondered, "will there ever be a time when a broken glass will be only that, just a broken tea glass, and not a symbol of loss, death, chaos, disruption, distrust, fear, and nightmares?"[9]

People worldwide would soon be transfixed by the dramatic images of wounded and dying people being treated on the street, and horrified by the images of wounded and dead children. The rescue personnel who braved the unstable environment of the Murrah Building were horrified by bodies crushed beyond recognition, the "rivers of bodily fluids," as one rescuer recalled, and the unforgettable smells and sounds of a mass disaster.

Certain images stuck in the minds of those tasked with rescue and recovery. Some recalled hearing telephone pagers going off all over in the rubble, as frantic family members tried to reach relatives already dead. Some recalled

This view of the Murrah Building became familiar to millions of people. (David Allen, Oklahoma City)

Scenes like this reminded people of horrific scenes of terrorism in remote places, like Beirut, Lebanon. (Oklahoma County, Sheriff's Office)

Looking toward the Journal Record Building, charred remains of cars surround what became known as the Survivor Tree. Note car parts in the tree. (City of Oklahoma City)

The interior of the Journal Record Building. The clock on the floor is stopped at 9:02. (June Ranney)

This area was called "The Pile," where nine floors had "pancaked" together. (Boldt Construction, photograph by Rick Schultz)

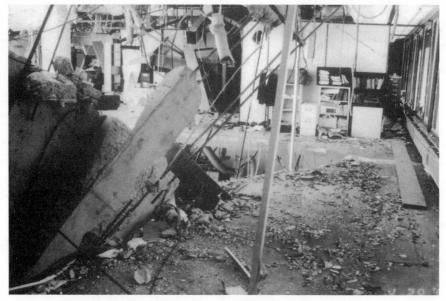

A floor of the Murrah Building clearly shows where the bomb scooped out the building. Note the coat still hanging on a rack and several bookcases still standing. (City of Oklahoma City)

seeing, amid the destruction, a suitcoat hanging neatly on a rack, near the jagged precipice where the building had ceased to exist. Some recalled the cold rainy weather and the forty-five mile-per-hour wind that descended that first night, as searchlights lit the area with an unearthly glare. And some remembered how, much too soon, rescue attempts turned into the long and arduous task of the recovery of bodies, a job so difficult that even some of the rescue dogs grew depressed at only locating the dead and would not work until their handlers hid themselves and let the dogs find them amid the rubble.[10]

Raymond Washburn, blind since childhood, ran the snack bar on the fourth floor of the Murrah Building. He thought of himself as one of the "lucky ones, I wish there were more lucky ones.... I knew just about everyone in the building. I knew the children; they came to the snack bar sometimes.... I heard people screaming below me in the building.... That's one day I was glad I couldn't see."[11]

David Allen's photograph of Skip Fernandez and Aspen became a familiar image from Oklahoma City. (David Allen, Oklahoma City)

FALLING INTO HISTORY

Compare to 9/11 class

Convictions of Innocence

"Things like this aren't supposed to happen in places like Oklahoma City."

"Downtown Oklahoma City looked more like Beirut than America."

Whether in immediate reaction or in comments people offered some years later, incomprehension characterized people's response to the bombing, which violated the assumed security and sanctity of the "heartland." Perhaps, people would say, this kind of thing might be expected to happen in New York or Los Angeles, hybrid cities at the nation's periphery, but not in middle America.

The sense of astonishment at the violation of the nation's interior was accompanied by incredulity at how evil could strike down innocents, and, within several days of the bombing, by the stunning news that Americans were responsible. For example, appearing on *CBS This Morning* the day after the bombing, Oklahoma Senator Don Nickles said, "to think that somebody could be so criminal, so evil that they'd be willing to do such a...a cowardly thing as destroy human...innocent lives, it's...it's almost beyond comprehension." Several years later, on June 14, 1997, the day after Timothy McVeigh was sentenced to death, one of the jurors said, "I mean, this is an American killing an American. You don't think that about somebody in your country doing this."[1]

How, in the last years of the twentieth century, so prominently stained by the deaths of millions of innocents through war, genocide, political torture, human slavery, and state-sponsored famine, could the bombing seem to reveal some as yet untapped revelation of human evil? And how, given the rich history of American violence, could there be such widespread disbelief about yet another enactment of mass murder on American soil? As we have seen, the bombing was immediately proclaimed the single worst act of domestic terrorism in the nation's history. What seemed incomprehensible was not the act itself, but that Americans were responsible for it.

The public saw the stark reality of the bombing on television—the ruins of the Murrah Building and the surrounding area, the bloodied adults and children who survived, the shock, despair, and anguish of family members looking for loved ones—but these "facts" did not immediately make sense. There was, seemingly, nowhere in the storehouse of American meaning to place the bombing, to make sense of it. It was, quite literally, "out of place." Through some murderous alchemy, Oklahoma City had become Beirut.

Life magazine expressed this reaction. Accompanying photographs of victims and personal items recovered from the site—a child's sneaker, the remains of a silk blouse—the editors observed,

> Even in a world accustomed to acts of violence on a battlefield that has no rules, we still harbored a few comforting assumptions. The bombing swept them away. *This can't happen here*—far from the country's urban edges, deep in the farm belt, a quintessentially secure and American landscape. *This can't happen to children*—children as young as three months, about to drink their breakfast juice in the day-care center that lay at the epicenter of the blast. *This must be the work of sophisticated international terrorists*—not, as alleged, of a crew-cut young ex-GI armed with fuel oil and a load of fertilizer, a man as nondescript as the building he is accused of bombing.[2]

The bombing activated enduring convictions that Americans were peaceable citizens of an innocent and vulnerable nation in a largely wicked world. Thus the evocative power of headlines: "Myth of Midwest safety shattered"; "After bombing, we'll never feel the same"; "American innocence buried in Oklahoma," where the "new tomb" was characterized as a grave for both "American innocents" and "American innocence."[3]

Throughout the nation's history, of course, Americans often understood their human nature and their world as something new. Unsullied by other nation's vices, the American could begin the world anew, be it through the Puritan mission to build the kingdom of God in an "empty" land or through the regeneration of the human species through a new creation: the American individual. R. W. B. Lewis characterized this original personality as "an individual emancipated from history, happily bereft of ancestry, untouched and undefiled by the usual inheritances of family and race; an individual standing alone, self-reliant and self propelling." In American newness, Lewis observed, is found innocence. "Moral position," he wrote, "was prior to experience."[4]

Throughout the nation's history, a whole host of events were widely pronounced to have brought an end to the state of innocence: controversial wars widely viewed as imperial ventures (e.g. the Mexican-American War and the Spanish-American War) industrialization, which transformed the rural identity of the nation and exacerbated class tensions, slavery and the mass slaughter of the Civil War, the enduring problem of racial violence, any number of examples of the nation's domestic failure to live up to its ideals, the advent of the nuclear age, and most recently the war in Vietnam, through which, as cultural analyst Morris Dickstein observed, "the 'idea' of America, the cherished myth of America" was damaged, perhaps beyond repair.[5]

Convictions of innocence endured, however, to be activated yet again when a people seemingly liberated from history and tradition greeted new crises as unprecedented. They also helped locate the bombing as Americans understood themselves as citizens of an innocent nation in a wicked world. If Oklahoma City had become Beirut, it was the fault of aliens. Consequently, the bombing became comprehensible as an expression of imported violence.

Immediately after the bombing it was, as David Nyhan predicted in the *Boston Globe*, "suspect time" in America. What follows "will not be nice." There was an immediate and widespread call to arms against Muslim terrorists. Editorials called for a military response, perhaps even against foreign governments that sponsored this act of terrorism. If the terrorists were unknown, and thereby safe from the nation's rage, there were those who resembled them in our midst, and that rage fell on them.[6]

"We Have Met the Enemy—and He Is Anyone but Us," wryly observed

Richard Goldstein of the *Village Voice*. Motivated in large part by reckless and irresponsible journalistic accusations that satisfied the convictions of innocence, Muslims were terrorized throughout the nation. For example, a mosque in Stillwater, Oklahoma, was damaged by a drive-by shooting, other mosques were vandalized or received bomb threats, and Muslims were physically assaulted and called "sand niggers." Shouting "it's a bomb," someone threw a bag into a playground at a Muslim day care center in Dallas, Texas.[7]

Nightline's Ted Koppel reported on the evening of April 19 that the Oklahoma City Police Department was looking for "two Middle Eastern men," and a host of self-proclaimed terrorism "experts" joined prominent administration officials, politicians, and journalists in blaming Islamic terrorists for the deed. For example, William Webster, former director of the CIA and FBI, observed that the bombing had the "hallmarks" of Middle Eastern terrorism. CBS's Connie Chung informed viewers that "U.S. government sources told CBS News that it has Middle East terrorism written all over it." Steven Emerson, who produced the controversial program *Jihad in America* for Public Television, characterized Oklahoma City as "one of the centers for Islamic radicalism outside the Middle East" and asserted that the bombing's purpose was to "inflict as many casualties as possible. That is a Middle Eastern trait."[8]

Even after sketches of two white men were publicized on April 20 as possible perpetrators, CNN's Wolf Blitzer said "there is still a possibility that there could have been some sort of connection to Middle East terrorism. One law enforcement source tells me that there's a possibility that this may have been contracted out as freelancers to go out and rent this truck that was used in this bombing."[9]

Stereotyping of Muslims continued incessantly on talk radio shows. Those listening to one of the most virulent, the *Bob Grant Show* on WABC in New York City, heard a caller declare that "we're going to have more bombings, and we can't stop it, because these people—like you said, it's a violent religion." Grant replied, "It is violent, it is violent. . . . They preach violence, for heaven's sake!" Practicing his own kind of rhetorical violence, Grant responded to a caller who objected to blaming Muslims: "the indications are that those people who did it were some Muslim terrorists. But a skunk like you, what I'd like to do is put you up against the wall with the rest of them, and mow you down along with them. Execute you with them. Because you obviously have a great hatred for America, otherwise you wouldn't talk the way you talk, you imbecile."[10]

Muslim groups in Oklahoma City and throughout the nation issued statements condemning the bombing and pleaded for the media not to fan the flames of violence. Muslim physicians in Oklahoma City volunteered at area hospitals, and Muslim groups nationwide sent letters of condolence to the mayor's and governor's offices, and they held blood drives and fund-raisers. Oklahoma governor Frank Keating, one of the few who cautioned against the rush to blame Islamic terrorists, wrote Nihad Awad, executive director of the Council on American-Islamic Relations, thanking him for the council's relief efforts. "I am immensely proud of Oklahomans of all races, creeds, and faiths," the governor declared. "May Allah bless you always."[11]

Also coming under suspicion as being capable of carrying out an act of retribution were the nation's own "aliens," the survivors of the federal government's attack on the Branch Davidian compound near Waco, Texas, on April 19, 1993. Davidians in federal prison were taken out of the general prison population and placed in confinement; several were questioned about the bombing and had their cells searched. Branch Davidian survivor Clive Doyle, joining approximately forty survivors and others at the Mount Carmel compound for a memorial service the morning of the Oklahoma City bombing, said "in no way are the Branch Davidians connected with the bombing. . . . The date is the only connection."[12]

The arrest of Timothy McVeigh and Terry Nichols, as well as mounting evidence against them, within a few days of the bombing abruptly ended most anti-Muslim violence. Interpretive strategies portrayed McVeigh and Nichols as "in" but not "of" America, peripheral beings who did not threaten convictions of innocence. Harper's publisher John MacArthur was skeptical of such efforts. "They are going to turn them into oddball crazies, caricaturing McVeigh as a trailer park terrorist, which is no better than the caricature of the Arabs." Indeed, portraying both men as "animals," "monsters," "drifters," "loners," "right-wingers," "robots," "mutated creatures," served to separate them from "real" Americans.

Their acts, it was argued, had made them domestic aliens. George Will assured readers that "paranoiacs have always been with us but have never defined us," and *Time*'s Lance Morrow declared that the bombing occurred at the "delusional margins."[13]

The need to distance McVeigh and Nichols from the national body was evidenced in June 1997, when the *Denver Post* revealed that despite his crimes, McVeigh, who received a Bronze Star in the Gulf War, was eligible for military burial benefits: "a grave site, perpetual care of the site, a headstone, a presidential memorial certificate and burial flags." Tom Blackburn, the commander of a Veterans of Foreign Wars Post in Oklahoma City responded, "The only military thing he deserves is a military firing squad." Another Oklahoma veteran disagreed, saying that because he "served his country honorably and received an honorable discharge," McVeigh had earned the right to be buried in a military cemetery but should not receive military burial honors. (On Friday, November 21, 1997, President Clinton signed "without comment" legislation "barring McVeigh from burial in a national cemetery because of his conviction.")[14]

In contrast to McVeigh and Nichols, "real" America, pundits declared, was represented by citizens—survivors, family members, rescuers—who demonstrated courage in the face of such searing loss. For example, even as it worried about the "soul and character of America," *U.S. News and World Report* assured its readers that while the perpetrators represented a "strain of evil in American society," the lesson to take from Oklahoma City "says something important about the American character: It's still incandescent." Utah Senator Orrin Hatch declared that the perpetrators "are not Americans in my book. The true Americans are the men, women and children who were killed.... Americans are the rescue workers.... Americans are all of us who share the same moral outrage."[15]

Another interpretive strategy, however, took direct aim at the convictions of innocence. Far from being an innocent nation in a wicked world, America was diagnosed as suffering from a potentially terminal case of spiritual rot, "heartland pathology," an illness of the civic body that mass-produced the Timothy McVeighs and Terry Nichols of the culture. "We are, and we have always been," observed the *New Republic*, "an ugly people, fascinated by force, uneasy about difference, enchanted by absolutes. A great country with a darkness to match."[16]

This interpretive take, far from viewing McVeigh and Nichols as domestic aliens, understood them as quintessentially American, securely located in the nation's tradition of populist violence. This dark vision resurrected alternative histories and paid attention to violent values and events that were understood to be as defining of the American experience as were the virtues revealed in rescue and recovery efforts in Oklahoma City.

Connecticut College historian Catherine McNicol Stock, beginning her study with Bacon's Rebellion in 1676, argued that rural radicalism is "older than the nation itself." Some recalled the history of terrorist acts against Native Americans and African Americans, who had long known there were no zones of safety in America. Cheyenne memories turned to the slaughter of Cheyenne people at Sand Creek on November 29, 1864 or Lt. Col. George Armstrong Custer's controversial attack on the Cheyenne village of Black Kettle on the Washita on November 27, 1868.[17]

Others recalled white terrorism in the Reconstruction South, the enduring terrorism of the Ku Klux Klan, the Haymarket Riot of 1886, the Tulsa Race Riot of 1921, and the September 15, 1963 bombing of the Sixteenth Street Baptist Church in Birmingham, Alabama, which killed four young girls. The Oklahoma City bombing also resurrected memories of the 1927 bombing of a schoolhouse in Bath, Michigan, by a farmer angry that a tax increase for the school would force him to foreclose. The blast killed forty-five people, including thirty-eight children. Still others thought of the killing of students at Kent State University on May 4, 1970.[18]

The rush to blame Muslims for the bombing was seen, in this interpretation, as clear evidence of the nation's propensity to violate its stated ideals of fair play, as well as an expression of darker national traditions. Two days after the bombing, for example, the popular writer Tom Clancy warned that "until the criminals are apprehended, we need to remember that prejudging anything is contrary to American tradition. Respect for religion is one of America's core principles, and if we depart from that, the terrorists win something important and we lose something even more important." News commentator Daniel Schorr thought that anti-Muslim hysteria illustrated "how easy it is to yield to xenophobia," and others suggested that after the collapse of Communism, Muslims had become the new "red menace." An editorial in the *Chicago Sun-Times* declared that Americans had lowered themselves "to the levels of terrorists, striking out blindly at whatever demon that was handy," and the *Sacramento Bee* wondered if "the very rhetoric that casti-gates immigrants and foreigners isn't encouraging the bombers we grow at home."[19]

Besides xenophobia, scapegoating, and terrorism against the nation's immigrants, many located anti-Muslim hysteria within the enduring tradi-tion of American racism. An angry editorial in the Springfield, Missouri, *News Leader* declared that "American racists can easily disappear into the background in places like the Ozarks, Kansas farm country or northern Michigan. . . . The fight against international terrorism is difficult and beyond the control of most of us. The fight against racism is much easier. It begins at home." And in the *Village Voice,* Richard Woodward lamented that one of the "unearned privileges of being a straight WASP male in this society is that, whatever atrocities I may commit or troubles I may suffer, I won't be forced by the dominant culture to represent my group."[20]

That racism was at work was clear to the American Jewish Committee's Kenneth Stern, program specialist on anti-Semitism and extremism, who told a congressional committee investigating domestic terrorism that he was "haunted" by how different public reaction would have been had black mili-tants been responsible for the bombing, and if there were "10,000 to 40,000 armed black men practicing rhetoric about war with the Government." We would, he said, "be dealing with this differently."[21]

Princeton historian Nell Irvin Painter also saw a double standard in the tepid public reaction to "white purveyors of hatred" compared with the much harsher reaction to the anti-Semitic rhetoric of the Nation of Islam's Louis Farrakhan and former aide Khalid Abdul Muhammad. "A year ago," she observed, "condemning them was de rigeur for anyone claiming citizenship in the American republic." Why, she wondered, were there not demands in Congress for the censure of militia members who "publish libraries full of hate literature, who run paramilitary camps, terrorize the Forest Service and regurgitate bigotry on computer networks," as there had been for Farrakhan and Muhammad? "On the one hand," she said, "we have white hate groups with actual histories of terrorizing federal agents in the West. On the other, we have two black men whose language is mean but who lack literal firepower. Yet it is the white neo-Nazis who have been dealt with gingerly, while a wall of condemnation came down on Messrs. Farrakhan and Muhammad."[22]

McVeigh and Nichols were also Americanized when their motives were linked to the tradition of the "inspired maverick," to their experience in the military, to class resentments, and more ominously to a resurgence of reactionary violence in post-Vietnam America. For example, Jonathan Friedland, the Washington correspondent for the *Guardian*, told a National Public Radio audience that McVeigh struck him as "wholly American," from his belief in government conspiracy to his infatuation with guns, and even to his "loner" persona. "Timothy McVeigh," he wrote, "saw himself in that kind of John Wayne tradition of the rugged individualist who knows best. And the rest of the country who are still taking their orders from Washington, they're too blind to see what this kind of inspired maverick can see. And that tradition . . . [is] deeply rooted in American popular culture and shared by both left and right."[23]

Both McVeigh and Nichols were deeply rooted in the traditional initiation into American masculinity—service in the armed forces. So, remarked Northwestern University's Carl Smith, McVeigh was a "crew-cut native son with good cheekbones and a firm jaw whom we ourselves had trusted and trained to defend our country." Writing in the *Nation,* Katha Pollitt offered this blunt assessment: "Timothy McVeigh is not some libertarian free spirit gone astray. He felt at home in the Army . . . he won medals for his Gulf War service. . . . If we're seriously interested in understanding how a young man could blow up a building full of hundreds of people, why not start by acknowledging that the state he now claims to oppose gave him his first lessons in killing?"[24]

The perpetrators were also understood as victims of the harsh impact of social and economic powerlessness. (And it was McVeigh, much more than Nichols, who seemed to command attention.) In the *New Yorker,* Joyce Carol Oates characterized him as a "marginal personality," emerging from upstate New York, where people understood that they were "distinctly marginal; wherever the fountainheads of significance, let alone power, they are surely not here." McVeigh, she believed, turned to "paramilitary groups" where "one is at the very center of power: the 'power,' at least, to destroy." And, in the *Los Angeles Times*, Michael Kazin portrayed McVeigh as a victim of the disruptions that seemingly disempowered blue-collar American men in recent decades.[25]

More ominously, McVeigh and Nichols were viewed as reactionary terrorists spawned by the corrosive legacy of the Vietnam War and energized by resentments similar to those that gave birth to the German Freikorps after World War I. These Germans, angered by the harsh terms of the Armistice of 1918, blamed the Weimar Republic for stabbing Germany in the back. They formed their own paramilitary force and fought against their domestic enemies, tilling the soil for the rise of the Nazis. "In the mythology of the New War," James William Gibson argued, "the U.S. government and, more generally, the political power structure across the country are seen as liberal, weak, and corrupt; the system no longer has legitimate moral authority."[26]

Consequently, McVeigh and Nichols did not appear as solitary killers but as harbingers of a new domestic threat, the post-Vietnam American Freikorps, the militias. The Oklahoma City bombing revealed a toxic American landscape, teeming with alienated and embittered antigovernment groups who understood themselves as remnant patriots guarding endangered American freedoms. The news that McVeigh and Nichols had attended meetings of the Michigan Militia sparked an intense fear that the bombing was the first salvo in a war against the government, a war that would be fought not on foreign battlefields but in the streets of the nation.[27]

Images of men in military garb on "training" exercises in the backwoods of America, links between some militia groups and neo-Nazis, widespread proliferation of the virulently anti-Semitic ideology of Christian Identity, alarmist rhetoric about invading U.N. troops using black helicopters for intelligence gathering and preparing to murder "true patriots" in secret extermination centers after said patriots had been rendered helpless by gun control, culminating in a "one world government," meshed with the horrific images coming out of Oklahoma City.

The militias were viewed as home-grown and alien at the same time. The *Omaha World Herald* opined that the militias were "dark forces on the far edges of society. . . . A tiny minority, still a lunatic fringe group." In *Vogue*, Julia Reed spoke of her visit to a paramilitary group, the Covenant, the Sword, and the Arm of the Lord, that had contemplated a missile attack on the Murrah Building in 1983 in retaliation for the killing of Posse Comitatus member Gordon Kahl. "In the best case scenario these guys vote for David Duke or buy 'the truth about Waco' videos at militia meetings: in the worst, you get guys holed up in the Ozarks with tanks plotting to overthrow the government and kill all the Jews, or guys who vent their rage on a federal building full of men, women, and children."[28]

There was anger that these groups had appropriated the terms "patriot" and "militia" from the nation's sacred story of revolutionary beginnings. For example, Jim McManus, a member of the Concord Minutemen, who dress in colonial Minuteman garb and take part in commemorative ceremonies each April 19 in honor of the battle at Concord Bridge, said, "It's an insult to the men and woman who fought here in order to start our country." His colleague, Steve Olsen, the captain of the Concord Minutemen, observed that "we built a nation and apparently they're trying to overthrow one." An editorial in the St. Petersburg Times declared, "The notion of patriots who are violently opposed to their own democratic government takes some getting used to. Where I'm from, we used to call such people 'traitors.'"[29]

Although some militia members tried to distance themselves from cultural demonization, they often followed statements of regret for the bombing and even categorical rejection of responsibility for it with references to a larger governmental conspiracy that was "really" responsible. While unfortunate, the bombing was a balancing of the scales of justice for federal actions that resulted in deaths at Ruby Ridge or at the Branch Davidian compound at Waco.

Militia spokesmen tried to reassure the public that they were not on the fringe, not (by and large, anyway) violent. Rather, they were "real" Americans with legitimate grievances against the federal government. Some of their analogies were strained, to say the least. John Trochmann, founder of the Militia of Montana, told a Senate subcommittee that the militias were much like a "giant neighborhood watch." Three days after the bombing, Ted Olson, a commander in the Michigan Militia, told an ABC Nightline audience that his fellow militia members had "shown Americans that they can stand up and they can speak out against their federal government." He linked the militia's work with the work of Sojourner Truth and the Underground Railroad. Just as black people who made their way to Michigan "escaped a tyranny," the militias, he argued, represented a new "pathway of hope."[30]

Responding to criticism from the Concord Minutemen, Edward Brown of New Hampshire's Constitutional Defense Militia declared, "We are absolutely identical to George Washington, Paul Revere, and Thomas Jefferson. . . . We're really a bunch of Boy Scouts." Popular talk show host Rush Limbaugh assured his audience that "weekend militia groups" were "just a bunch of weekend bubbas who go out there with their guns and play army, but they mean no harm."[31]

In addition to trying to reassure citizens that they had no more to fear from militias than from members of a Neighborhood Watch group or Boy Scouts or good-natured weekend social groups of bonding males, and (even better) that they traced their ideological lineage to the nation's Founding Fathers, militia members envisioned themselves as victims, trapped in the same precarious situation as Jews in Nazi Germany. This time, however, they pledged that they would not be disarmed and led passively to their deaths. Their fevered rhetoric warned about the "gestapo mentality" of the federal government and about the interstate highway signs, which (for those in the know) were really directions for vehicles transporting patriot-victims to the concentration camps and extermination centers supposedly already waiting for them. "Within the next two years," a militia member declared in 1995, "you will see the Constitution suspended. . . . Christian fundamentalists will be the first to go under fascism this time. Just like the Jews were last time."[32]

Some who studied militia cultures, however, argued that the same hysteria that stereotyped Muslims now inaccurately tarred all militia members with the same brush. Lou Prato, adjunct professor of journalism at George Mason University, observed that McVeigh and Nichols had only "fringe" connections with the Michigan Militia. Whatever their connection, however, there was not "a shred of evidence that the militias per se had anything to do with the bombing." Writing in *Washington Monthly*, Paul Glastris cautioned that "most members of the patriot movement are less obsessed with guns than with laws. . . . For every camouflage-wearing amateur soldier drilling on weekends there are several amateur lawyers sitting at home reading federal statutes." Also objecting to the image of a monolithic militia culture was Barbara Dority, who told readers of the *Humanist* that in addition to some violent militia subcultures, this "amorphous populist movement" included "tax protestors, constitutionalists, gun collectors, hunters, and ranchers, farmers, and loggers upset by federal land-use controls."[33]

The Oklahoma City bombing was situated within starkly contrasting convictions about the essence of American identity. Did it reveal an innocent nation victimized by an evil world or, conversely, a diseased nation revealing once again a virulent strain of violence? Convictions of innocence did not require any fundamental readjustment of American identity in the wake of the bombing. Rather, it called for eternal vigilance and, occasionally, righteous vengeance for those who would violate the sanctity of national boundaries.

Those disabused of the convictions of innocence understood the bombing as another horrific manifestation of a violent nation in a violent world. For them, protestations of innocence revealed a woeful, almost infantile failure to recognize that violence was an essential part of American identity. For them, enduring legacies of racism, xenophobia, and violent populism represented virulent cancers emerging from the national body, with the Oklahoma City bombing seen as a tumor, an indicator of more profound internal disease.

Like some science fiction story, the bombing threw the nation into a dizzying confusion of space and time. Oklahoma City became a Middle East war zone. America became Weimar Germany in its last tortured days. Or, for militia members and their sympathizers, America was Nazi Germany. Summoned like angry apparitions from the nation's past were dark episodes that both situated the bombing in a grim history and threatened the cherished national conviction of moral progress in history. Oklahoma City was to the 1990s what the Birmingham bombing was to the 1960s, what Wounded Knee was to the 1890s, what Sand Creek was to the 1860s. Most ominously, the toxic legacy of the Vietnam War created a mutant offspring, the militia threat, with Oklahoma City widely viewed as a declaration of war against the government.

The Oklahoma City bombing was much more than a crime, a tragic event, a terrorist event; it sparked a crisis of American identity in which much was at stake. Discussion about what it "meant" had little to do with Oklahoma City and everything to do with American worlds seemingly threatened by the bombing. It would continue to resonate richly and contentiously in the culture.

Falling into History

Despite the tenaciousness of the convictions of innocence, the bombing was widely felt as a fall into history, as if a contemporary Pandora's box had been opened. Contending public voices struggled not only with the meaning of the bombing but with its envisioned social and political consequences. There were voices that strained to find something "good" in the ruins of the event. Many, however, thought the bombing would create a pervasive climate of fear, further impoverishing any sense of civic community and altering the cultural geography of the nation. Just as interpretation of the Oklahoma City bombing became enmeshed in diverse readings of American identity, so too it became part of contentious debates over appropriate civic behavior in post-Oklahoma City America.

Perhaps, some suggested, the widespread feelings of vulnerability, helplessness, and rage were, in fact, signs of an initiation into a newer and wiser domestic order. "Our world has been smashed, which makes us angry as hell," declared a Missouri editorial. But, it added, "anger is good, if it helps us build a new sense of control, balanced between fear and a foolish sense of invulnerability, and tempered by the image of the Oklahoma City firefighter, framed by flames, carrying the limp body of a diapered infant."[34]

Political columnist David Broder was among those who hoped the bombing would bring positive social change in its wake. He envisioned a new focus on "children, family and community," an appreciation of the "positive value of government," and a "revulsion to extremist rhetoric." The *Christian Science Monitor* thought it a timely opportunity for "Americans to respect and love their country anew as a corporate whole," and the *Nation* hoped that the "social ethic of solidarity" would triumph over the "dehumanizing anger of the right." Otherwise, they feared a "helter-skelter descent further into fear and rage."[35]

Many public voices pointed sadly to the reality of such a "helter-skelter descent" as an enduring legacy of the bombing. Walter Truett Anderson, director of the Meridian Institute on Global Governance, worried that America would soon become a place where "we put more locks on our doors, hire more guards, and break out the guns." Others noted that "weapons, technology and speed-of-light communications are now available to fanatics as well as the sane and harmless."[36]

Increasing fears of the dangers of public spaces and the elusive search for security led marketing executives to project that on-line shopping would grow more popular and that retailers situated near federal buildings would often choose to relocate. CNN's Bill Schneider offered a gloomy vision of a nation of "walled and gated communities. Private security forces.... Private cars, not public transportation. Home entertainment, not public theaters and celebrations. Private beaches and parks, not public spaces."[37]

In August 1995, *Management Review* carried a "primer" for businesses on how to prepare for bombings, and two days after the bombing the *Des Moines Register* informed its readers that "Life in Iowa may forever be altered." That same day, *USA Today* envisioned "new architectural styles that offer asylum over aesthetics. Reminiscent of medieval castles, new buildings will face away from the street and be surrounded by an electronic shield. Corridors will have more angles to make it harder to shoot a target. Parking lots will be above-ground and removed from buildings. Physical obstacles everywhere. Concrete planters, tire shredders, crash beams and pop-up steel barricades will become common."[38]

The national landscape did, in fact, "remember" the bombing through physical alterations. In Washington, D.C., a section of Pennsylvania Avenue near the White House was closed, creating "a dispiriting place, an abandoned boulevard," according to Benjamin Forgey, architectural critic for the *Washington Post*. The city—"both the actual and symbolic center of American democracy"—looked, he thought, like "a capital city under an eerie siege." Grieving already over the loss of close access to the White House, an editorial in the *Omaha World Herald* recommended a memorial plaque: "Motor vehicles once traveled here until they were banned for fear of irrational terrorism. This mall is dedicated to the day when such monstrous violence is merely the stuff of legends."[39]

The bombing also altered the federal landscape throughout the nation, as over $600 million was spent to improve security in federal buildings. Placement of day care centers in federal buildings also came under scrutiny. Would —or should—people continue to bring their children to such vulnerable places? Should these be in less visible and accessible areas of buildings in order to lessen the possibility of attack? Trade journals discussed the possibilities of blast-resistant design in public buildings, the use of new kinds of safety glass, secure ventilation systems to protect against chemical and biological attack, and sophisticated recovery programs in case an attack succeeded.[40]

The bombing became a useful ideological commodity in the intense and enduring arguments over how to strike a delicate balance between personal liberties and civil order. It figured prominently in arguments over the necessity of new antiterrorism legislation, and in arguments about appropriate limits to First Amendment liberties, specifically whether the bombing revealed a need to curtail certain kinds of inflammatory public rhetoric.

In an interview with CBS's Mike Wallace nine days after the bombing, President Clinton said that the challenge of terrorism demanded a new civic discipline in order for civil liberties to survive. "We still will have freedom of speech. We'll have freedom of association," the president declared. "We'll have freedom of movement. But we may have to have some discipline in doing it so we can go after people who want to destroy our very way of life."[41]

This civic discipline was envisioned as crucial to the life of the nation, and the balancing act between the preservation of civil liberties and the need for security precarious. Anthony Lewis of the New York Times reminded readers of the nation's "faith in constitutional democracy" and the need to "redouble our commitment to reason." Carl Rowan of the Chicago Sun-Times believed that citizens must step "delicately around the tender flowers of freedom, as we try to stamp out the noxious weeds of insane violence and callous terrorism."[42]

Public fears led to increased pressure for President Clinton and Congress to pass antiterrorism legislation that had simmered since the bombing of the World Trade Center in 1993. Within a week of the Oklahoma City bombing, as polls showed that "by a 3-1 margin, Americans support sterner measures against terrorist groups even if some civil rights are infringed," the president asked Congress to pass his Omnibus Counterterrorism Act.[43]

After months of heated congressional debate, during which both liberal and conservative lawmakers expressed wariness of expanding federal surveillance powers, President Clinton signed an antiterrorism bill on April 24, 1996, a bill that was derided for being too "watered down" (not having, for example, provisions for more expansive FBI wiretap capabilities) and feared because it resurrected memories of previous illegal federal invasions of citizens' civil rights. Interestingly, the president's description of the bill's benefits focused on the threat of foreign terrorism, not the threat from domestic extremists. He assured the nation that legislation meant "we can quickly expel foreigners who dare come to America and support terrorist activities. From now on, American prosecutors can wield new tools and expanded penalties against those who terrorize Americans at home or abroad. From now on, we can stop terrorists from raising money in the United States to pay for their horrible crimes."[44]

Two contending public voices became evident in postbombing debate over the virtues and vices of antiterrorism legislation, each envisioning diametrically opposed futures for the nation. One voice envisioned a nation transformed by the violent actions of terrorists, with domestic tranquility a distant memory as social paralysis ensued from an increasing orgy of blown-up buildings and body counts. This nightmarish vision was dramatically portrayed in the popular and controversial film *The Siege*, in which Islamic terrorist cells kill hundreds in a series of bombings in New York City, forcing the president to declare martial law and resulting in a dramatic confrontation between an FBI agent (played by Denzel Washington) devoted to sacred civil liberties and an army general (played by Bruce Willis) whose job it was to restore order at any price, even torture and murder.[45]

Some believed this legislation too little, too late. The *National Review*'s Eugene Methvin angrily denounced liberal opposition to such legislation as part of a "twenty-year campaign that has destroyed the nation's domestic intelligence capacity and left Americans pathetically vulnerable to atrocities like the one in Oklahoma." Also in *National Review,* Conor Cruise O'Brien warned that liberals were incapable of responding adequately to terrorism, believing as they did that "terrorism can be rooted out by concessions and compromise. . . . The terrorist mind is absolutist and unappeasable."[46]

A very different public voice envisioned not an America besieged by terrorism and social disruption but an increasingly repressive state in which the demands for safety would upset civic balance and lead to a loss of civil liberties, dangerously expand governmental power, and fundamentally transform the nation. "We may be willing," declared the *Atlanta Constitution*'s editorial page editor Cynthia Tucker, "to sacrifice our right to privacy and our protections against intrusive searches and unwarranted access by government to the details of our personal lives. But we would not honor our Oklahoma dead by doing so." A "terror-proof America," the newspaper declared, "would no longer be America." Perhaps, as Great Britain's *Economist* argued, maintaining American freedoms meant another Oklahoma City would be possible. This, it declared, "is liberty's price."[47]

Not all commentators believed that a loss of freedom was inevitable. Objecting to the many comparisons of the chaotic scenes of Oklahoma City with those of battle-scarred Beirut, Thomas Friedman of the *New York Times* argued that "in Beirut, the car bomb was a symptom of a Lebanese way of life that had broken down. In Oklahoma City, the car bomb is an assault on an American way of life that is still thriving." Sounding the call to Clinton's ideal of civic discipline in a post-Oklahoma City nation, Friedman said, "There is an ongoing battle that all Americans must wage within themselves—a battle against the fear that destroys the foundation of a free society."[48]

Numerous editorials worried that it was antiterrorism legislation itself that threatened this delicate balance, and still another set of historical memories was resurrected. The *New York Times* argued that "Washington too quickly forgets the brazen violations of American freedoms committed by the F.B.I., the Central Intelligence Agency and other security services in their misguided efforts to control domestic political dissent in the 1960s and 1970s." Political columnist David Broder warned that Oklahoma City should not "usher in a return to Big Brother government."[49]

Fear of "Big Brother," however, resurrected memories of the Palmer raids in the 1920s, the internment of Americans of Japanese ancestry in the 1940s, the McCarthy hearings of the 1950s, and the FBI's wiretapping of Martin Luther King, Jr. in the 1960s. It also led to gloomy visions of daily life in a repressive state. *USA Today,* for example, thought that "fallout" from the bombing could include "stepped-up security at government and corporate offices, including more metal detectors, surveillance cameras, employee I.D.s and electronic access cards [and] electronic screening devices that can identify an employee's fingerprint or pupil."[50]

Still others objected to the president's declaration that new laws were needed to protect citizens against those who were unfairly tarred with the epithet "un-American" because they disliked the government. "Suspicion of state power is a long American tradition," observed the *Nation*. "Laws most often protect the interests of corporations and the wealthy. Politicians and generals send teenagers to be killed in pointless military adventures. Long before Waco, the police were known to murder citizens, like the Black Panthers' Fred Hampton, in their beds." Writing angrily in the *Humanist*, Barbara Dority recalled the Vietnam War protest. "Yes, we hated the government for what it was doing. We hated it with the passionate intensity of youthful outrage.... The president says that Americans who feel as we did then are dangerous enemies of the state and should not be voicing these beliefs."[51]

Several commentators representing diverse ideological positions worried that harsh antiterrorism legislation would in fact *increase* the danger by stifling dissent. "It appears," said Richard Barnet of the Institute for Policy Study, "that the government is increasingly basing indictments on what suspects say rather than what they do, and that government informants may be encouraging them to engage in criminal conspiracy. All this strengthens the views of the militiamen that they have found the right enemy."[52]

Echoing Barnet from the right was the *National Review*'s Angelo Codevilla, who envisioned a governmental witch hunt as a first step "down a well-worn path to civil war." Also worried about potential conflict based on government intrusion was the *Daily Oklahoman*, which argued that the given the popularity of the militias and "open hostility toward government," the lesson of the bombing "is not that we need greater limits on liberty and privacy...but for government to back off."[53]

The bombing also sparked bitter debates about whether the government should enforce civic discipline by regulating inflammatory public speech, specifically rhetoric from politicians and radio talk show hosts accused of creating a climate of hate within which domestic terrorism flourished.

Anger at talk radio, for example, was expressed by an agent of the Bureau of Alcohol, Tobacco, and Firearms who helped in the rescue effort at the Murrah site. "We started our shift at midnight with the recovery of a woman's shattered body by Oklahoma City firefighters and a search of the area for evidence," he wrote. "Our conversation turns to militias of self-proclaimed patriots, bomb threats received at federal buildings, so-called talk show hosts telling their listeners to shoot federal agents in the head. [He was referring to the highly publicized words of former Watergate figure G. Gordon Liddy, who instructed his radio audience on how to kill federal agents: "They've got a big target there on their chest.... Don't shoot at that because they've got a vest on underneath that. Head shots, head shots.... Kill the sons of bitches."] He is talking about those sitting around me, people from around the country I have come to know well in the past few days. Tired, covered with concrete dust, mud, and, in some cases, the remains of fellow Americans, I am depressed and angry."[54]

President Clinton focused attention on talk radio on April 23, 1995, in a speech to the American Association of Community Colleges. He spoke of the "many loud and angry voices in America today whose sole goal seems to be to try to keep some people as paranoid as possible and the rest of us all torn up and upset with each other. They spread hate. They leave the impression that, by their very words, that violence is acceptable." The president reminded the audience that freedom brought with it responsibility. "It is time we all stood up and spoke against that kind of reckless speech and behavior.... When they talk of violence, we must stand against them. When they say things that are irresponsible, that may have egregious consequences, we must call them on it. The exercise of their freedom of speech makes our silence all the more unforgivable."[55]

Reaction was immediate. Some pundits believed that the link between talk radio and the bombing was direct. Others argued that while it may not have led directly to violence, it helped create a poisonous climate conducive to violence. Still others angrily protested that there was no link at all, that the president was shamefully using the bombing as an excuse to smear his opponents. And there were those who wondered if, in the wake of the bombing, the fundamental contours of the First Amendment should be revisited so that certain kinds of violent rhetoric would no longer be protected.[56]

Making the case for a direct link was Jonathan Alter. Writing in *Newsweek*, he declared, "When Liddy tells listeners to murder agents... or laughs about using pictures of the Clintons as target practice; when self-styled 'patriots' plot armed rebellion on short-wave radio or pass along bomb recipes on computer bulletin boards; when Bob Mohan of KYFI Phoenix says of handgun-control advocate Sarah Brady [the wife of James S. Brady, assistant to the president and White House press secretary, severely wounded in the assassination attempt on President Ronald Reagan on March 30, 1981] 'She ought to be put down. A humane shot at a veterinarian's would be an easy way to do it'; when gun shows sell bumper stickers that say FIRST LINCOLN, THEN KENNEDY, NOW CLINTON?—then it's time to draw a line."[57]

The Minneapolis *Star Tribune* focused its anger on the National Rifle Association, arguing that its spokesmen had violated the line separating legitimate dissent from hate speech. "You can't say the outrageous things the NRA says, then claim innocence when federal buildings get bombed and people get killed. It doesn't wash; the Oklahoma City bombing is a bloody shirt that the NRA and lots of others are going to have to wear for a long time." The *New York Times* reminded its readers that the language of segregationist governors George Wallace, Ross Barnett, and Lester Maddox "created the climate that produced a flurry of murders by gun and bomb. The lesson of that era is clear. When leadership figures use violent language to warn of apocalyptic developments, borderline personalities interpret this as permission for violence."[58]

Michael Lind, senior editor of *Harper's*, did not see such a direct link but declared that mainstream conservatism helped "legitimate the world view of the Oklahoma City bombers and the Michigan Militia." Frank Rich of the *New York Times* declared that this worldview was not one held only by the "lunatic fringe" but was moving into the mainstream, largely through the activities of Pat Robertson and the Christian Coalition. And prominent conservative Kevin Phillips, editor-publisher of the *American Political Report,* also worried that the Republican party was "failing an old but critical test of U.S. politics: the need for a would-be majority to keep firm control of its fringe groups and radicals."[59]

The link between increasingly popular racist and conspiratorial worldviews and the bombing was described by the *New Yorker's* Adam Gopnik. "The point, of course, isn't that Limbaugh or Pat Robertson or G. Gordon Liddy caused the killing. It is that they seemed never to have given a moment's thought, as they addressed their audiences, to the consequences of stuffing so much flammable resentment into such tiny bottles." Gopnik argued that in fifty years, historians would be unlikely to write "'In the mid-nineties, politicians and talk-show radio hosts created an atmosphere of poisonous hatred against the national government. Also in a completely unrelated development, somebody blew up the federal building in Oklahoma City.'" They would, he said, be more likely to write, "'In the mid-nineties, an atmosphere of poisonous hatred of the national government was allowed to grow in America; a few right-wing extremists even went as far as to bomb a federal building.'"[60]

Hate speech was considered both a constitutive building block and a poisonous by-product of this conspiratorial worldview, and its impact, some argued, was widespread. An editorial in the *Toronto Star* argued that toxic speech marked "the death of civility and rational debate . . . the dangerous and final blurring of the line between disagreeing with someone's ideas, and calling for their head." Jonathan Alter called attention to the dangerous impoverishment such speech brings in its wake: "anger breeds withdrawal breeds profound alienation and a new lonelier civic existence." Similarly, the *Village Voice* turned to the purported lessons of the Holocaust to argue that "hate speech is a weapon in the breakdown of liberal society, if only because it shatters the capacity for empathy."[61]

Most objections to any linkage between conservative critique of "big" government, the rhetoric of talk radio, and the bombing came from the right. The *National Review* characterized Clinton's attack as "McCarthyism," dismissed as more "damp than inflammatory" the rhetoric of talk show hosts, and argued that the bombing represented "anarchic terrorism," not "conservative governance." In the *Washington Post*, Charles Colson declared that it was an "egregious and irresponsible—indeed, fanatical—stretch to suggest that whoever committed the Oklahoma City atrocity is somehow linked to religious conservatives." An angry editorial in the *Seattle Times* thought that any linkage with the world of conservative government was like "blaming civil-rights leaders such as Martin Luther King for the racial violence of the Black Panthers in the 1960s."[62]

Responding directly—since it was widely assumed that the president's words were directed at him—was Rush Limbaugh. He linked himself with his audience, declaring that "whenever I am attacked as a purveyor of 'hate' or as somebody who spreads a so-called 'climate of anger,' the same charges extend to my audience." His audience, he observed, was made up of the "rescue teams who tried to save lives in Oklahoma . . . the law-enforcement officials who are trying to bring the lunatics ... to justice ... of people who've lost loved ones, who've had members of their families injured."[63]

The *Detroit News* saw the president's words as tactical. "Scratch a Republican, the insinuation runs, and you'll find a militia member." It also reminded readers of antigovernment rhetoric and violence from the left: Oliver Stone's conspiracy theory-laden film *JFK* and the bombings of the Weathermen in the 1960s, for example. However, the argument that "the left did this too" proved problematic. In the pages of *New York*, for example, Jacob Weisberg and Jeffrey Goldberg found the right's anger "a bit rich [since] the blame game has been a major mode of conservative discourse for years. ... It's hard to find a social ill or evil that some conservative won't try to attribute to the permissiveness and moral relativism taken to be an adjunct of Democratic liberalism."[64]

Attempting to move beyond partisan volleying were Millsaps College historian Robert McElvaine and Vanderbilt political scientist Jean Bethke Elshtain. Conservatives, McElvaine wrote, had long argued that mass media sex and violence promoted real-life violence, and liberals had long called attention to the violent rhetoric of hate radio. "Conservatives," he noted, "now react with anger to the suggestion that hate-filled, right-wing radio shows might push some people to violence. ... Many of the liberals who have long defended Hollywood's right to present any images that sell and have generally insisted that there is no connection between those images and social pathology are now quick to detect such a connection with talk radio." The danger, McElvaine said, "is in the message of hatred and violence, not in which medium carries them."[65]

Writing almost two years after the bombing, Elshtain recalled that "civil rights protestors were told that their rhetoric itself constituted violence because it cast fear into the hearts of defenders of segregation." She thought the most appropriate honor to those killed in the bombing was to "cease and desist the facile deployment of 'Oklahoma City' as an all-purpose club to discredit one's opponents as terrorists or the coddlers of terrorists."[66]

A few voices also wondered if a healthy civic discipline called for restricting further the kind of speech protected under the First Amendment. During the Red Scare era of the early twentieth century, many states adopted statutes that made it a crime to advocate violence to bring about political change. Since the Supreme Court case *Brandenburg v. Ohio* (1969), which overturned the conviction of a Ku Klux Klan member for uttering violent speech at a Klan rally, however, the Court held that "the constitutional guarantees of free speech and free press do not permit a State to forbid or proscribe advocacy of the use of force or of law violation except where such advocacy is directed to inciting or producing imminent lawless action and is likely to incite or produce such action."[67]

Appearing on the PBS *Newshour*, Robert Bork, former federal judge and solicitor general of the United States, thought the violence of the time called for a rethinking of the expansive limits of free speech. The Supreme Court, he thought, might need to go back to an "older view . . . which I think was more sensible." Stuart Taylor, Jr., opinion columnist for the *National Journal* and contributing editor for *Newsweek,* also argued for revisiting *Brandenburg*. Taylor defined hate speech as "speech that advocates killing or other use of violence against human beings (outside the context of killing enemy soldiers in war)."[68]

Taylor focused on two issues: the direct targeting of doctors who performed abortions and the publication of a "hit manual" used by a hired murderer. In February 1999, an Oregon jury ruled against antiabortion activists in the amount of $107 million. They had listed the names and addresses of doctors with a message, "One day we may be able to hold them on trial for crimes against humanity," along with names of doctors who had been murdered crossed out. Such rhetoric, Taylor argued, is not "political hyperbole" or "generalized, abstract advocacy of violence," and it should not be protected speech. He questioned whether proof of "imminent" action was needed, since, he said, "What was at most a remote possibility in 1969 is now very real: violent rhetoric that can foreseeably lead to violent action months or years after its initial publication."[69]

Taylor also informed his readers about a judgment against Paladin Enterprises, Inc., which published *Hit Man: A Technical Manual for Independent Contractors,* used by a hired killer to murder three people—one of them an eight-year-old quadriplegic—so that the father could collect insurance money. Agreeing with the words of Harvard Law School champion of free speech, Zechariah Chafee, Jr., "When A urges B to kill C and tells him how he can do it, this has nothing to do with the attainment and dissemination of truth," Taylor argued that a murder manual—which might lead to violent action, even if not "imminent"—should not be protected by *Brandenburg*. He asked readers if the First Amendment should protect those who publish a manual about how to smuggle bombs onto planes or one that teaches "how to steal nuclear materials from Russia, build a nuclear device, smuggle it into New York City, and blow up a few million people? How imminent would the intended explosion have to be to satisfy Brandenburg? Is the Constitution a suicide pact?"[70]

It was widely believed that William Pierce's infamous novel, *The Turner Diaries*, was McVeigh and Nichol's how-to manual for the Oklahoma City bombing. Writing under the pseudonym Andrew MacDonald, Pierce (founder of the neo-Nazi National Alliance) tells the story of Earl Turner, the leader of a group carrying out terrorist acts against a Jewish-controlled American government. After establishing a racially pure state in California, the group initiates a nuclear war designed to purify the world. Pierce's description of a terrorist attack against the FBI building in Washington, D.C., using a truck fertilizer bomb was chillingly similar to what happened in Oklahoma City.[71]

The Turner Diaries figured prominently in McVeigh's trial, as U.S. special attorney and lead prosecutor Joseph Hartzler told the jury that photocopied text from the novel was in McVeigh's possession when he was stopped. Indeed, he had never made a secret of his fascination with the book. Making the strongest case for a direct linkage was psychologist Robert Jay Lifton, who argued that the book took the place of a "guru" for McVeigh; in fact, the text *became* his guru. It provided him, said Lifton, with "entree to the equivalent of a radical cultic experience." By early 1996, Pierce enjoyed royalties from the sale of approximately 200,000 copies of *The Turner Diaries*, and its notoriety after the bombing led to its mass release in 1996, angering those who thought Pierce should be held accountable for writing a fictional "textbook" for the bombing.[72]

An editorial in *Legal Times* bemoaned the fact that this "perverse outcome" is permitted by an interpretation of the First Amendment that requires that "we pretend not to know what we intuitively understand to be true: that there is a link between what is depicted and what is done." Survivors, the editorial argued, should be able to sue Pierce not because of his unpopular political views but because he, like everyone else, should be "held responsible for the natural and foreseeable consequences of our actions."[73]

Military historians are fond of using the phrase the "fog of battle" to illustrate how the chaos of war often renders a familiar landscape beyond recognition, how armies blunder through this fog disoriented, desperately searching for points of orientation. Contemporary culture wars produce their own fog of battle, as citizens faced a bewildering spectrum of voices explaining and interpreting the bombing. The danger, the public was immediately told, came from foreign terrorists. Never mind, they were told only a few days later, the danger was from within, but where, exactly? Did it emerge from the bosom of the nation, from the poisonous world of the militias, from a cultural climate fostered by the power of violent language? Or was it an act disconnected to any larger national trait, only to be explained by the pathology of two loners? Did it represent the inevitable outcome of a weak government too soft on terrorism for too long or the toxic legacy of post-Vietnam American militarism?

As the public contemplated the range of internal causes, antiterrorism legislation focused largely on the specter of external threat. Such legislation, the president said, would safeguard the nation. No, said others, arguing that the legislation was either too weak or too strong. In either case, the nation was at risk. Some argued that the gravity of the bombing called for a reformation of enduring civil liberties. They believed that American civil identity would have to change in the twenty-first century to survive.

As these public struggles over the meaning of the bombing raged, members of the bereaved community of Oklahoma City struggled to situate the bombing in narratives of civic renewal and religious redemption, as well as a toxic narrative of an unfinished bombing.

TELLING THE STORY: THREE NARRATIVES

During our meeting in January 1998, Charles Van Rysselberge, president of the Oklahoma City Chamber of Commerce, spoke with justifiable pride about Oklahomans' outpouring of generosity in response to the bombing. He hoped that widespread respect for these efforts would transform what many in Oklahoma believed was an enduring national image of "ignorant Okies" and that the same civic energies evident in response to the bombing would spark a revitalization of the city. "This tragedy," he wrote several months after the bombing, "has been a defining moment for Oklahoma City. ... The world has defined/branded us as America's Heartland ... and Oklahomans may have found a reason to have the strongest dose possible of self-pride and to be proud to be Okies!"[1]

As I left Van Rysselberge's office, I thought of Holocaust scholar Lawrence Langer's idea of "preferred narratives." Some events threaten bedrock convictions so severely that we engage them only by softening the story, reducing the sheer horror of an event (be it the Holocaust or the Oklahoma City bombing) by grasping for comforting and reassuring story lines. I recall wondering if what I had just heard, which seemed a "progressive narrative" about the bombing, "yes, it was horrendous but ..." was such a story.[2]

It is, I decided, not an easy question to answer. Clearly, people were heartened by the many expressions of human caring after the bombing. There was an outpouring of generosity for family members and survivors. Rescue workers from around the nation speak movingly about how they were treated in Oklahoma City, about the enduring relationships they established with those they helped rescue, with the families of those killed.

This, however, is only one way of telling the story of the bombing and its aftermath. While we will not make the mistake of discounting it, we should also not let it register as *the* story, for there are several other narratives through which the story has been told.

There is a redemptive narrative that emerges from religious communities' struggle to mobilize the sacred resources of their traditions to respond to the crisis of meaning engendered by the bombing. Indeed, the event threatened to subvert the convictions deeply held by many in this overwhelmingly conservative Protestant city, that God is loving, just, and all-powerful, and directs human history, through which God's will can be discerned. Someone lived because she had gone to the break room for a cup of coffee or to the restroom. Someone was late because he overslept or had a dentist's appointment. Some died because they were early, because they were talking to a colleague in another office, or had gone to work despite not feeling well. Random chance, impersonal fate, good or bad luck seemed to make as much sense—or more—than the purposeful workings of a providential God.

Not all religious responses offered "answers" for making sense of such horror. All of them, however, sought to give members of particular religious communities theological contexts through which they could locate the bombing religiously through an understanding of evil's place in the world and God's role in human life. Such responses offered grieving people assurance that there was an afterlife in which their loved ones resided and assured them that one day they would be reunited with them.

Both of these narratives sought to recover from the ruins of the bombing some evidence of people's resiliency and some sense of coherence. They sought, in Hannah Arendt's words, to "reveal the meaning of what otherwise would remain an unbearable sequence of sheer happenings." There is, however, a third narrative that does not speak of acts of civic reconstruction or affirmations of the human spirit, but concentrates instead on the impact of the "sheer happening" of mass murder.

This story focuses on the bombing itself, and how it was imprinted on

the bodies and in the minds and spirits of so many. It is a story of an unfinished bombing, one that still reaches out to claim people through suicide, to
shatter families through divorce, substance abuse, and the corrosive effects of
profound and seemingly endless grief. It is a toxic narrative, and it exists
alongside of, and intermingled with, the other story lines. As Pam Whicher,
whose husband was murdered, said to me after reading a draft of this section, "all of the narratives seem to live within my experience, some to greater
or lesser degree, from day one to now."[3]

Her remark helped me appreciate that these narratives not only helped
shape political rhetoric, editorial response, or other expressions of public
culture but were at work in the lives of individuals. She recalled, for example,
"the progressive Pam," "determined, absolutely determined, that my family
would not be weakened by this experience. In fact, it was my goal, even my
expectation, that we would emerge stronger." She remembered "the redemptive Pam," "always a deeply religious person. The morning of the bombing I
was to be a speaker at a Bible study I regularly attended. But I felt so abandoned by God, so angry. I still believed in God, I still even loved God, I even
felt his presence in my mourning."

She recalled as well "the toxic Pam." "There is the before and after me.
The before me had a simple faith in God. The after me questions everything.
The before me rarely smoked; the after me is *still* smoking a pack a day
[started April 19, 1995]. The before me was simpler, a housewife, a mother, a
person who saw life in clearness, in innocence. Now each day . . . every day
without disaster is a day to be thankful for. Today, five years later, I have rede-
fined myself . . . incorporated pain has made me a new person. More cynical,
less tolerant, but I also feel somehow richer for the experience of pain and
loss. . . . Watch TV and there is the Murrah Building. Read the paper, and
there, casually, the words Oklahoma City bombing appear; and the pain in
my heart resurfaces."

The Progressive Narrative

Bob L. Blackburn, executive director of the Oklahoma State Historical Society, observed that Oklahomans' reaction to the bombing cannot be under-

stood without appreciating the "personality" of the state, a personality, he believes is "based on disasters—natural, manmade . . . economic. . . . It's very natural in our personality to react to disasters, to say 'yes this happened, but tomorrow's going to be brighter.'" Many Oklahomans, said Blackburn, are only one generation removed from the rural values and traditions that led people to help neighbors build a barn after it burned down or plow the fields when they were sick. It was these values, he believed, that led so many to rush back into the building immediately after the bombing. Blackburn's words echoed often as I listened to people recall their feelings when they first heard about the bombing: "I had to do something, I had to find a way to help." There was little comfort in being a bystander in Oklahoma City.[4]

Many Oklahomans possess a fierce pride in their pioneer heritage, largely stemming from the great land run of April 22, 1889, when Oklahoma City became a tent city of 10,000 in one day. Blackburn spoke of the "spirit of '89," which has as its legacy an infectious spirit of optimism that engendered agricultural energies, urban renewal, and oil "boom" periods. Oklahomans also feel pride in surviving the disasters Blackburn mentioned: the Dust Bowl of the 1930s and the Great Depression, devastating tornadoes, the corrosive effects of economic "busts" when oil prices fell sharply, and, of course, the bombing.

Alongside this pride in their pioneer and survivor traditions, Oklahomans still speak of how the rest of the nation (when they would think of the state at all) draws on enduring Dust Bowl images of ignorant and impoverished "Okies," dramatized in John Steinbeck's *Grapes of Wrath*. Blackburn, for one, does not believe that Oklahoma's image problem stems from Steinbeck. On the contrary, he observed, "Steinbeck celebrates the resilience of these survivors, it is really the John Ford movie adaptation that gave rise to a negative image." He traced the state's problem to a different source: the "long tradition of exploitation in the state, beginning with the dispossession of native Americans which made many rich, and our long history of slavery. Alongside our hardy optimism runs a pessimistic strain that emerges from our exploitation of others. It says, 'expect the worst, and before you get slapped in the face, get prepared.'"[5]

With national and often international media attention fixed on Oklahoma City for weeks after the bombing, Oklahomans had the opportunity to show and tell the world that their pioneer and survivor legacies continued to serve them well, that traditional values were not outmoded in the modern world, and that the negative stereotypes of Oklahoma and Oklahomans did great injustice to a people whose humane response to the bombing impressed so many. Governor Keating addressed the negative image directly. "To emerge from this muscular, attractive and lionized is something quite candidly that surprised people. The 'Grapes of Wrath' are gone," he said. "Oklahoma has an opportunity to step into the first tier of states. The good will generated by this tragedy is a door-opening opportunity for us and one we fully wish to enjoy."[6]

Some celebrated the perceived values of the "heartland." Writer and storyteller Carol Hamilton, who became poet laureate of Oklahoma in 1995, exclaimed in "Braced against the Wind":

> *Nothing gentles down from*
> *A mild Heaven here.*
> *We are always braced*
> *Against the wild wind.*
> *We were ever hand in hand*
> *As far as the eye can see.*
>
> *Cataclysms are the story.*
> *Our cities sprang up overnight,*
> *Are flattened at a tongue-lashing*
> *By clouds, and bush-whackers and*
> *Bonnies and Clydes*
> *Struck fast and hid against*
> *The Land, stretched and pegged*
> *Flat to the Four Corners*
> *Of the Earth. We do not cower*
> *At disaster.*
>
> *We join hands, sing hymns.*
> *We share tears, and*
> *Bend our backs, raising*

A neighbor's barn.
Do not think your
Abrupt terror will
Destroy us.

Wide horizons stretch our
Vision. We do not believe in limits.
We shift with the red dust,
Dance golden like the wheatfields.
We believe. We move on.
We bend and dance
On the tallgrass.

The prairie sings our pain.
The land shouts our praise.
The wind calls us together.[7]

NBC News anchor Tom Brokaw also drew on comforting images of rural values to celebrate Oklahomans' response to the bombing. "As a son of the Great Plains, I knew instinctively the response of the people of Oklahoma.... Oklahomans may feel more vulnerable now, a little disoriented by what's happened to them, but in their response to this madness, they have elevated us all with their essential sense of goodness, community, and compassion." It was these values, Brokaw and others declared, that brought about an explosion of goodness and revealed the character of the people of Oklahoma. If the bombing was an act that threatened everyday feelings of safety and security in presumed zones of safety such as offices and day care centers, these values promised to restore moral order. If the bombing was an event that would be remembered as a terrorist act of mass murder, the response would be recalled as a heroic saga, a moral lesson to be told and sung and celebrated for generations to come.[8]

And there was much to tell. If focusing solely on the progressive narrative leaves out an essential part of the story—the horror and enduring impact of the bombing itself—ignoring or discounting it as a soothing rhetorical strategy of civic boosterism would be a cynical evasion of a caring response to horror. "Evil does not produce good but sometimes evil circumstances can reveal a deep reservoir of goodness that was just waiting to be expressed," said First Christian Church's senior minister Don Alexander.[9]

The progressive narrative tells of nurse Rebecca Anderson, who rushed into the building to help, was struck by falling concrete, and died four days later. Her heart, liver, kidneys, and eyes were transplanted. It focuses on the many coworkers who escaped into the street and then rushed back to search for friends and colleagues; and on the real danger faced day after day by those involved in grim and taxing rescue and recovery efforts. Thousands of workers from various organizations responded to the bombing including those trained to respond to disasters, such as Red Cross volunteers, and those from other organizations, such as the Oklahoma Restaurant Association, which was holding its annual trade show on April 19. Its members immediately began preparing to serve rescue workers. "For the next ten days, they served 15,000-20,000 meals per 24-hour period, with food service being available 24 hours a day."[10]

This narrative tells the story of Dr. Andy Sullivan, who had to amputate Daina Bradley's right leg without anesthetic while lying on top of her in the basement of the Murrah Building in six inches of water. It tells of several hundred HAM radio operators "who worked with the Army to get calls out from the site to a base of operators...who could tell the Army immediately what was needed in supplies"; of the work of the Salvation Army, United Way, Feed the Children; of lawyers, doctors, funeral directors, clergy, businesspeople, musicians who donated services and money; of sixty-seven massage therapists who offered their services to the rescue workers, many of them working "18-36-hour shifts and getting only four to six hours of sleep"; of the services of Southwestern Bell Telephone, whose headquarters near the site became a vital center for law enforcement agencies, a site for rest, food and telephones—free telephone usage and cellular phones were provided for rescue workers; of many churches, some of them badly damaged, that helped in any number of ways; of the Oklahoma Veterinary Medical Association which set up twenty-four-hour medical care centers for rescue dogs, which often suffered cuts working in the sharp glass in the rubble and needed daily baths and saline treatment for their eyes after working amid the dust and blood; of a Dallas group that "sent therapeutic mattresses for the dogs" and the "owners of a tack and harness shop in Anchorage, Alaska" who made dog booties. When "Federal Express could not guarantee overnight service from Alaska to Oklahoma City, the owners' daughter, an airline flight attendant, took a day to fly them...personally."[11]

This narrative highlights the memories of those involved in the day-to-day rescue and recovery. They tell stories of how their memories of Oklahoma City were so different from the experiences of those who worked during the World Trade Center bombing in New York City, where vendors hiked the price of bottled water and some rescue workers had to sleep in automobiles. In Oklahoma City, hundreds of volunteers made sure each worker had a cot made fresh each day with a flower and a piece of candy or chocolate on their pillow, as well as clean clothes. The walls of the Myriad Convention Center were adorned with thousands of letters from school-children from around the nation thanking them for being "heroes." Rescue workers often recalled the generosity of the community by telling stories about the "Oklahoma dollar." "I left home with only a few dollars," I would hear over and over again, "but no one would let me spend a dime. I went home with those same dollar bills in my wallet."[12]

People lined up by the thousands and waited hours to give blood. If there was a need for boots or batteries or gloves or blankets, the media would mention it, and the site would be inundated as people went to buy whatever they heard was needed. "One such request for rain gear," the city's *Final Report* noted, "was aired at noon on April 22. By 2:00 P.M., cars and trucks formed a three-block line that slowly moved to the north entrance of the Myriad Convention Center, where volunteers received hundreds of donations." Before food service was regulated, individuals would come to the site with homemade sandwiches and baked goods. One rescue worker recalled with tears in his eyes the first night of rescue and recovery operations when an old car arrived at the site, and an obviously poverty-stricken couple brought food to those working.[13]

The community's response to the bombing, an outpouring of generosity by tens of thousands of people, was characterized as the "the Oklahoma Standard." Governor Keating defined this model of civic behavior on July 4, 1995, when standing on the steps of the state capitol, he ordered flags across Oklahoma raised after seventy-six days at half-mast. "Oklahomans have always been capable of greatness.... The spirit of April 19 was not an accident. It will carry us into the next century and make of Oklahoma what we always knew was possible. Good enough is no longer acceptable...we know we are capable of the very best."[14]

Well before this speech, however, Oklahomans were celebrating the Oklahoma Standard. On May 11, for example, community volunteers and rescuers were honored at the state capitol. "For nearly two hours the rescue workers—whose uniforms varied from those of the Salvation Army to the National Guard to those in priestly attire—stood in the front of the chamber and filled the walkways between the desks of representatives and senators."[15]

The Oklahoma Standard was viewed as beneficial in several ways. It allowed people to envision a new era for Oklahoma City. Citizens, it was hoped, would be inspired by the invigorating energies of decency. Governor Keating likened the postbomb era to postwar euphoria. "When you're in the war, it's anguish-strewn and horrible and hopeless. But once it's over, and you've won, it's a source of pride and optimism."[16]

Pride in the Oklahoma Standard sometimes turned into the rhetoric of civic boosterism. Oklahoma City's Mayor Ronald Norick hoped that the Oklahoma Standard would translate into economic benefits for the city. Major companies, he said, were considering Oklahoma City as a site for relocation or expansion. "The companies want to go where they can get a good labor force, competent people. And they saw that in the bombing response." Others also noted that the city's response offered a grand opportunity for the state and city to transform its image. Robert DeRocker, vice president of Development Counselors International in New York City, who contracted shortly before the bombing to provide public relations services for Oklahoma City, seemed to turn the tragedy into a commercial benefit when he said, "I think someone in the media...banged out 'Terror in the Heartland' very early in the whole process, and suddenly it became institutionalized: Oklahoma is the heartland of America. And I have to tell you that's a beautiful image.... If you're trying to attract distribution facilities, who wouldn't want to be in the heartland? So that's another gift to come out of this."[17]

A renewed commitment to urban renewal was a tangible way in which a demonstration of character and a new image would be imprinted on the city.

In 1993, two years before the bombing, voters had approved a sales tax to support a $300 million renovation of downtown Oklahoma City, the Metropolitan Area Projects (MAPS), which included plans for a new baseball stadium for the city's minor league team, an indoor sports arena, a riverwalk canal similar to San Antonio's famed riverwalk, arts and convention centers, and a new library. A chamber of commerce brochure declared in 1998 that MAPS had already "triggered substantial private sector investment (hotels, restaurants, clubs, shops), and will continue to catalyze growth."

There was widespread hope that postbomb commitment would accelerate the MAPS program and that other renewal projects emerging directly from the bombing would be tied to it. Garner Stoll, the city's planning director, observed that "the blast was so psychologically devastating that you almost have to find ways to tie in the most important public projects we have now to something that has affected the whole community."[18]

The envisioned memorial planned for the Murrah site was considered a crucial element in the projections of urban renewal. The Oklahoma City National Memorial, the chamber noted, would add "even more to the capital infusion downtown." Even before the bombing, the area around the Murrah Building was economically depressed. The impact of the bombing was devastating to area business owners, some of whom were underinsured, many of whom had difficulty obtaining disaster loans to rebuild or repair. Many worried that the relocation of approximately five hundred federal employees in the Murrah Building and state employees from their ruined offices in the Journal Record Building would affect their businesses dramatically. Plans for a memorial, it was hoped, would convince businesses to remain downtown, attracted by the prospect of tens of thousands of visitors.[19]

The memorial task force also expected the memorial to become a new urban "anchor" in the area. In their design competition materials, the task force envisioned a "memorial district" that would provide the neighborhood with an "evolving theme," one of "healing and rebuilding." The task force declared that "the memorial complex can be a catalyst for redevelopment of the district [and] form the core of a current and future redevelopment as well as provide the focus for a 'renewed' neighborhood in the city." Several urban renewal proposals echoed the task force's conviction that the memorial could become a crucial element of civic reclamation and revitalization.[20]

Design competition materials also informed participants that the memorial district would contain a "memorial zone," bringing people from "secular" urban space into a memorial environment identifiable by a certain aesthetic quality imprinted on the streets. "Lighting, street furniture and signage guidelines should provide an appropriate quality of environment consistent with the quality of design expected for the Memorial." Competitors were told that intersections should be "paved with specialty paving that informs the driver that he/she is arriving or passing through the Memorial Zone." Walls at the edge of the zone might include "messages or memorial-supporting exhibits."[21]

Many groups contributed to this new era of urban planning. Eight days after the bombing, for example, Mayor Norick and Garner Stoll attended the Mayors Institute in Charleston, South Carolina. Sponsored by the National Endowment of the Arts Design Program (NEA), the institute brought selected mayors to a symposium with city planners, architects, and urban design experts. Samina Quraeshi, director of NEA's program, offered to help Oklahoma City "restore not only its physical fabric but also the spirit and identity of the community." She proposed a "charette," a "brainstorming/idea event with designers from various disciplines . . . focusing on a specific design problem." The goals of the project were to "create hope and encourage reinvestment in the damaged areas, provide a design context to rebuild the area . . . provide a forum for broad community involvement," and to "place the memorial planning process in a broader context." Six design teams made up of local "architects, engineers, planners, property owners, residents, community leaders and representatives of financing institutions" examined different sections of the city and made recommendations for various renewal programs that were presented at a July 24-25, 1995 public design workshop in Oklahoma City that was sponsored by NEA and included nationally recognized urban design professionals.[22]

The NEA and the National Building Museum in Washington, D.C., celebrated the new vision for Oklahoma City by cosponsoring a museum exhibition entitled "We Will Be Back: Oklahoma City Rebuilds," which ran from November 17, 1995, through March 17, 1996. It took its title from the popular photograph of an American flag unfurled on plywood covering broken windows of the Walker Stamp and Seal Company, located only blocks from the

Murrah Building. Alongside the flag was spray painted the defiant message, "We Will Be Back."

Walker Stamp and Seal suffered $120,000 in damage, and three employees suffered minor injuries. Contractors had come late on the evening of April 19 to board up the building. Kenny Walker, the company's vice president, recalled coming to the building the next day with employee Gary Poole, who had put up the flag and spray painted the message. "I received copies of newspapers with the photograph from all over the country, I even got a call from Germany," said Walker. "Looking back now, we should have saved the plywood, but it was taken down by the contractor who installed new windows six weeks after the bombing, and I'm sure it was destroyed. I suppose it became a symbol of resilience, and people wanted to hear that message from us." Gary Poole reenacted the spray painting of his message on a sheet of plywood during the exhibit's opening, and visitors were invited to sign it with magic markers.[23]

The exhibition celebrated the progressive narrative. It located the bombing and the city's response in Oklahoma's pioneer and survivor traditions, informing visitors of the boom and bust history of Oklahoma City, the phys-

An icon of the "progressive narrative," at the Walker Stamp and Seal Company. (*Fort Worth Star Telegram*, photograph by Carolyn Bauman)

ical destruction of the bombing, and the envisioned future for a revitalized downtown. It illustrated, according to cocurator Sharon Blume, how civic renewal could aid in the "the emotional rebuilding of the city."[24]

The progressive narrative of the bombing invites people to focus on possibility, opportunity, healing, rebuilding. It celebrates what is perceived as the essential goodness of Americans, revealed in response to the bombing. It hopes for a revitalized civic life in the collective energies of citizens inspired by their own deeds. Its most powerful theme, expressed in the language of civic renewal, is one particularly familiar to members of religious communities in Oklahoma City: New life springs from death.

The Redemptive Narrative

A poem written in November 1995 sadly observed:

> *And we have suddenly become*
> *An International City*
> *Our Insulation instantly torn away.*
> *We are ordinary no longer.*
> *Now we are the heartland struck deep and hard,*
> *A wound running black and red,*
> *And nothing is clear anymore.*[25]

The bombing engendered a crisis of meaning, as people struggled to locate it in an ongoing religious narrative. Many worship services held in the days and weeks after April 19 turned to the plaintive verses of the Psalms and to Jesus's despairing words on the cross in the face of God's seeming abandonment to give voice to contemporary voices of anger, despair, and bewilderment.

Dr. John Rusco, dean of the chapel at Oklahoma City University, held a prayer vigil in the university chapel at noon on April 19. "We read from the book of worship, from scripture, had some readings on grief, and a good deal of silence," he recalled. "Individuals would lift up their prayers, and the community would respond, 'God in your mercy, hear our prayers.' It was a ministry of presence with each other." The First Christian Church, site of the Family Assistance Center, where family members waited for days for information on their loved ones, held a community prayer service on the evening of April 20. After singing a hymn, "O God, Our Help," grieving relatives joined in a litany that confessed, "When a disaster over which we have no control is unleashed our frail humanness is exposed. We are breakable, we are not in control, we are submerged in our own loss...our own humanness."[26]

In addition to commemorative services in churches, temples, and mosques, a "Christian Native Evangelical Prayer Gathering," was held in Oklahoma City on May 13, and a native American healing ceremony "offering memorial songs, a smoking ceremony, and prayers for all the victims, families, rescue workers and anyone else who feels the need for healing" was organized by the Good Medicine Society.

There was hope among the ecumenically minded that the "we are all in this together" community response would lead to new relationships between faith communities in Oklahoma City. Toward that end, a group of mainline Protestants, Jews, Muslims, and Bahais created Interfaith Disaster Recovery of Greater Oklahoma City. They saw an opportunity to break down religious barriers and create programs that would begin by assisting bombing victims, and remain as models of interfaith activity. Dr. Rita Newton, the executive director of the Oklahoma Conference of Churches said, however, that while "the level of caring for bombing victims in the first couple of years was tremendous," there was little sustained interest in interreligious dialogue. "In Oklahoma City," she said, "there is no ministerial alliance, and it is difficult to get religious communities to work together." She lamented the fact that "we missed our chance. At the time of the bombing we had something to come together for; now the perception of urgency is just not there." Eventually, boundaries between faith communities prevailed over membership in an ecumenical organization.[27]

Just as a vast array of material resources was mobilized in order to establish some measure of control at the site, and those at the Family Assistance Center began the painful task of systematizing the process of death notification, religious communities mobilized resources to address enduring questions of meaning.

There is a small Jewish community of about 2,500 in Oklahoma City:

"Our Jewish population is smaller than the statistical error in the city's census," observed Rabbi David Packman. "But we responded in a number of ways." Packman did not encourage people to ask "why did God do this" but "for us to come together for selfless giving and doing." For him, the response to the bombing was a "magnificent statement, it was America at its best. As a rabbi, I try to highlight that, because part of our remembrance is that we're a city which has met the challenge."[28]

Packman recalled being asked to offer reflections for people working in the makeshift morgue shortly after the bombing. He found it so traumatic that "I have blacked out what I said." Many Jewish volunteers were active in various parts of the rescue and recovery effort, he said, and Jews from all over the world sent approximately $600,000 to Oklahoma City's synagogues and to the Jewish Federation of Oklahoma City, funds that went directly to victims, $250,000 going to the Memorial Foundation. Packman also invited to Oklahoma City Rabbi Harold Kushner, author of *When Bad Things Happen to Good People*. In a June 1995 meeting with family members and survivors on the grounds of the governor's mansion, Kushner asked them not to think of God as "cause," but to find God "in one's own ability to survive and accept the response of the community."[29]

Inevitably, the bombing revealed to some Jews the enduring nature of murderous hatred also present in the Holocaust. A special candle was lit for victims of the bombing during the Days of Remembrance ceremonies in late April 1995. Edie Rodman, director of the Jewish Federation, declared that "the senseless loss of men, women, and children in Oklahoma City underscores that the cruelty and blind hate which were so much a part of Nazi Germany still exists today." In New York City, President Clinton linked the Holocaust and the bombing, telling a crowd of 6,000, "As we have seen, hatred still flourishes where it has a chance."[30]

The vast majority of responses came from various Christian communities, many of them theologically and socially conservative. Half of the state's population, observed The *Oklahoma Gazette*'s Phil Bacharach, "identifies itself as born-again Christian. About 65 percent of Oklahomans attend a house of worship at least once a week, nearly double the national average."[31]

In Christian communities throughout Oklahoma City, the Sunday after the bombing began a prolonged period of struggle with agonizing questions of faith: how could any deity allow this to happen? Was there a religious answer regarding why some lived and some died? How, in the face of such an atrocity, could the language of forgiveness be used without belittling the evil done?[32]

Religious responses sought to assure people that they did not live in a cold, unfeeling, empty universe in which such acts simply happened, that lives ended for no reason, that there was, finally, no redemptive ending to this story. That a loved one survived the bombing registered as miraculous, and God was thanked for intentionally saving a life. Or God was sorrowfully acknowledged as having the right to "call home" a child to a more peaceful heavenly world. Guardian angels were praised, and many steadfastly held to their faith, insisting that although they could never know "why," their religious convictions assured them that there was an ultimate reason, known only to God, a God who did not, it was said, measure out more suffering than an individual could bear.

In services of worship, clergy offered the resources of scripture: the trials of Job, the passion story of Christ, and the story of doubting Thomas. Some clergy cautioned their communities about seeking refuge in simplistic answers. Reverend Don Alexander, senior minister of First Christian Church, delivered a sermon on April 30 that called attention to the power of language. "Words, words, words. Have you ever heard so many words as in this last week?" he asked his congregation. He gently but directly criticized certain ways of making sense of the bombing religiously. It was not, he believed, part of God's plan. "When chaos erupts, that is not what God wants; that's not in God's plan." And he cautioned them to use the word "miracle" with care. "If you use the word . . . to describe an unusually marvelous event, then that was a miracle." To characterize it as a "supernatural act, God's intervention," however, means that "God acted capriciously—saving some, killing others. . . . We worship a God who is neither fickle nor capricious."[33]

Reverend J. Pat Kennedy, pastor of St. Andrew's Presbyterian Church, told his congregation that in the New Testament, death was "always interrupting what God has given—life." This means, he said, that "we will not say that God needed or wanted anyone to be with God in heaven. For God is with us wherever we are here on earth, and God is with us out of love, not out of need. So let us not say or think that death is something God arranges for us, for death is not God's will."[34]

Many clergy reminded their congregations that God was still in control but that human beings had free will to practice good or evil. Dr. Robert E. Long, senior minister of St. Luke's United Methodist Church, a church near the site that became a Red Cross center and a blood bank, objected to those who called the bombing part of God's will. "I don't believe it was all those people's time. I don't believe that God wanted those people to die.... God has created us and set us free, and in our freedom we can choose to hate and hurt and destroy, and in our freedom, we can chose to love and build up and heal." The evil that people do, however, does not break the bond between God and suffering humanity. God was with those who died as well as those who lived, Long said. "That's the message of Easter—God is with us when we live and God is with us when we die."[35]

Joining Long and many others who steadfastly proclaimed God's continuing love and presence, Dr. M. L. Jemison, pastor of St. John's Missionary Baptist Church, who served as a volunteer chaplain at the site, echoed the words of the Psalm 46:10: "Be still and know God is able. Be still and know God is sovereign. Be still and know our extremity is God's opportunity. Be still and know that earth has no sorrow that heaven cannot heal."[36]

The argument that the bombing resulted from human misuse of free will was a popular one, seemingly short-circuiting any questioning of God's goodness or justice, doubts that could potentially weaken faith. Some clergy told their communities that misuse of free will was an unmistakable sign of the reality of evil, and evidence of the presence of an evil one: Satan. Reverend William Simms, pastor of Wildewood Christian Church and a volunteer chaplain at the site, told his congregation that "when somebody gets the devil in him, he will do anything.... The person who did this was operating under the influence of Satan." He strongly objected to the bombing as evidence of God's will. "No! No! No! The Bible tells us that Satan, the devil, comes like a thief to steal, to kill, and to destroy." Cautioning his parishioners not to weaken, he declared that Satan "wants you to blame God, he wants you to question God, and he wants you to make God responsible for what has happened."[37]

Reverend Nick Harris, pastor of First Methodist Church, directly across the street from the Murrah Building, also rejected the bombing as any work of God. "It's our thing," he said, "it's our responsibility." He recalled talking with the media and being asked "why did God let this happen." He responded, "My God doesn't kill kids." Harris did not think Christians should be surprised by the bombing. "Evil goes with living in this world, evil has a right to be here. The dominion of earth was surrendered by Adam to evil, so evil has been invited here by human actions, and we must recognize the fact of sin."

Harris understood the bombing as part of an ongoing struggle in the cosmic warfare between God and Satan. He did not record his usual Wednesday morning radio program on April 19 and was quite probably saved from death, given the destruction in that particular area of his church. He did not speak of being "saved" by God but being "kept," because "there is a purpose for my life, not because my life is special. I'll never be done with this, in my commitment to fight evil."[38]

Despite warnings about the power of evil, it remained curiously faceless. Dr. Robin Meyers of Mayflower Congregational Church was one of the few to place blame directly from the pulpit. "In our country, the hate speech never rests.... If you're angry and scared...there are plenty of entrepreneurs out there who will take your money and in return, give you someone to blame, someone to hate."[39]

For religious communities used to reading contemporary events through apocalyptic lenses, the bombing was evidence of cosmic warfare and a sign of the end times. For example, literature from the Heritage Baptist Church informed readers that God wanted his people to fight his battles on earth, and those killed in the bombing were casualties of war as surely as those killed in World War II. "Because the U.S. government does not recognize it as such, they will never be honored with Purple Hearts. But they deserve them, for their physical and spiritual wounds are the result of the physical and spiritual warfare waged by the great enemy of God."[40]

Working from scripture such as 2 Timothy 3:1, "This know also, that in the last days perilous times shall come," end-time messages offered comfort and cultural critique. In *Prophecy in the News*, J. R. Church declared that "the hope of resurrection keeps us all going. The soon return of our Savior helps us to cope with the tragedy." He informed his readers that McVeigh was "not the product of Christian values, a church, or a Christian school. He is the product of a government sponsored school-system that took God, prayer, the Bible, and moral values out of the public school-system . . . and is now reaping what they sow." Church reminded his readers that Nero took advantage of the burning of Rome to persecute Christians, and he asked them to pray that the federal government would not go on a "witch hunt" against Christians who hold the "blessed hope" that "Christ is coming soon."[41]

Many clergy were forthright in their inability to make sense of the bombing. FBI chaplain Joe Williams recalled speaking at the FBI Academy, and "everyone wanted to know 'why.' I said, 'I don't know.' My belief in the sovereignty of God is that he could have prevented it but he didn't and I don't know why." Legitimating a sense of divine mystery was Reverend Billy Graham, who spoke at a public memorial service, "Time for Healing," at the Oklahoma State Fair Arena, Sunday, April 23. Joining approximately 11,000 people in the arena were an estimated 30,000 outside, and the service was viewed by thousands more in churches throughout the city. "I have been asked on hundreds of occasions why God allows tragedy and suffering. I have to confess that I can never fully answer to satisfy even myself." A sense of profound, uncomprehending awe in the face of the event was also communicated to those attending the community prayer service on April 20 at the First Christian Church by Rabbi Dan Shevitz of Emanuel Synagogue. He spoke of telephone calls he received from Israel. He expected them to say, Now you understand. What they said instead was, Now you don't understand. "We cried together and I said, 'Yes, now we don't understand like you.'"[42]

In response to "where was God?" questions, artists joined area clergy in locating Jesus Christ among the victims and the rescue workers. (Michael Vance)

Assurances were given that God or Jesus or the Holy Spirit had been and would continue to be present. Interestingly, despite the large Christian population of the city, during the Time for Healing service, Governor Keating emphasized the God of civil religion, a God available to all: "He is not a God of your religion or mine, but of all people, in all times. He is a God of love, but he is also a God of justice." In the midst of this public crisis the god of civil religion was defined by the personal and civic virtues of love and justice.[43]

THIS WORSHIP IS DEDICATED TO THE CHILDREN AND OTHERS BRUTALLY MURDERED IN OKLAHOMA CITY AND AROUND THE WORLD THIS WEEK

Jesus on the Cross

Name: Scott Steven   Age: 8

Eight-year-old Scott Stevens portrayed Jesus in the form of the murdered children on the cross. Credit: reproduced with permission from Scott Stevens, Scott's family, and the Carrollton, Missouri First Christian Church.

The Christian God was perceived to be working in Oklahoma City, either alongside rescue workers and grieving family members, sharing their heartache, or as a victim, broken and suffering, like Christ on the cross. Christians of all persuasions were reminded that resurrection followed death, and that this was the ultimate promise of a redemptive ending.

Reverend Don Alexander located God grieving with his people. "God's heart," he said, was "the first to break." Dr. Meyers spoke of how the bombing reversed the sacred rhythm of the Christian calendar. "Sadly, only three days *after* Easter, Oklahoma City found itself immersed as never before in the world of Good Friday. . . . Instead of signs of the Risen Christ, we stared into the face of death in disbelief."

Meyers told his congregation the story of doubting Thomas recounted in the Gospel of John. The disciples, fearing Roman soldiers, hid in a room and felt the presence of Jesus, who offered them the power of the Holy Spirit to return to the world. The disciple Thomas was not present, did not believe, and said he would only believe when he touched Jesus's wounds himself. Jesus allowed Thomas to touch him and said, "Have you believed because you have seen me? Blessed are those who have not seen and yet believed."

Meyers asked his congregation, "Do you think that we need to reach out and touch the side of Christ to know that he is risen? . . . You do not have to tell us about a distant apparition, a statue that is said to be weeping blood, or a cloud that was photographed and showed the head of Christ. It was our fireman who lifted children, some bleeding, some already dead. . . . We became the bleeding body of Christ." Meyers assured his congregation that "as Christians we have looked into the face of death before and said, 'This is not the final victory. . . . God has the last word.'" For Meyers, God did not just grieve alongside his people; the community, united in grief and suffering and embodying Christian virtues in their response, was transformed into the suffering savior.[44]

Many clergy focused on the extraordinary response of so many at the site to proclaim the presence of God. The focus shifted from the horror of the bombing to religious renewal: the "Lord's work" of rescue and recovery. A theology of the cross was the basis for messages of hope. Reverend Lee Benson, associate minister at St. John's Missionary Baptist Church, was asked by the ministerial alliance in the black community to contact families and assess their needs. He recalled how difficult it was for so many who had lost primary breadwinners, but, he remarked, "the gospel of Christ is the gospel of hope. We didn't have to deviate from our message, that message just lived a little more."[45]

For Father Joseph Ross, priest at Christ the King Church, and a chaplain for the National Guard, scripture came alive in new ways. He offered "accessible interfaith" prayers at First Christian Church in the days immediately following the bombing. "We prayed the Psalms, and I noticed that they had new meaning for me." He offered mass at his parish in Norman, Oklahoma, the first weekend after the bombing and worried that the scripture selections wouldn't fit the time. One was from the Gospel of John, once again the story of doubting Thomas. "I usually thought of this as an act of authenticating wounds," Ross said. "But after the bombing I thought of it as illustrating that despite fatal wounds, Christ was still present. The terrorists can't end life."[46]

For some evangelical Christians, the presence of God was obvious. It was as if the bombing had ripped open the veil of secular illusion about the nature of the world to reveal a transcendent world enveloping the site as miracles were plentiful, angels populated the site, and the comforting presence of Jesus and the Holy Spirit was indisputable to those who saw through the eyes of faith.

The reality of the transcendent world was certainly the message of KQCV/KNTL radio general manager Robin Jones, who wrote *Where Was God at 9:02 A.M.?* "A powerful spiritual presence pervaded the whole incident," Jones declared. "People all over the world comment on it. Even agnostics admit something unique happened; those who believe in God are certain what it was. The movement of what Christians call the Holy Spirit. In a word, God among us." For her, miracles included not only those of supernatural origin but also the very human "miracles" of an "expert response," of "ordinary people doing the extraordinary," of "comfort to servants on the edge," of "unity despite differences."[47]

Anecdotal evidence of, for example, sightings of angels confirmed a divine presence. A woman driving on the freeway spoke of a "brilliant" white

Artistic expression often tried to provide solace to the horror of the murder of 19 children by illustrating both their ascension to heaven and their transformation into angels, and angels gently carrying them to heaven. (Right) Bev England, N.B., Canada; (Left) Kathy Creed.

cloud "filled with hundreds of angels wings!... All the angels were facing west. Long wings of incredible dimension trailed gracefully behind their backs." Jones told readers about sightings of the "spirits of the souls... of some of the ones whose bodies were destroyed by the blast," still "hovering, sort of suspended, above the area of the Alfred P. Murrah building." She reported confidently that voices of the dead reassured living relatives that they were all right. For example, a mother traveling out of town saw the face of her dead daughter "basked in a radiance no one else seemed to notice." The daughter said, "Mom, I'm okay."[48]

Other extreme situations—notably the crisis of war—have engendered a thirst for the presence of the transcendent. Paul Fussell wrote that the conditions of both world wars provided fertile ground for a "plethora of very unmodern superstitions, talismans, wonders, miracles, relics, legends, and rumors." In particular, he mentioned the legend of the Angel of Mons, reputed to have protected the British in their retreat in August 1914. And he said that no "front-line soldier [in World War I] or officer was without his amulet, and every tunic pocket became a reliquary. Lucky coins, buttons, dried flowers, hair cuttings, New Testaments, pebbles from home, medals of St. Christopher and St. George, childhood dolls and teddy bears, poems or Scripture verses written out and worn in a small bag around the neck like a phylactery.... So urgent was the need no talisman was too absurd."[49]

The presence of a sacred world populated by divine beings in which miracles were commonplace offered a way to contain the bombing through a particular religious reading of the "evidence." In the midst of such tragedy, discernment—the ability to see through horrible but ultimately transient suffering—was crucial. "American Christians," wrote historian Colleen McDannell, "want to see, hear, and touch God." In Oklahoma City, many wanted and needed to feel, hear, and see the palpable presence of a sacred material world that, like the theology of the cross, assured grieving people that death did not have the last word.[50]

Not all interpretations of angels spiriting away the children were soothing, however. ("Oklahoma City, April 19, 1995," a tribute to the bombing, by a young artist, Ragen Mendenhall)

The aftermath of the bombing was also seized upon as a unique opportunity for religious revival. Billy Graham cautioned that the bombing "reminds us that we never know when we too will be called into eternity. I doubt that even one of those people who walked into the Federal Building last Wednesday morning thought that it would be their last day on earth. That is why we each need to face our own spiritual need and commit ourselves to God and his will now." Reverend Tom Elliff, former president of the Southern Baptist Convention and senior pastor of the First Southern Baptist Church in Del City, Oklahoma, understood the bombing as a "wake-up call." "This society has lost a sense of God consciousness," he told me, "and we will suffer greatly if we do not regain it."[51]

Some saw the bombing as offering the opportunity to refocus their lives. Fireman Chris Fields, who held Baylee Almon in his arms in a photograph that communicated the horror of the bombing around the world, declared on *The Newshour with Jim Lehrer*, "I was a good Christian on the outside, but the inside, it wasn't there. But this makes you reevaluate it. . . . God put me where I was that day for a reason."[52]

Some, however, used this "opportunity" inappropriately. Dr. Robert Allen, senior minister at Wesley Methodist Church at the time of the bombing, coordinated chaplains' activities at the Murrah site and recalled that of the 500-600 ministers on-site, "we pulled about 20 tags or less, just because they were doing inappropriate things. Our job was not to . . . evangelize or hand out our own denominational literature. Our job was to be there—to be the presence of God—to be ministers. . . . If they could not follow the rules . . . we pulled their tag and had the police officer who was assigned to us escort them off the property."[53]

Some clergy cautioned their parishioners about the danger of spiritual degeneration if they allowed hatred to overcome them. At the First Christian Church's community prayer service the night after the bombing, a prayer was offered for the perpetrators, "for those whose view of life is so dark and empty that they would willingly and knowingly waste the life of another. We pray that they might come to know the awfulness of what they have done."

Forgiveness, especially without evidence of remorse, was difficult. Reverend Gene Garrison, pastor of First Baptist Church in Oklahoma City, said, "I know I'm supposed to pray for the people who did this, but I'm finding that very hard to do when I look at these little babies." Yet, on the first Sunday after the bombing, Reverend Nick Harris told his congregation, worshiping in the auditorium at Oklahoma City University, "if we are going to be a church and not a social club . . . we must pray for those who did this."[54]

Others worried that their own humanity could be impoverished by any stoic acceptance of the horrific scenes they witnessed at the site. Reverend Robert Wise, a bishop in the Communion of Evangelical Episcopal Churches, said, "I always wear a clerical collar, so I thought I would go to the site, be recognizable and help in whatever ways I could. Someone told me, 'we'd like you to stand where we're going to bring bodies out and say a prayer.'" Reverend Wise spoke of the impact of seeing the bodies and body parts of children being brought out of the building. "Nothing in the world prepares you for that. We are not made to understand," he said. "We are not supposed to see a child dismembered, to see a man turned partly into charcoal. If I could accept that, I would have lost part of my humanity."

For Reverend Wise, "trauma" meant that there were some things human beings were not supposed to see, and being traumatized by such sights was a sign of spiritual violation. Rescue and recovery teams treated each body with respect to remind one another that this body was a person, not just "matter." Reverend Tish Malloy, senior minister at Village United Methodist Church, worked for two weeks every night in the morgue and triage area and recalled that work stopped and people would take off their hard hats when a body was found. The stretchers were always taken out of the south side of the building away from cameras and onlookers to the temporary morgue at the First Methodist Church. "I felt protective of the bodies when they came out," she said. "This person had a life, and we needed to respect that even in the midst of the recovery work."[55]

Reverend Wise also mobilized liturgical resources to help rescue workers move beyond the horror. "If a person is raped, abused, or in this case, thrown into a terrible situation, their memory is frozen in that event. It inhibits their growth." He offered a service entitled "Healing of the Memories" at the Church of the Redeemer. "The service brought the horror into the context of prayer. With their eyes closed, participants were led to realize the presence of God and his ability to restore what was broken."[56]

One of the highly publicized instances of spiritual transformation occurred in the life of Bud Welch, whose daughter Julie, a translator in the Social Security office, was killed. Welch, who owns a Texaco service station in Oklahoma City, grew up in a large family on a dairy farm in Oklahoma and remembered hearing his grandfather talk about an innocent black man executed in the 1920s. "My opposition to the death penalty ended when Julie was killed," Welch said. "I could have killed them with my bare hands, and I felt this way for months." One day, however, while he was at the site, he recalled a conversation he had with his daughter while driving home from Milwaukee and she reacted to a story on the radio about an execution. "She said to me, 'they are only teaching their children to hate,' and I began to realize that what took her life was an act of vengeance and hatred, and to put McVeigh to death would also be an act of vengeance and hatred. I decided to honor Julie's convictions by speaking up about this issue. I made a decision not to let hate and anger transform me into someone whom Julie would not recognize if she were here."[57]

Welch, a member of the board of directors of the Memorial Foundation, rooted his passionate, articulate, and public opposition to the death penalty in his Roman Catholic tradition. Speaking to the National Association of Criminal Defense Lawyers on November 1, 1997, several months after McVeigh's conviction and shortly after he was sentenced to death, Welch said, "The question is for me not just one of deterrent or the necessity of accepting the ultimate penalty from one of the most horrendous crimes in history; the question is whether or not this so-called Christian nation cares to wrestle honestly with the seemingly impossible demands of the Gospel." How, he asks "can we live in the Gospel's message to love our neighbor if we deliberately kill him? Would Jesus pull the switch or inject the needle?"[58]

Bud Welch on the first anniversary of the bombing. His daughter Julie was murdered in the bombing, and he became an articulate, nationally-known opponent of the death penalty. (David Allen, Oklahoma City)

For Bud Welch, the Christian imperative to forgive is not part of a promise of cheap grace, offered through a simple-minded rhetoric of forgiveness. Rather, it is part of a lifelong spiritual process in which he sees himself moving away from the vicious cycle of hatred and revenge that perverts a human being. He is forthright about his current inability to forgive McVeigh and Nichols. He hopes that they will live long enough to express remorse, certainly a first stage in any conversation about forgiveness.[59]

In a powerful act of reconciliation, Welch traveled to Buffalo, New York, in September 1998 to meet with Bill McVeigh, Timothy's father, and his sister, Jennifer. "I had seen him on television, seen the pain in his face, and I knew then I wanted to talk with him and tell him I cared about how he felt. I spent two hours with him, and when I left I hugged Jennifer, and both of us were crying. I told her that I didn't want her brother to die and I would do everything I could to prevent it." In his *Guideposts* interview, Welch recalled that at that moment "I was thinking that I'd gone to church all my life and had never felt as close to God as I did at that moment."

The religious landscape of downtown Oklahoma City was also transformed by the power of the bomb. Reverend Nick Harris's First Methodist Church was closed for three years. During this time, they met at Trinity Baptist Church, rotating worship services and Sunday school schedules. "There was never a cross word," Harris said. "This spoke to me about what the Christian ethic should be." On Easter Sunday 1998, seven hundred people gathered at Trinity Baptist and walked to their new building, which included the outdoor Heartland Chapel (whose altar included granite from the Murrah Building), built in 1995 with financial support from the Jewish and Muslim communities to offer shelter and reflective space for the many visitors to the Murrah site. The Roman Catholic St. Joseph Old Cathedral, across the street from the site, was reopened in December 1996 and dedicated a nine-foot marble sculpture, *Weeping Jesus*, on April 19, 1998, on a corner directly across the street from the site. The nondenominational City Church and First Baptist Church also suffered extensive damage.

Rebuilding these churches was understood as both an act of physical resurrection, as religious communities were reborn in this wounded area, and an act of protest and defiance. Reverend Harris, for example, said "there was some consideration given to moving out of downtown, but I wasn't going to let a terrorist drive me off the corner."[60]

The religious landscape of downtown Oklahoma City was transformed by the bombing. In addition to massive renovations in a number of churches, the "Heartland Chapel" was constructed near the First Methodist Church, and the "Weeping Jesus" near St. Joseph's Old Cathedral. (David Allen, Oklahoma City)

The community of St. Paul's Cathedral (Episcopal), several blocks from the site, also incorporated the bombing into its new life. The cathedral was closed for two years, and renovation was still ongoing when I visited in the summer of 1999. Dean of the cathedral George Back spoke of the enduring presence of the bombing. "There are so many reminders in our everyday lives," he said. "We still find pieces of glass in our library books."[61]

I asked him about his memory of that day. He replied, "Memory is not something one recalls. That day is more present to me than the present moment. I can feel it in my body. It is much more than mental images, but sounds, smells, that are sparked in so many ways every day." He did not understand this as necessarily positive. "There is a dark side to this. There are too many people trapped, who may never leave April 19." He too turned to scripture, particularly the Gospel of John, with, he said, "its many mansions, its many stopping places. The bombing was a stopping point, a meeting of life and death, horror and grace, the absolute contrasts of life."

St. Paul's has incorporated these "absolute contrasts" into its rebuilding. The cross on top of the cathedral was shattered by the bomb, and pieces of the broken cross are now built into the wrought iron gateway of the new cloister. Many parishioners also wear a memorial chain with a silver broken cross "as reminders of communion of the heartbrokenness with resurrection." "The bombing is a part of us," said Back, "and we are forever marked by it."[62]

Also seeking to incorporate the bombing into her life as a survivor and member of St. Paul's community was Susan Urbach, regional director of the Oklahoma Small Business Development Center with the University of Central Oklahoma, whose office was in the Journal Record Building, directly across the street from the Murrah Building. She bears scars from the flying glass that lodged in her face and upper body, requiring more than three hundred stitches. For her, as for so many, April 19 became a moment of transformation. She wrote in her journal, "I really can hardly remember before April 19. It doesn't matter what was happening, for that life no longer exists. And the Susan who is present today is a Susan modified from that life. . . . The Susan of pre-April 19th knew her strengths. . . . Post April 19th Susan is one who is acquainted with her vulnerabilities and weaknesses."

On May 21, just over a month after the bombing, Urbach offered a message to the congregation at St. Paul's. She spoke of how her wounds went far beyond physical ones to the wounding of her downtown community. "There is no normal for me to return to," she said. "The only way for me to return to any kind of normalcy is to build a new normal, and in being an active part of that...rebuilt community."[63]

Urbach spoke both of personal and community transformation in familiar terms of death and resurrection: "There has been and will be good that will come out of the situation if we will but look for it. It has a horrible price tag of tragedy and loss.... We cannot change the action and the outcome, but through God's grace and mercy we can redeem the outcome for ourselves, not by increasing in hate and anger, but in reevaluating what it means to live and to love, and to do that more fully."

Urbach envisioned those powerfully affected by the bombing as part of a "remnant community." "We must remember," she wrote, "we must be transformed, for a more horrible tragedy would be to have lost family, friends and colleagues and not be changed to redeem their loss to us."

Pain, death, struggles for meaning, compassion, transformation, remnant communities, and redemption: all concepts through which the bombing could be read religiously. Back and Urbach spoke forcefully of how the bombing continued to impact the lives of so many, and indeed it did. Even in his message of hope, Billy Graham declared, "That blast was like a violent explosion ripping at the heart of America, and long after the rubble is cleared and the rebuilding begins, the scars of this senseless and evil outrage will remain." Susan Urbach wished her scars to become a "sacrament—an outward and visible sign of an inward and invisible grace" that would help her be more sensitive to the pain and suffering of others. For so many, however, visible and invisible scars were not sacramental but toxic. For far too many, the bombing was unfinished, having left in its wake people struggling with enduring pain and loss.

The Toxic Narrative

"It's almost five years now," one survivor said to me, "and I still have glass and small pieces of rubble from the building working their way out of my scalp, back, and my ears. I know other people who have the same experience," he said, "and it seems an apt metaphor for how the bomb lives on in us."

The governor's office estimated that in addition to the 168 people killed, approximately 850 were injured, 30 children were orphaned, 219 children lost at least one parent, 462 people were left homeless, and 7,000 lost their workplace. Over one-third of the population—approximately 387,000 people—knew someone killed or injured, and approximately 190,000 people went to funerals. Many of the 12,384 volunteers and rescue workers were exposed to the horrors of the site, approximately 100 were injured, and nurse Rebecca Anderson died.[64]

The authors of the study "Population Effects of the Oklahoma City Bombing" observed that "the exposure to the bombing was widespread, including more than half the adults in the metropolitan area surrounding Oklahoma City. The psychological effects were high and, while decreasing, persisted more than a year after the bombing. Primary care practitioners should screen their patients, who may normally not be considered victims, for exposure to the effects of a terrorist disaster for an extended period of time."[65]

The bomb lived on in the disabling injuries and chronic pain of survivors, some of whom continued to undergo surgical procedures years after April 19. One young woman, for example, had approximately two-thirds of the bones in her body broken. She became addicted to the narcotic pain medication she was taking, was taken off the medication too quickly, and turned to buying crack cocaine on the street to deal with the pain. As she struggled to recover from both her injuries and her drug addiction, a colleague observed that "she was a beautiful woman who is not beautiful anymore. She can't even look in the mirror."[66]

The bomb lived on in the intense and enduring mourning for loved ones lost. Jannie Coverdale, for example, whose grandchildren Aaron and Elijah were killed in the day care center, still maintains their room in her apartment. Beds are made, with dolls and bears resting on the covers, and a whole cabinet of angel figures—many of them sent from people throughout the nation—stands in her dining area with the boys' shoes on the bottom. "I lived in the Regency Apartments," Coverdale said (the high rise building near the Murrah Building badly damaged in the bombing), "and I moved back in October 1995 still believing that the boys were coming back." She recalled that some people who lost loved ones preserved all sorts of remembrances: voices on answering machines, hand prints or footprints on wall or floors. "When I moved back, all traces of them were gone. Everything was painted and repaired."

In her new apartment, Coverdale still goes into their bedroom to "talk" with "her babies," as she calls them. "They were here, part of my life. I'm not going to forget them, or put them in a closet. Looking at all this reminds me of how important it is to keep asking questions, to know why my boys died." Her hearty laugh and warm smile make her words all the more painful, as she spoke despairingly of her future. "They were my reason for getting up in the morning. They were my happiness."[67]

Just as the bomb brought the community and many families together, it also strained relations in offices and homes. Laverna Williams, the director of the Social Security Administration in Oklahoma City, had begun her job on April 17, 1995. She observed that "April 19 was a totally different day for me than for others who had many friends killed. I was totally disoriented, and I started thinking about what I needed to do to be a responsible manager."

Jannie Coverdale and portraits of her grandchildren, five-year-old Aaron and two-year-old Elijah, both murdered in the bombing. (David Allen, Oklahoma City)

The Social Security office opened in a new location five weeks later, and Williams recalled the complex relationships between new employees and those who lived through the bombing. "While many of the new people were supportive, they had a difficult time. Some felt guilty because they were hired or promoted due to someone's death in the bombing." She recalled as well the tremendous challenge of managing an office staffed by so many who were struggling to work so soon after April 19. "Some people couldn't stay long, some threw themselves into work, some grieved openly for months and months, and some moved to other offices. For several years now, we've often had to shield survivors from work that had been done by someone who died. Now, many of them are able to handle picking up a case evaluation folder and reading through it even though it might have been written by a close friend who was killed." Still, she said, "after more than four years, we have people who have never returned, some still in therapy, some who can't work much. It is still very much a wounded office."[68]

There were the almost imperceptible toxins that affected families. Who—parents or spouse—would be the official spokesperson for those lost? Some divorced parents of children argued bitterly over viewing the remains, about funeral arrangements, about invitations to memorial services. Plans for the physical memorial also sparked controversy. As we will see in chapter 5, many people were moved by the memorial plan that envisioned 168 named empty chairs on the Murrah site to commemorate those killed. Should the wishes of parents of divorced children killed who wanted their family sur-

After the bombing, some family members kept rooms of murdered loved ones intact for various lengths of time. This is the room of three-year-old Chase and two-year-old Colton Smith. (David Allen, Oklahoma City)

name on the chairs be honored if ex-spouses did not agree? And who would have the privilege of telling the story of their murdered loved ones and selecting a personal artifact for the planned memorial center museum exhibition?

FBI chaplain Joe Williams spoke of how his daughter-in-law grieved the murder of her father so deeply that her mourning led to divorce. He recalled his son saying to him, " 'You know, if it weren't for Timothy McVeigh, I'd have a child now.' That's pretty tough stuff." Doris Jones, who lost her pregnant daughter, Carrie Lenz, and became very active in memorial work, spoke movingly of how her relationship with her son-in-law was also a casualty of the bombing. Eventually, she said, he started living with someone else. "I was angry. She was using my daughter's dishes, looking in her mirror, sleeping in her bed. He got to move on, but I don't get to have another daughter." Speaking gently, and with great sadness, Jones said, "I don't blame him anymore, he's entitled to his life, but it is hard."[69]

A study by the University of Oklahoma's Health Sciences Center in Oklahoma City reported that mothers of the murdered children spoke of being robbed of the "role of parenting [their] child throughout life and had a sense that [they] should have died first." Most were advised not to view their children's bodies. "One woman had been told her child's body was 'mostly there,' and she chose not to view the entire body; however, she did see and kiss one extremity." Often, mothers and grandmothers took solace in some part of the body that was intact. " 'At least his face was untouched.' . . . All spoke of getting some of their child's clothes back, perhaps a single sock or shoe, and then of going out to search for the other. Some were told details of the condition of the bodies or read the medical examiner's report. All wished they had not received this information."

Some of these women who appeared often on television became celebrities. "One woman was stalked and total strangers from distant parts of the country came to Oklahoma City to find the graves of the children or otherwise behaved in a manner suggestive of an intimacy that did not exist. . . . Many of the women found themselves angry at the parents of living children and rifts soon developed. . . . At times, this led to formerly close knit families no longer holding family gatherings."

Grandmothers grieved for the loss of their grandchild but also worried about how their own children were coping. "One father began to drink and use drugs. An adoptive father who felt pushed into the background at the child's funeral by his wife's ex-husband, who was the biological father, soon separated from her. One mother withdrew into herself in serious depression. 'I lost both of them,' reported the grandmother." Few of them found counseling helpful, often because they resented being labeled as "ill," or being treated as little more than a "victim," or as being cast within a particular "stage" of grief. "Some in fact," the report observed, "found such treatment actively destructive."[70]

Children, of course, were profoundly affected by the bombing, and not just the few who survived the Murrah day care center or those injured in the YMCA day care. Children who were glued to the television for days after April 19 also suffered. A child psychiatry group at the University of Oklahoma Health Sciences Center identified a "strong correlation between the emotional distress of children and the amount of television coverage of the bombing they watched." Dr. James Allen and Dr. Barbara Allen reported that for days after the bombing "the blown up building was often shown during the cartoon hours, and many young children watch television alone, without adults to comfort them and assure them of their safety or to correct their fantasies and misunderstandings." Preschoolers, they reported, thought that each time they saw the ruins of the Murrah Building a new building had been destroyed, and "some still kick the walls of the buildings they go into— just to make sure they will not fall down." A child psychologist in Oklahoma City told me, "We didn't do a very good job of protecting our children from information they didn't have to have."[71]

Even very young children, those who were one or two in 1995, may have received an "imprint" from the event. Dr. Robin Gurwitch, director of early childhood intervention programs at the University of Oklahoma Health Sciences Center, observed that some of these children were showing problems almost five years after the bombing, and clinicians were left to puzzle out whether it was from their parents' trauma or their own. Gurwitch spoke as well about older children's nightmares, sleep disturbances, and those who would talk about it over and over. Children aged ten to twelve were curious about "who got squished, who lost heads," their way, she said, of engaging the bombing, although "it made adults very uncomfortable." Younger children, she observed, would reenact it. One child had his play action figures, the Power Rangers, come to the rescue. A five-year-old rescued from the Murrah Building would put dismembered Lego pieces of people on a bed by themselves in a play hospital. "After a year," Gurwitch recalled, "all the pieces were whole, and someone was with them. There were also Christmas trees that symbolized happiness."[72]

The bombing continued to resonate in the ongoing work of support organizations. Debbie Hampton, deputy executive officer of the Red Cross, served on April 19 as a local disaster volunteer and said that "there is a different kind of gravity about the way we do our work. There hasn't been a single work day in the past four years that I haven't dealt with the bombing, whether it be for mental health concerns for people, legal issues, or various other problems."[73]

The event continued to affect the lives of professional and volunteer rescuers as well. Those who dedicated themselves to saving lives in mass disasters were forced to turn almost immediately from the act of rescue to the job of recovery. Celebrated as heroes in Oklahoma City and beyond, the word grated for many, as they considered themselves having failed because so many died, and they were helpless to do anything about it.

Cindy Alexander, the manager of Mercy Mobile Health, had been trained in critical incident stress work and was in charge of the incident command system set up for rescue workers at the site. She recalled that many rescuers expressed anger, vulnerability, and guilt about not being able to protect those who were killed. And rescuers soon learned of the suicide of Robert O'Donnell, the paramedic who rescued Jessica McClure, "baby Jessica," from an abandoned well in Midland, Texas, in 1987. He had experienced great difficulty dealing with the vicissitudes of celebrity status and killed himself only a few days after the Oklahoma City bombing.

"After he heard about Oklahoma City," Alexander said, "Robert O'Donnell told his mother he knew what the rescuers in Oklahoma City would go through. Four days after the bombing he laid his fire department uniform on the ground and shot himself. When we heard about this, it drove us even harder to make sure we got everyone help. I was committed to see that we did not have a suicide."[74]

Tragically, the bombing reached out and claimed more lives. Police chaplain Jack Poe reported that by the end of 1997, "there had been more than thirty successful suicide interventions of local firefighters and members of their families. At least six people involved in the bombing recovery and prosecution have committed suicide." In addition, the police department "had experienced an increase in the domestic violence rate among its officers," EMSA teams "weathered a rise in the alcoholism rate of its employees," and "divorce rates for Oklahoma City police, fire, and FBI personnel have climbed dramatically." In 1999, the Memorial Foundation's Families and Survivors committee added the word "rescuer" to its name, signifying recognition of what some called the "trauma club."[75]

And it was not just rescuers who struggled with their experiences. Many in the "helping professions" (e.g., mental health workers, clergy, funeral directors) were affected, as well as others such as the National Guardsmen who provided security at the Family Assistance Center, especially those assigned to guard the elevator on the fourth floor, which brought family members to receive official notification of a loved one's death. Police chaplain Jack Poe told me a story that captured vividly the continuing power of the bomb among these people. In spring 1996, a minister who had worked at the site came to see Poe. He told him that he had been conducting a christening at his church but could not bring himself to hold the baby in the birthing blanket. He had run out of the church without understanding why, and he was scared. When Poe asked the minister what he had done at the site on April 19, he remembered bringing out dead children and children's limbs in blankets. Poe's eyes moistened as he told me this story, and he said, "Even with all the help he can get, I don't think he'll ever be able to hold a child without triggering the bombing."

The toxic narrative also complicates the comforting image of the Oklahoma Standard. Almost immediately after the bombing, hospitals in Oklahoma City received bomb threats and "at least 15 federal buildings scattered across the country were briefly evacuated." While the *Daily Oklahoman* carried a special column on acts of kindness for many days, it also offered tips to help people avoid scam artists seeking to cash in on the tragedy.[76]

Many residents of Oklahoma City of Middle Eastern descent and African American Muslims bore the brunt of the nation's initial rage at "Muslim terrorists." KFOR television's coverage of the bombing informed viewers that a member of the Nation of Islam had taken credit for the bombing. They cautioned that it might be a crank call but repeated this "story" throughout the day's coverage, with one reporter noting that similarities with the World Trade Center bombing were "eerie." KFOR also mistakenly identified an Iraqi resident who was a citizen of Oklahoma City as "John Doe 2." Following the accusation, and even after the FBI cleared his name, he was subjected to public harassment and lost his job.[77]

The bombing claimed another victim when Sahar Al-Muwsawi, also an Iraqi resident living in Oklahoma City, had a miscarriage after her home was attacked on April 20. According to the Council on American-Islamic Relations: "The woman heard the screech of brakes and the breaking of a number of windows in her house. Unknown assailants also pounded on the woman's door screaming anti-Islamic epithets. The woman retreated to her bathroom with her two-year-old daughter and another child in her care. She then felt a pain in her abdomen and began bleeding uncontrollably. She miscarried a stillborn baby boy several hours later. . . . The child was named 'Salaam,' or 'peace.'" Another Oklahoma City resident, Abraham Ahmad, a computer technician, gained dubious fame when he was placed in handcuffs in London and returned to the United States. When his name was released to the press, his family endured verbal threats and someone spit on his wife.[78]

In the wake of numerous incidents of harassment, including suggestions on the radio that all Arab Americans be put in internment camps, on April 20 the Oklahoma City Police Department offered leaders in the Muslim community whatever protection they deemed necessary. National Public Radio's Daniel Zwerdling observed that a good opportunity for a public gesture toward the Muslim community was lost during the planning for the "Time For Healing" service. "While the planners of the service took great pains to be inclusive and to include Jews, Catholics, Evangelical Christians among the religious leaders at the service, Islamic groups were excluded." Dr. M. A. Shakir, president of the American Muslim Society of Oklahoma, said, "We have been insulted. Our children have been scared to death, and no one has even said they're sorry. That's what hurts most. How can we begin the healing work?"[79]

Also dividing citizens of Oklahoma City and the nation were various conspiracy theories, to which a few family members subscribed. Four days after the bombing, the *Daily Oklahoman* noted that the Internet had become a rich repository of such discussions. "Part news medium, part community bulletin board, part researcher's clearinghouse, part rumor mill, part fanatics' soapbox, the Internet has seethed with information, rumor and innuendo." Among the most popular theories was that the bombing was planned and carried out by the federal government to "divert attention from domestic problems, and to destroy key federal documents implicating President Clinton and U.S. Attorney General Janet Reno for 'murder' in the 1993 fire at the Branch Davidian compound in Waco, Texas."[80]

The federal grand jury indictment of McVeigh and Nichols, charging that they had conspired with "others unknown," provided fuel for conspiracy fires. According to the *Gallup Poll Monthly* of August 1995, "almost one in ten Americans believe that federal government officials were involved in a conspiracy to bomb the building." Glenn and Cathy Wilburn, whose two grandsons, Chase and Colton Smith were killed, became the most highly publicized family members who believed there was a wider conspiracy, perhaps involving members of far-right groups in Oklahoma. They joined more than three hundred people who asked attorney Johnnie Cochran (who had gained dubious celebrity status during the trial of O. J. Simpson) to file a lawsuit against the Bureau of Alcohol, Tobacco, and Firearms, the America's Kids Day Care Center, McVeigh and Nichols, and an explosives company, claiming that "the bureau had prior warning of . . . the bombing and that officials of the day care center . . . knew or should have known about the attack," and that ICI Explosives and subsidiaries "were negligent in the manufacturing of ammonium nitrate, which prosecutors say was used in the truck bomb that destroyed the building."[81]

In the fall of 1997, a successful petition drive to form a grand jury to investigate the bombing was led by Glenn Wilburn and Republican state representative Charles Key. "I want the grand jury to investigate whether there was complicity on the part of federal authorities to keep information from the public about prior knowledge or warning of the bombing," Key said. "There is clear evidence that is being ignored or hushed that shows there were others involved. We have a right to know." On December 30, 1998, the grand jury "found no additional perpetrators and dismissed suggestions that the government had prior knowledge about the blast."[82]

Other tensions in the community emerged in the aftermath of the bombing. State senator Angela Monson, state representative Kevin Cox, and Oklahoma City councilwoman Willa Johnson spoke of subterranean resentment in the African American community about national news reports that portrayed the bombing as a "majority hurt," with little or no discussion about the impact on African Americans. Councilwoman Johnson also cast a skeptical eye on the comforting idea that the bombing had bridged the racial divide in Oklahoma City in any enduring manner. "There was no sea change after the bombing," she said. "After the crisis, most people just 'went home.' Not all, but most."[83]

There were, inevitably perhaps, differences of opinion and some bitterness regarding the distribution of support funds. The guardian of three children who were killed joined a lawsuit against Governor Keating and Mayor Norick over restrictions on emergency funds. Representative Kevin Cox declared in June 1995 that "all the red tape, the loopholes and the cracks that the victims and those adversely affected are falling through should not be there." His sentiments were echoed by Senator Monson, who said they were still hearing "horror stories" from those who needed support.[84]

I moved back and forth between these narratives as I met with people in Oklahoma City. I was struck by the power of human resilience in the face of mass murder. I appreciated the great importance of the community's religious resources. At times, however, I felt overwhelmed by the torrent of immediate religious interpretation of the bombing, as if so many words would somehow make some sense of the event. There seemed little room for silence, a kind of awe-filled, deeply silent sadness in the face of the power of such loss. And I began to appreciate, after Oklahoma City faded from the headlines, and other tragedies captured the public's attention, how deeply the bomb's impact would live on. Discordant but related stories continue to be lived out: a song celebrating the heroic saga of rescue and response, a prayer for transcendence amid the rubble, and a lament from those for whom April 19 is always today.

"A New World": The Inner Life of a Wounded Community

During my first visit to Oklahoma City in the spring of 1997, I was intrigued when Timothy O'Connor, executive director of Associated Catholic Charities said, "A new world began in Oklahoma City after the bombing." I am familiar with the rhetoric of new beginnings emerging out of the carnage of death and destruction. This is, after all, one of the dominant images used to interpret America's wars: a new nation emerging from the blood sacrifice of its warriors. Images of a new world certainly accompanied the dawn of the atomic age, and as O'Connor and I continued to talk, I thought about Herman Hagedorn's 1946 epic poem, "The Bomb That Fell on America," his attempt to emphasize how the atomic bomb that destroyed Hiroshima had profoundly transformed American life. The bomb, he wrote

> Erased no church, vaporized no public building...
>   did not dissolve their bodies,
> But it dissolved something vitally important to the greatest of them, and
>   the least.
> What it dissolved were their links with the past and with the future.
> It made the earth, that seemed so solid, Main Street, that seemed so
>   well-paved, a kind of vast jelly, quivering and dividing underfoot.[1]

The bombing in Oklahoma City certainly did not represent a quantum leap in technology, as did the splitting of the atom, nor did this terrorist attack threaten human existence itself, as do thermonuclear weapons. O'Connor's comment was, I thought, simply a way of emphasizing widespread feelings of horror and shock. The more time I spent in Oklahoma City, however, the more I came to appreciate how perceptive O'Connor had been. The city had indeed been "born again," it became "new" in important ways. It was a city that found itself in the company of other communities forever changed by acts of violence. "Sometimes," wrote sociologist Kai Erickson, "the tissues of community can be damaged in much the same way as the tissues of mind and body." Like the communities Erickson studied, victimized and defined by environmental disaster, the bombing became central to the city's identity.[2]

The bombing brought into being a new world of social relationships and groups. It gave birth to a commemorated community of the dead, a community of family members, survivors, and eventually rescuers, and to their subgroups, each with particular interests and issues to engage. "Trauma shared," observed Erickson, creates a "spiritual kinship," which functions as a "source of commonality in the same way that common languages and common cultural backgrounds can." There is no better place to appreciate "trauma shared" in a new community than the Family Assistance Center (FAC), also known as the Compassion Center, at First Christian Church, which was created only several hours after the bombing.[3]

Ray Blakeney, director of operations for Oklahoma's Office of the Chief Medical Examiner, recalled that early reports from the site projected perhaps five hundred casualties. Blakeney, who had attended and then taught a course in preparedness for mass death situations at the National Emergency Training Center in Emmittsburg, Maryland, said, "I knew that unless we found a place to gather information and inform people of their loved one's fate, it would be a chaotic situation. We needed someplace big with parking, near downtown but separate from the site." Among those he asked to look for an appropriate location was Tom Demuth, president of the Oklahoma Funeral Director's Association, who had been certified by the Federal Emergency Management Agency (FEMA) as a mass casualty disaster coordinator. Demuth talked with Don Alexander, senior minister of First Christian Church, several blocks north of the Murrah site. The church has a domed sanctuary, a large hall and theater, and several floors of offices and class-rooms. Demuth asked, "Could we use your dining room to interview family members for assistance in gathering identification materials and taking missing person reports?" By late afternoon of April 19, two hundred people were at the church, by early evening there were over five hundred. "We set up some tables," Demuth recalls, "and twenty-five funeral directors were there. We all felt overwhelmed. We had no earthly idea that it would grow as it did."[4]

Funeral directors met families as they arrived at the church, and some—desperate to believe that their loved one was alive and expecting only to fill out a missing person's report—reacted angrily. One woman complained to the media about "vulture funeral directors." "We were there as representatives of the medical examiner's office, not trying to drum up business for ourselves," Demuth recalled, "so we quickly took off our funeral director's badges. We were creating something new at the church. This wasn't an airplane disaster where people pretty much know everyone is dead. People weren't prepared for our presence."[5]

Many family members had been searching frantically at various hospitals, hoping for some news, and when they arrived at the FAC, they were asked to provide information that might help in identification. "It was chaotic," Demuth said. "It was indeed like another world in the church, with hundreds of people confused, in shock, angry, frightened, starving for any morsel of information. People were stoic, they were hysterical, it was an unforgettable and painful scene. People begged us for information, but we didn't have much, and we were almost as shell-shocked as they were."

By the morning of April 20, the church had become a major crisis center, with the Red Cross, Salvation Army, and other services setting up to assist families. The National Guard and Oklahoma City police provided security in the parking lot and the building. The media, already numbering in the hundreds, were sequestered in the theater, and family members could decide whether to talk with them or not. (The previous evening, some reporters had wandered freely, asking what were widely perceived as intrusive questions, angering many. Even after the press was isolated, however, a well-known talk show host tried to sneak into the family area dressed as a priest.)[6]

Hundreds of clergy, mental health workers, church volunteers, members of the public, the media, and the inevitable gawkers threatened to over-whelm any orderly process. On Wednesday evening, for example, there were approximately thirty-six people working with families; by Thursday morning there were more than three hundred. Blakeney met with representatives of every agency that morning. "I had to lay down the law. I said that funeral directors had more experience than anyone there in working with families, and if you can't work with them, leave." (One person did.) That morning, the Red Cross took over the minute-to-minute managing of the FAC and the process of death notification took shape.

Blakeney spoke with family members at 9:30 Thursday morning. "By that time the parking lot was completely full, there were well over a thousand people in the meeting area. I stood up on a chair in the middle of the crowd with a microphone, and told people that my presence did not mean that their loved ones were dead, but that there were many deaths. I told them about the recovery process. There was not a sound in the room. The emotion was overwhelming, and I began to cry and as much as I told myself, 'Ray, you have to be strong,' it didn't work. It was an overwhelming moment, and I cried for a couple of minutes. Of course, almost everyone else started crying as well. In retrospect, perhaps it was the most human response at that time. The families knew how much this had affected those of us burdened with working through this disaster. I told them that some of them might be at the church for a very long time, perhaps two or three weeks, and I promised that I would come daily for morning and afternoon briefings, and that they would get information before anyone else, and I kept that promise."

The medical examiner's office wanted to begin releasing bodies to family members and funeral homes on the afternoon of April 20 (only eighteen bodies, mainly children, were recovered on April 19). Consequently, it was imperative that a notification process be put in place quickly. The military did their own notification for families. For others, information went to representatives at the FAC. Families checked in each day when they arrived at the church, were assigned tables and escorts (Red Cross volunteers), and were taken on an elevator to small rooms on the fourth floor to be told their loved one had been identified. Death notification teams usually included two representatives from the medical examiner's office, a mental health professional, and a member of the clergy. Tom Demuth was a member of the team that made the first notification—to the family of Pamela Argo, who had been a customer in the Social Security office. "We all agreed on the language we should use, that their loved one had been 'positively identified as dead.' I told the family how she had been identified, and we began releasing bodies to the funeral home of their choice. We took extraordinary care not to be funeral directors at that point. We were doing a job for the medical examiner's office. As funeral directors, when we meet families, they know that their loved one is dead, but in the bombing, we were telling them this news, and it was difficult." Families soon learned, of course, what a call to go upstairs meant, and others with whom they had shared the long vigil would say to them, "your wait is over."

Dr. Elinor Lottinville, an Oklahoma City psychologist and past president of the Mental Health Association of Oklahoma City, had helped in the aftermath of the murder of postal workers in Edmond, Oklahoma, several years earlier, and she had gone through disaster training herself. She matched up death notification teams and described how jarring it was for families when a long and agonizing vigil was transformed into an intense process of death notification. "All of a sudden we would receive word that a family was on the elevator coming up. None of us had ever done anything quite like this before, so we were scrambling to find what we needed: plastic wastebaskets for people who got sick, medical people for those who passed out, telephone directories so people could call funeral homes (they had twenty-four hours to decide what they wanted to do with the body) and we had to set up special telephone lines so people could call relatives or friends anywhere in the country."[7]

Several unfortunate incidents were caused by reckless rumormongering among the media, reports that persons had been identified who in fact had not been. On several occasions family members had their hopes raised by hearing on television that their loved one was alive in a hospital, only to find out it wasn't so. "I had to go to the press and read them the riot act," said Blakeney.

After a few days, people began to ask whether or not remains would be found, not if someone would be found alive. "I had a real fear that we would not find all the babies," Blakeney recalled. "We knew that they were in the cribs, almost directly over the Ryder truck, and every day during my visits, a mother would raise her hand and ask, 'Mr. Blakeney, did you find any babies today'? We found her baby on the fifteenth day, and everyone was relieved. We knew that if we found one, we would find others, and by ten that evening we found the last two babies." For parents, the agony of dealing with the bodies of their children did not always end with death notification. Six months after the bombing, Blakeney had to call Kathleen Treanor, whose in-laws and four-year-old daughter, Ashley, had been killed in the bombing. Ashley's hand had been identified well after her burial, and Blakeney had to ask Treanor what she wanted to do. "We decided to bury it in an urn near the body. Even though it was a horrible episode," Treanor recalled, "it was also a blessing from God. I didn't yet accept that she was really dead and I told myself I needed to eventually look at the photograph of her body. After this, I didn't need to." Given the grim condition of many of the bodies, Treanor said, "This saved me from something I probably couldn't have handled."[8]

At 11:30 P.M. on May 4, Oklahoma City fire chief Gary Marss halted rescue efforts, with three bodies still remaining in the rubble. The area in which they were located could not be reached safely, and they could not be recovered until the building was imploded on May 23. "We recovered many on that last day and night of work, but not everyone," Blakeney said. "It was the worst night of my life. I was supposed to tell people who had waited so long that we could not recover their loved ones. I told Tom Demuth, 'Tom, I can't do it,' and he said he would."

Demuth talked with the families of Christy Rosas and Virginia Thompson, both of whom worked in the Federal Employees Credit Union. "I told them that we knew that bodies had often fallen straight down, so we knew where they were, but we could not reach them safely." The area was spray painted fluorescent orange so that when the building came down, recovery teams would know where to look. The Thompson family had been the first to arrive at the FAC on April 19, and for Demuth, "telling them that they had to wait was the hardest thing I've ever had to do. I said a prayer and went in the room. All three of the Thompson children came up and hugged me. And then they waited for seventeen days." On May 6, 1995, the day after official recovery efforts ended, family members were brought to the site for a memorial service. Phillip Thompson recalls that his family was allowed a short time at the site alone, and fire chief Gary Marss showed him where they believed his mother's remains were buried. He and his brother put on hard hats and walked on a layer of roses to lay a cross of flowers on the spot. "I recall the most intense pain and grief," Thompson said, "and I began a kind of healing the next day." After the implosion, the area was dug out by hand, until the remains of Thompson's mother, along with the other two people, were recovered.[9]

Many of the family members with whom I spoke emphasized the extraordinary nature of the community at First Christian Church. People usually sat at the same tables each day, often adorned with photographs or flowers. Families offered support to each other. Even though family members were required to leave the church immediately after going through the notification process, several quietly returned later to remain with those still waiting. For two weeks, there were over five hundred people in the church each day, taking part in a process designed by various professionals, who were often waging their own turf battles while carrying out their responsibilities to family members.

Dr. David Hockensmith, Jr. senior minister at the Village Christian (Disciples) Church, served on death notification teams and escorted families from the fourth floor to their car to protect them from the media. He recalled that the Red Cross and some mental health workers ignited a controversy by insisting that clergy would not be part of the notification teams. Finally they relented to include clergy who had a seminary degree. However, "Jack Poe, chief of chaplains for the Oklahoma City police department, insisted that family members needed their clergy whether they had seminary degrees or not, and he won that battle."[10]

Issues of quality control and professional hierarchy also plagued mental health workers. "We were overwhelmed with people claiming some sort of expertise in mental health," Lottinville remembered, "and we had to be very careful about credentialing people to work with us." Dr. John Tassey, an Oklahoma City clinical psychologist and director of the Health Psychology Clinic at the Oklahoma City Veterans Affairs Medical Center, worked at the Murrah site and also helped set up the process at the FAC. He recalled someone arriving from another state and insisting that he be assigned to a death notification team because he had written about it and therefore was an authority. Unwilling to take "no" for an answer, he had to be escorted from the church by police. "We found that any number of people, particularly some of those who came to Oklahoma City [disaster vultures, Tassey called them], wanted to gain credibility by working here. Their credibility in the future would be their claim to have worked in Oklahoma City."[11]

The behavior of some of the mental health professionals at the FAC was harshly criticized. Tom Demuth, for example, said that "while we were trying to develop the notification process, who should be there, how should we handle this, some of the mental health workers were busy counseling each other in seemingly endless debriefing sessions." David Hockensmith, Jr. and Don Alexander have similar recollections. "I remember lots of early turf battles among mental health workers," said Hockensmith, "and I remember one instance when they left a family alone so they could debrief with each other." Alexander spoke of some mental health people passing out cards among families, "like money changers in the temple," he said.

In fact, a grief industry descended on Oklahoma City immediately after the bombing. Some local psychiatrists and psychologists—Elinor Lottinville, for example—welcomed the support, albeit with mixed feelings. "We needed outsiders to come in, because often we didn't know when we were completely exhausted. There were problems, however, because in addition to many well-trained people, we had quasi-mental health folks arrive, and in the chaos of those early days, there was simply no way to weed out all of them."

Others, however, offered a harsher assessment. Dr. James Allen, professor in the department of psychiatry and behavioral sciences and chief of child-adolescent mental health services at the University of Oklahoma Health Sciences Center in Oklahoma City, was "horrified" by the grief industry that grew "after the first puff of smoke." Groups rushed in, he said, "determined to teach us how to take care of this. I recall a group that had just come from their own traumatic experience working an air disaster. They were in no condition to help anyone. They came here to help and ended up doing therapy on themselves. Their good intentions were greater than their clinical abilities and sometimes made things worse."[12]

John Tassey was also critical. "Too many people didn't wait to be asked if we needed them. It was a real problem, logistically. How do you deploy them? What were their motives for coming? It was offensive for many of us to hear outside people assume the role of oracle," Tassey said, "for example, 'we did this and this after the earthquake,' and we reminded them that we had not had an earthquake, that the problems we were facing were altogether different." One psychologist, Tassey recalled, "had worked in the aftermath of Hurricane Andrew and insisted that women here drink lots of cranberry juice to avoid urinary tract infections. We hadn't been in a hurricane either, and somehow it escaped him that we were not bereft of essentials, like clean water."

Medicalized Grief[13]

Various mental health resources were available to people immediately after the bombing through churches, through the Red Cross, individual practitioners (both those whose professional lives were rooted in Oklahoma and those who brought various "specialties" to the city), and the federally funded Project Heartland, which was, according to the American Psychological Association, "the first community mental health program funded by FEMA/CMHS [Federal Emergency Management Agency/Center for Mental Health Services] that was designed to intervene with the survivors of a major terrorist event in the United States."[14]

Project Heartland's final report, issued in May 1998, illustrates the massive mental health response to the bombing. The project's life had three phases. The immediate services grant phase (May 9, 1995-October 31, 1995) offered "crisis counseling, crisis intervention, support groups, outreach, consultation, and education to individuals who were affected by emotional or physical proximity to the bombing." In the outreach/recovery phase (November 1, 1995-December 31, 1996) the project offered services to "specific, targeted populations" through subcontracts with various organizations, for example, public school systems, counseling centers, Associated Catholic Charities (which provided services to Asian and refugee communities), Cope, Inc., which offered services to African Americans, and the Latino Community Development Agency. The criminal trials phase (January 1, 1997-February 28, 1998) helped family members, survivors, and rescue workers prepare for "potentially upsetting trial testimony and evidence or the possibility of 'not guilty' verdicts, as well as assisting in the development of coping skills which would enable the clients to better handle upsetting information which was to be presented during the course of the trials." By February 1998, "an unduplicated count of 8,868 individuals received counseling, support group, and crisis intervention ... totaling 41,419 sessions and 51,319 hours of service."[15]

There were, some thought, far too many mental health providers in Oklahoma City. James Allen recalls "caregivers fighting over patients" because "there were simply not enough to go around." John Tassey observed that the great challenge—sometimes met, sometimes not—was ensuring "access, quality, and confidentiality." Indeed, Project Heartland's report noted that many young counselors "had no experience with death or its related issues. Their previous employment had been as case managers with the seriously and persistently mentally ill. . . . To say they were traumatized by the stories they heard is an understatement."[16]

The dominant diagnosis of and treatment for the invisible wounds caused by the bombing was expressed through the language of psychology, which provided a traumatic vision for treatment of the impact of violence. This vision transformed an act of mass terrorism into the source of a disease, posttraumatic stress disorder (PTSD). The condition was recognized in the late 1970s, emerging out of the work of Vietnam veterans and several prominent antiwar psychiatrists and psychologists convinced that this particular war gave rise, in psychiatrist Robert Jay Lifton's term, to "atrocity producing situations" that sparked intense trauma among veterans, with severe ramifications both for themselves and the society to which they returned. The condition was accepted as an "official" mental disorder by the American Psychiatric Association in 1980, when it listed PTSD in the third edition of its *Diagnostic and Statistical Manual* (DSM-III). In an era that witnessed the growing power of identity politics, a segment of the antiwar movement could organize around PTSD with war-related trauma as the defining experience.[17]

PTSD quickly became a template to treat those suffering from the impact of various forms of violence. For Judith Herman, associate clinical professor of psychiatry at Harvard Medical School, the experiences of Vietnam veterans illustrated the reality of PTSD and made it possible to uncover the hidden life of the disorder among survivors of rape, domestic abuse, and incest. "The most common post-traumatic disorders," she argued, "are those not of men in war but of women in civilian life." In recent years, the term has expanded to include not only the aftereffects of acts of violence but also other stressful situations: divorce, loss of job, or even loss of a pet.[18]

In Oklahoma City, some mental health professionals thought the diagnosis was used too often. It seemed too indiscriminate. It lumped together not only people traumatized by loss of a loved one or those who faced horrific work at the site, handling body parts, for example, but also those in the community and beyond who had no direct link to the horrors of the event but were seemingly "traumatized" in some fashion. It was convenient for professionals to find an epidemic of PTSD. One Oklahoma City psychiatrist said, "There was grant money galore to study PTSD, so naturally, the numbers of those diagnosed with the illness grew. There was no grant money to study the chronic suffering that this event brought about, however."

Oklahoma City psychologist Kay Goebel, a long-time member of the board of directors of the Oklahoma City National Memorial Foundation, worried about how a diagnosis of PTSD could create illness out of what could also be understood as a normal human reaction to violent loss. "When the memorial task force was put together in the summer of 1995," she recalled, "I spoke strongly against naming one of the committees 'families, survivors, and victims.' I thought the use of the term 'victim' was not in anyone's best interest. We should not be about creating more victims through the power of diagnostic names, because people can live out a diagnosis they are given. I think that being labeled as suffering from PTSD made some people more troubled than they otherwise would have been."[19]

No one was arguing, of course, that people whose loved ones had died in the bombing had not suffered a horrendous loss—an experience that would qualify as "traumatic" by anyone's standard. At the same time, however, there was a growing sense of unease about the way in which the language of "trauma" and "PTSD" was increasingly used to describe the emotions and reactions of people who had no personal ties with the actual victims of the bombing. And there was unease with the idea that these experiences were being translated into an official or authoritative language of suffering by "trauma experts."

This "traumatic vision" of the events, experiences, and reactions offered an alternative or at least an adjunct to the language of civic renewal or religious redemption. Unlike more traditional languages of suffering, sorrow, and hope, it did not speak of sin or injustice but of damaged psyches and indigestible memories. This worldview, the "traumatic vision," was clearly the authoritative public "scientific" language of suffering. Consequently, the bombing was widely perceived to have engendered a crisis of memory, not soul or spirit, and it was only the new "priest" of our time, the medical expert, who laid claim to ownership—meaning correct interpretation—of the traumatic memory. PTSD, argued Arthur Kleinman, professor of medical anthropology and psychiatry at Harvard University, "medicalizes problems as psychiatric conditions that elsewhere and for much of human history in the West have been appreciated as religious or social problems."[20]

This traumatic vision revealed a self that was intrinsically weak, passive, seemingly helpless amid the onslaughts of traumatic events, "a mind waiting to be smitten," said Allan Young, historian of traumatic memory and medical anthropologist at McGill University. This sense of the passive self is a major component in the construction of the victim as a wounded and privileged voice.

This passive sense of self is also evident in the traumatic vision's transformation of those who have experienced political violence. Someone "first becomes a victim," Kleinman observes, "an image of innocence and passivity, someone who cannot represent himself. . . . Then he becomes a patient. . . . Indeed, to receive even modest public assistance it may be necessary to undergo a sequential transformation from one who experiences, who suffers political terror, to one who is a victim of political violence, to one who is sick, who has a disease."[21]

This transformation removes the consequences of political violence from the public world into the realm of intimate relations between a doctor and a patient. The focus is on the struggle within an individual mind, and the social dimension of violence is ignored. Would we think differently about the causes and consequences of violence if we understood people in Oklahoma City to be a "greatly heterogeneous category of social sufferers," rather than patients or victims? Perhaps we would not read their trauma stories as symptomatic of illness but as narratives of moral witness, as testimony.[22]

Henry Greenspan's comments about the testimony ("modes of recounting") of Holocaust survivors seems appropriate for many in Oklahoma City as well. Psychiatric approaches to survivors' symptoms, he writes, "are typically viewed as the sequelae of traumatic experience: the result to be explained." However, understanding these expressions as life stories, Greenspan writes, "symptoms stand at the beginning of our attempts to understand." If we do not perceive these individuals through the lenses of the traumatic vision—as passive victims or patients whose words of anger, sorrow, outrage, and confusion are reduced to illness narratives—their words might register as moral testimony—public rhetoric—about the shattering personal and social impact of violence.[23]

Social suffering is more than a problem of repressed and parasitic memories that haunt individuals; it is also evidence of what was widely felt as the traumatic loss of a particular way of being in the world. "The experience of suffering," Kleinman writes, "is interpersonal, involving lost relationships, the brutal breaking of intimate bonds, collective fear, and an assault on loyalty and respect among family and friends."[24]

In Oklahoma City, people grieved over the loss of life rhythms: waving to the same person on their way to work, sharing work space and personal relationships with friends and colleagues. People grieved over the symbolic loss of a city and an America that was no more. As we have seen, the bombing was perceived to have destroyed an era of innocence, and people grieved over its passing. Although expressions of innocence were breathtaking in their naïveté at the end of the twentieth century, a very real sense of loss was felt in Oklahoma City and beyond.

There was a sense of profound disorientation among those struggling to make moral sense of the bombing in a culture that both glorifies individual life and at the same time devalues it. American culture celebrates violence—murders in popular film, serial killer and victim trading cards, serial killer Web sites and heavy metal music, and "faces of serial killers . . . on T-shirts sold through a mail-order catalogue devoted to murder memorabilia"—yet is horrified by graphic spectacles of mass violence such as the bombing in Oklahoma City.[25]

Perhaps a sense of cultural disorientation is shared by those struggling with what Lawrence Langer called the "revision of the myth of civilized being" in the face of mass violence. Human nature, he wrote, "can no longer be set in opposition to inhuman nature, as if one were the norm and the other a correctable atrocity. Atrocity in the form of violence . . . has become a 'normal' rather than a pathological expression of the self—not all selves, to be sure, but enough to cause us to question ancient premises about moral instincts and spiritual purpose."[26]

To raise questions about the traumatic vision is not to minimize the searing loss experienced by so many in Oklahoma City or to question the benefits that mental health professionals brought to many. But even among the "core constituency" of those most at risk for the "disease" of PTSD, the labels "victim" and "patient" did not always sit well. Conversely, some let these labels define their postbombing identities, impoverishing their sense of self. Too many life histories were conveniently erased by the bombing, many people's troubles seemingly emerging only after April 19, 1995. Too many were characterized too easily as suffering from PTSD. But the traumatic vision could not account for the distinctively local context in which the bombing took place, nor could it account for the wider cultural struggles that emerged.

The traumatic vision was also alluring because it promised resolution: suffering can end, traumatic memories can be engaged and robbed of their assaultive power. In this view, suffering was seen as abnormal, and a prolonged state of grieving as pathological. The widespread notion that PTSD was a disease that could be cured (that there was, in fact, little that could not be "fixed" after the bombing) led to a simplistic pop psychology. Solemn media pronouncements referred to "the healing process" that would eventually lead to "closure" (a word many in Oklahoma City came to detest). Popular cultural metaphors of disease (e.g., drugs are a cancer destroying the nation) were replaced in the case of Oklahoma City by the image of a traumatic wound. Wounds, of course, are treated differently than cancer or viruses.

The implosion of the Murrah Building on May 23 led to numerous suggestions that the city had "healed," that the event was "over." *USA Today* informed its readers that "for residents, demolition will mean closure." The host of National Public Radio's *All Things Considered* told his audience that "true closure is still far away" (implying that it is clearly attainable). Trade journals were full of the language of pop psychology. *Demolition Age* reported that the implosion "helped bring the nation some closure." *Construction News* told its readers that the implosion laid the "Oklahoma City nightmare to rest." The *Engineering News-Record* observed that the implosion was a "catharsis for the American People" and that it was "time to begin the healing process and start a new chapter in Oklahoma City."[27]

Reporting for ABC News on July 4, 1995, Dean Reynolds combined the language of exorcism ("on the seventy-seventh day after the bombing that shook America, the people of Oklahoma City tried to expel the ghosts of April 19 by raising the flag") with the astonishing judgment that "the mourning process is over here.... The healing process has really just begun." And after Terry Nichols was sentenced on December 23, 1997, a CNN correspondent asked Bud Welch, whose daughter had been murdered, "can you get closure out of this?"[28]

Psychologist John Tassey offered the most charitable interpretation of the media's use of these terms, suggesting that news people had an interest in writing about the psychological dimension of the event but no real understanding of how to do it. Consequently, they took refuge in simplistic terms. Others were more critical. According to columnist Ellen Goodman, these words had "spread across the post-mortem landscape like a nail across my blackboard." These words suggested, she argued, that "loss is something to get over—according to a prescribed emotional timetable." In *City Business New Orleans*, columnist Errol Laborde wrote, "In a culture that gives priority to the quick cure, the hard truth is that there are some wounds that will just never heal."[29]

The language of healing and closure revealed a need to systematize and regulate mourning, particularly after violent mass death. In the days following the bombing the *Daily Oklahoman* showered readers with the "stages of grief," telling them to look for signs of normal or abnormal grief. The newspaper passed on one of the problematic assumptions of traumatic culture, that Elizabeth Kubler-Ross's description of the stages of dying—helpful in working with the terminally ill—constitute a template that also applies to those who suffer the effects of any number of events that might register as traumatic.

The widespread conviction that grief has "stages," that "healing" (a free-floating term that can mean getting on with one's life, satisfaction that the perpetrators were brought to justice, or relief that the pain is becoming less overpowering) is a "process"; and that suffering can neatly be brought to "closure" often had insidious consequences in Oklahoma City.

Government agencies each had their own regulations regarding leaves of absence for survivors. While some agencies were patient when their people returned and struggled in their jobs, others expected them to be "over it" when they came to work. There seemed throughout the city—indeed throughout the culture—an unspoken statute of limitations on mourning. The failure to "get on with it" or "be back to your old self" after a prescribed period indicated, according to the traumatic vision, the presence of an illness and the need for treatment. However much time the bereaved was "given," in Oklahoma City moreover, the unspoken message was, "your grieving process should be over by such-and-such a time. If it is not, you are not grieving intensely, you are ill."[30]

The need to regulate mourning led not only to pathologizing any condition of mourning that violated term limits but also to labeling as "normal" expressions of grief that were emotionally contained. By contrast, explosive manifestations of grief that violated the behavioral protocols of public culture were labeled as abnormal. During a death notification at the FAC, for example, "an African American family came into the room and was informed of a positive identification," David Hockensmith, Jr. remembered. "The mother fell to the floor, wailing and writhing on the ground in her grief. The mental health folks thought immediately of sedating her. They literally went to get the needles, but we were able to stop them."

Perhaps what I have characterized as the traumatic vision is really another kind of consolatory narrative. As we have seen, the story of both civic renewal and religious redemption envisioned a newly redeemed society emerging out of the wreckage of the bombing. So too the traumatic narrative offers a form of redemption for individual trauma. But only the toxic narrative deals with the reality of the chronic affliction. Only it is willing to consider that, in Lawrence Langer's words, violent mass death is "an event to be endured, not a trauma to be healed." (Compare that sentiment with the upbeat words of a Project Heartland publication one year after the bombing: "Resolution means you will be able to put your life back together and feel more like yourself again.") If we have learned anything from those struggling with the impact of violence it is that there is rarely an "old" self to be put back together, only a new self to be shaped out of the mix of newly shattering experience that blends with one's life history, a condition characterized in Oklahoma City as the "new normal."[31]

In a sensitive portrayal of his family's struggle in the aftermath of the attempted rape of his wife, Jamie Kalven reflected on the inadequacy of the traumatic vision to engage the reality of the chronic condition. "Literature deals uncertainly with endurance. Matters of sustained effort, of staying put and standing fast. Daily efforts that build into weeks, months, years, life-times. The conventions by which we recognize and understand stories—dramatic conflicts and defining moments, reversals of expectations and denouements—are poorly adapted to the task of rendering that which is strenuously ongoing.... And a violent act fascinates us in a way that the life-time of grieving and healing (or failing to heal) it sets in motion does not."[32]

Some family members and survivors quite consciously rejected being transformed into a patient or victim. One survivor recalled feeling "an abyss opening in the months after the bombing and I almost succumbed to its seductiveness. I caught myself because I remember my fifteen-year-old cry-ing, saying, 'Dad, you sound different.' Hard as it was, I had a responsibility to my children and wife not to be a victim!" Dr. Brian Espe, a veterinarian for the Department of Agriculture widely recognized because of his dramatic descent from the wreckage of the Murrah Building on a fire truck ladder, never attended meetings of various survivors' groups. "They didn't fill a need for me," he said. "I am a survivor and not a victim, and my philosophy is to get on with life."[33]

Some family members resented the overwhelming presence of the grief industry. Pam Whicher, for example, said that "when counselors and 'trauma sessions' descend en masse to people affected by this kind of horror there is not time to let individuals deal with their feelings in their own way. I wanted and needed time to sort out for myself what I was feeling. The intent I am sure, is to ease mental anguish and prevent psychological 'damage.' You can-not incorporate this type of experience if people are telling you 'we're gonna fix it.' Early intervention should leave people the heck alone for a little while."[34]

Many grieving people in Oklahoma City understood that there would be no resolution to the suffering brought about by mass murder. They also understood, however, that they had the option of making suffering meaningful by rejecting the passive sense of self nurtured by the traumatic vision and taking an active role in the reshaping of self and community.

Active Grief

Active grief was expressed in many ways. Some people both grieved—and postponed grieving—by returning immediately to work. Some turned to the creative arts to express themselves. Some used the media for commemorative purposes as much as the media used them as cultural commodities. Many sought solace in joining new communities of the bereaved, and some became active in the victims rights movement, in habeas corpus reform, and in implementing critical incident stress management techniques for those who might face disasters in the future. Some practiced active and private forms of mourning, and some turned to the work of creating a national memorial.

Florence Rogers, the CEO of the Federal Employees Credit Union, began a meeting with seven members of her staff in her office in the Murrah Building at 8:40 A.M. on April 19. "I don't recall an explosion," she said, "although I do remember a lot of noise. A whirlwind jerked me around with its force. It sucked me out of my chair and slammed me against the floor and wall where the credenza had been. . . . Walls and ceilings had disappeared. My employees vanished. My desk was gone. Everything had dropped into a gaping abyss just inches away." Eighteen credit union employees and two board members were killed in the blast, and ten injured. Miraculously, Rogers escaped with minor injuries and attended an emergency board meeting that afternoon.[35]

Immediate action was necessary because the credit union served more than 15,000 members around the world from the Oklahoma City office, but its information technology had been destroyed. "Hundreds of thousands of dollars in checks, traveler's checks, and cash vanished into the smoldering rubble." For Rogers, "money was not high on my priority list when I limped into that meeting a few hours later. My heart ached for all my lost coworkers and closest friends, yet we had to find the funds entrusted to us. . . . Our members would need access to their accounts; money to see them through the crisis of funeral expense, emergency bills, groceries and living expenses."

With the help of comptroller Raymond Stroud and data processing specialist Brad Grant, volunteers from other area credit unions, and the FBI, which recovered most of the money from the rubble, Rogers opened the credit union at a new location forty-eight hours after the bombing. Stroud recalls "the phones were ringing off the hook throughout the whole day, and five hundred members visited the emergency site." Rogers and others worked and went to many funerals. She "didn't cry until early August."

Not surprisingly, Rogers, who serves on the board of the Oklahoma City National Memorial Foundation, became a symbol of courage and endurance, and she has traveled throughout the United States, Canada, and Australia talking about her experience. "People ask me, 'How did you go on, how do you come to work every day after losing so many people?' It's a fair question, I suppose. How do you go on? Yet at times it also seems like a silly question. If the alternative is not to go on, then there is no alternative."

One of the cultural casualties of the bombing was the annual Festival of the Arts in Oklahoma City, which attracts more than 700,000 visitors and approximately 150 artists from around the nation. Its cancellation ignited intense controversy. Betty Price, executive director of the state Arts Council, recalled "a lot of people felt as if it would have been dancing on the graves of those killed. Some of us believed that the arts could help people deal with the bombing. The arts can be a wonderful way to express oneself, but it was premature to think about this within days of the bombing." Jackie Jones, executive director of the city's Arts Council, agreed, observing several weeks after the bombing that "we've certainly seen how critical the arts are to a situation like this, how necessary they are to help people express themselves in picture form, in poetry, in song."[36]

Exactly six months after the bombing, 127 family members had the opportunity to grieve through the arts. They had responded to an invitation from the Oklahoma Arts Institute to attend a four-day workshop with professional artists from around the nation at Quartz Mountain retreat center in Lone Wolf, Oklahoma. Participants wrote personal essays and poetry, learned Cherokee basket weaving, made memory boxes, and created music and dance. "The goal," observed Dr. James Allen, "was not to do therapy but to help people transform their experiences and to give them significance.... It gave them permission to mourn and to get on with their lives, to connect with the health in themselves, to use their own resources and those of the community, and to integrate back into their communities without defining themselves as 'mental patients.'"[37]

In one of the workshops, for example, artist Tim Rollins—who works with at-risk teens in the Bronx, New York—asked his group of teenagers to read the first and last chapters of Stephen Crane's *The Red Badge of Courage* before the workshop began and then asked them to paint their own badges of courage: "heraldic shields, flags representing the nations of the heart—all self-portraits. Some used dark, moody colors, others chose bright, celebrating colors. I had thought they might paint their wounds but instead the images which evolved were more like planets or suns." Reflecting on the significance of Quartz Mountain, Rollins wrote, "We made something beautiful out of something that was horrible. It is very important for us to make beautiful things in times of tragedy, as only beauty can change things. The most direct way we can make beauty is to create art."[38]

The intense media activity in Oklahoma City lasted for weeks after the bombing and then reappeared at several anniversaries, particularly the first and fifth (when the outdoor memorial was dedicated), and during the trials of Timothy McVeigh and Terry Nichols. The horror stories about media behavior abounded: stories about, for example, the seemingly endless "how do you feel" questions that struck many as a blatant example of media insensitivity. Fred Anderson, whose wife, Rebecca, was killed during early rescue efforts, agreed to an interview with a Tulsa television reporter shortly before the implosion and was asked on camera why he was still wearing his wedding ring. "When I got questions like this, I just wouldn't say anything. I shouldn't have to do that." There were oft repeated stories of reporters and their cameramen sneaking through bushes at the medical examiner's office where bodies were taken, sneaking into hospital rooms or funerals. The image of "the media" was often that of a voracious shark, swimming through grief-filled waters, consuming and spewing out for its viewers the personal and communal agonies of the city. The media was sequestered in the FAC and was kept at some distance during anniversaries and the trials. Family members and survivors could agree to interviews in media space, but journalists could not mingle freely among those mourning.[39]

Some family members and survivors were, even in the early hours and days after the bombing, adept at dealing with the media. Credit Union employee Patti Hall, who endured sixteen surgeries and is on permanent disability, recalled early media attention. "Like others, I appeared on *Good Morning America* and talked with a variety of reporters. I was a commodity, and I knew it would end." Kathleen Treanor, who lost her in-laws and her daughter Ashley, received more than three hundred phone calls the Saturday after the bombing. "We were one of two families who had lost three people. The media could get one-stop shopping with us."[40]

Immediately after the bombing, however, when Ashley was still classified as missing, Kathleen and Mike Treanor turned to local television stations, which were willing to air Ashley's photograph. Subsequently, Kathleen appeared on *Oprah Winfrey* and a number of other national shows. "It helped me tell the story," she said. "I wanted people to know who Ashley was, and what had been taken from us." "Many people were offering a kind of public eulogy," recalled Cheryl Scroggins, whose husband, Lanny, was killed in the bombing.[41]

Indeed, some family members used the media to make their grief communal in the broadest sense. Jannie Coverdale, whose two grandsons were killed in the Murrah day care center, said, "I made up my mind that I would introduce Aaron and Elijah to the world." Edye Smith Stowe, whose two sons Chase and Colton were also killed in the day care center, described her connection with the media as a "source of solace and healing." "It was my way of sharing my boys with the nation." She chose to allow television cameras in the church for their funeral, attended by 1,500 people. "I wanted the funeral to be public. At that point, I didn't know if I could have children again, but if I did I wanted them to see the funeral of their brothers." Many members of the media were, of course, moved by the suffering in Oklahoma City. Both local and national reporters developed ongoing relationships with family members and survivors, some of whom have placed photographs of various media figures in their homes and still receive letters and telephone calls from them on birthdays or near the anniversary of the bombing.[42]

Public eulogies brought solace for some. Just as the highly publicized deaths of public figures—from JFK to Princess Diana—created a bereaved community without boundaries, so too did the heart-rending stories told by family members. And just as this media-sparked bereaved community was formed, family members and survivors formed new communities to offer support to each other.

Marsha Kight was one of the most outspoken family members, insisting immediately—and sometimes angrily—on family involvement in the work of the memorial task force formed in July 1995. Her daughter, Frankie Merrill, was killed, leaving behind a five-year-old daughter. "During the first six months," she told me, "I was trying to destroy myself with alcohol. I wanted to reach in and pull my heart out, it hurt so bad. Finally, I got involved with the memorial task force and I also formed Family and Survivors United." The group approached several foundations, attempting to secure financial help for people who were having trouble. Some family members, Kight contended, "felt like second-class citizens." The group commissioned a commemorative angel figurine that raised enough money to support travel expenses for nineteen people to the trials in Denver, and it sent a thank-you videotape to rescue units around the nation.[43]

Members of wounded agencies also started support groups. Dr. Paul Heath, a psychologist with the Veterans Administration, organized the Oklahoma City Murrah Building Survivors Association, which held its first meeting, a Help Fair, at the First Methodist Church in July 1995. Heath figured prominently in media coverage for several years after the bombing. He said, "I angered some people by doing so much, and I probably did more than I should have, but it gave me a chance to give the association some recognition." The survivors association continues to meet and offer various programs, although attendance has diminished in recent years. "The biggest mistake of my life was selecting the name of the organization," Heath said. "I did it because of name recognition, and the hope that we could do fund-raising to help survivors, but it was perceived as leaving out survivors who were not in the Murrah Building, and we certainly did not mean to do that." For many survivors of the close-knit community in the Murrah Building, however, the association offered them the opportunity to support one another, to mourn losses together, and to struggle together with a host of issues.[44]

The grief and anger of some family members led them also into activist roles in public policy issues. Marsha Kight, for example, became a highly visible spokeswoman for the victims rights movement, calling attention to the struggles of family members and survivors who wished to participate fully in the trial of Timothy McVeigh, struggles that intensified public and congressional voices calling for a constitutional amendment to ensure the rights of victims of crime.

Since the mid-1960s, increasing attention has been paid to the victims of violent crime at state and federal levels. California established the first crime victim compensation program, and there are now numerous state and federal victim assistance programs, support systems, and public policy organizations, for example, Mothers Against Drunk Driving (MADD), and the National Organization for Victim Assistance (NOVA). Civic calendars have been augmented by victims rights weeks and rituals of protest ("take back the night" marches against rape and other forms of violence). The first bill of rights for crime victims was passed in Wisconsin in 1980, and by the year 2000 thirty more states had passed such legislation.

There were a number of reasons for the increasingly popular focus on victims' rights. It was an era when violent crime was rampant, when "tough on crime" measures were increasingly popular, when voices of Americans collectively affected by violence were raised more insistently, when the terms "victim" and "survivor" engendered a widely held popular conviction that those who had been immersed in or affected by acts of violence had important stories—moral, cautionary, horrific—to impart. It was also a time when the "sentimental solidarity of remembered victimhood" was crucial to contemporary identity, not only for ethnic Americans but also for victims of crime. Consequently, activist groups like Parents of Murdered Children, MADD, and family members of those killed in TWA 800 or Pan Am 103 all sought to bring about social change through legislative or judicial action.[45]

Not surprisingly, there was a strong collective identity among family members and survivors in Oklahoma City, and their anger was evident when the trials were moved to Denver from Oklahoma, a distance that prevented many people from attending. In the spring of 1996, after Judge Richard Matsch dismissed a motion filed by Oklahoma City attorney Karen Howick to broadcast the trial via closed-circuit television to a site in Oklahoma City, family members and survivors went to Washington, D.C., successfully lobbying members of Congress to pass legislation allowing the closed-circuit broadcast to proceed. After legislation sped its way through the system, Howick then filed a motion on behalf of approximately one hundred family members and survivors to move the broadcast from a room in the Oklahoma City federal courthouse that held 150 to the Federal Aviation Administration's 330-seat auditorium at the Will Rogers World Airport. Any sense of the successful "enfranchisement" of victims was short-lived, however, as family members and survivors soon learned that no seats were reserved for them in the courtroom: forty-five seats were reserved for the media, thirty-seven for the public, and sixteen for the defense. The government did give families their twelve seats.[46]

Congress again intervened on behalf of family members and survivors in an even more celebrated issue of victims' rights. During a pretrial hearing on a motion to suppress evidence on June 26, 1996, Judge Matsch informed family members and survivors—who were planning to offer impact testimony (to tell the court, in their own words, the effect of the bombing on their lives) if and when the sentencing phase of the trial took place—that they could not observe courtroom proceedings because such participation might influence their testimony. He gave them the lunch hour to make the decision. Being forced to choose between attending the trial and testifying was agonizing for many. "I felt like my life was a puzzle. My border was intact, but my insides were scattered. The only way to put the pieces back together was with information, to attend the trials," said Diane Leonard, whose husband, Don, a secret service agent, was killed. Paul Cassell, professor at the University of Utah College of Law, represented family members and survivors. He observed that "despite the pleas from the victims, the Department of Justice, 49 members of Congress, all six Attorneys General in the Tenth Circuit, and a number of the nation's leading crime victims organizations," all appeals were unsuccessful. Some left Denver and returned home. Some chose to observe the trial and give up the possibility of offering impact testimony. Some, like Diane Leonard and Marsha Kight, lobbied hard for changes in the law.[47]

"We had to turn to Congress, since the courts said we had no legal rights as victims," Kight recalled. The Victim Allocution Clarification Act of 1997 "clarified" rights of victims set forth in the 1990 Victims Rights and Restitution Act (better known as the Victims Bill of Rights). Theoretically, it gave victims the right both to observe trials and to offer impact testimony. The legislation once again sped through both houses of Congress and was signed into law by President Clinton on March 20, 1997, who said, "When someone is a victim, he or she should be at the center of the criminal justice process, not on the outside looking in."[48]

This legislation, however, did not end the struggle, as Judge Matsch reserved the right to rule on possible prejudicial impact after the trial. "The Department of Justice . . . met with many of the impact witnesses, advising them of these substantial uncertainties in the law, and noting that any observation of the trial would create the possibility of exclusion of impact testimony."[49]

For supporters of a victims' rights amendment to the Constitution, the struggles of family members and survivors during the trial showed that legislation alone would not ensure victims' rights. And if people were treated so badly in a highly publicized trial, "the treatment of victims in forgotten courtrooms and trials is certainly no better," Cassell argued, "and in all likelihood much worse." The call for a constitutional amendment, he stated, "is rooted in the simple idea that victims of crime, no less than perpetrators, have rights in the criminal process. It would give victims of violent crime the right to be notified of court hearings, to attend those hearings, and to speak on such issues as bail, plea bargaining, and sentencing. The amendment would require judges to consider the victims' safety before granting bail. Victims would also be entitled to a speedy trial, notification of an offender's release or escape, and restitution from a convicted offender."[50]

Marsha Kight was not, of course, the only family member or survivor who was active in this regard, but she was certainly one of the most prominent. Since the conclusion of the trials she has continued to be a forceful spokesperson for victims' rights, testifying before the Senate Judiciary Committee several times and taking a full-time position with NOVA in 1999. "My hope," she wrote, "is that the good which comes from this tragedy will shine as a beacon of hope for all victims of crime everywhere, and that it will act as the catalyst for positive change in American laws on victimization. That hope has yet to be realized."[51]

Diane Leonard and Glenn Seidl, whose wife, Kathy, was killed, joined other family members shortly after the bombing in lobbying successfully for habeas corpus reform that would do away with what they considered an interminable appeals process. It seemed to have become a stalling tactic for those convicted of murder and sentenced to die rather than a necessary judicial safeguard. Republicans had promoted this for some years, but legislation had been stalled in Congress until the bombing gave the movement new impetus. The day after the bombing, Oklahoma senator Don Nickles told CNN, "We need habeas corpus reform." Surprising many Democrats, President Clinton stated on *60 Minutes,* on April 23, only four days after the bombing, "I hope the Congress will pass a review and a reform of the habeas corpus provisions." Leonard, Seidl, and others lobbied lawmakers and in June 1995 held an emotional press conference outside the Capitol. They expressed their outrage that too many sentenced to death were using habeas corpus provisions to delay execution indefinitely. (Family members pointed, for example, to Roger Stafford, who had been convicted of murder but was still carrying out appeals seventeen years later.) Some family members wanted to make sure that similar delays would not take place if McVeigh or Nichols were sentenced to death. "I'm thankful and glad I did it," Seidl said. "I honestly feel we did make a difference."[52]

As part of sweeping antiterrorism legislation, President Clinton signed the Effective Death Penalty Act of 1996 into law on March 24, 1996. It was bitterly opposed by those who believed that habeas corpus reform took away the federal safety net for those convicted in state procedure. Some family members, Bud Welch, for example, were absolutely opposed to this legislation, believing that it rushed people to their death and increased the possibility of executing an innocent person. For Diane Leonard, however, this public work was part of her transformation. "I had been a shy sales representative, very uncomfortable speaking in public," she said. "I spoke at Don's funeral, and God put the words in my head and showed me that I could speak in front of a group, and that there were things I should do." In addition to her activity on habeas corpus reform, she joined police chaplain Jack Poe in writing grant proposals to carry out critical incident stress management workshops, lobbied for the Victims Clarification Act, and accepted a job with Drew Edmondson, Oklahoma's attorney general, as his office's first victim witness coordinator.[53]

Leonard also helped teach death notification procedures to police departments in Oklahoma City and Norman. "We need to think about how we do this in order to avoid doing any more damage than the news of violent death has already done," she said. She recalls her former passivity in the face of a funeral director who urged her not to view the body of her mother some years ago, and how she had regretted it. "Like many others, I suspect, I was simply not strong enough at a time like that to argue. I didn't view her body, and I had nightmares for a long time. When my husband was killed, I was strongly advised against seeing his body, but I knew I had to do it. He was in bad shape. He had no face, in fact his head looked like it had been scooped out, only the back of the skull was there. But I sat and held his hand and talked to him. It was an important time and an important act for me. I've had no nightmares." As in the realm of public policy, Leonard and other family members belied the traumatic vision of a passive self in publicly invisible yet very active ways of engaging violent death.

A number of family members and survivors immersed themselves in a memorial process that took shape in the summer of 1995. Doris Jones, whose pregnant daughter, Carrie Ann Lenz, was killed, recalled, "I wanted to do something, and I called the mayor's office and was told to call another family member who told me about the memorial meetings. The memorial process has been my therapy." Like Diane Leonard, Jones had been shy about speaking in public. After the bombing, however, she said, "I believe that Carrie is the driving force with me. She can't speak, so I have to speak for her."

Polly Nichols, who served as the executive director of the Oklahoma Foundation for Excellence—a nonprofit private foundation supporting public schools—was in her office in the Journal Record building and was severely wounded by the blast. Badly bleeding, she was carried out of the building and lay waiting for an ambulance on Fifth Street. "I didn't have many minutes left," she recalled, "and I was fortunate that a thoracic specialist was walking down the hall at the hospital. He was one of the few who could have saved my life."

Involved with the memorial task force from the beginning, Nichols focused on the campaign to raise funds for the memorial, having been instrumental, for example, in organizing the 168 Pennies campaign, which has raised funds from schoolchildren around the nation to pay for the children's memorial area. "I don't want the image of the bombed-out building to be what they remember," Nichols said. "I want them to know that there was an outpouring of goodness and hope."[54]

Many family members and survivors recall having an initial interest in a memorial. Chapter 5 tells the story of the memorial process, which resulted in an outdoor memorial dedicated on the fifth anniversary of the bombing, April 19, 2000, the Oklahoma City National Memorial Institute for the Prevention of Terrorism, and the Memorial Center, which includes a permanent exhibition and archival resources, dedicated on February 19, 2001.

Before we turn to that story, however, I want to focus on the avalanche of memorial activities that took place around the nation immediately after the bombing, and the tremendous variety of memorial suggestions that poured into Oklahoma City. People from around the world felt enfranchised to enter the lives of family members and survivors as if they were intimately acquainted. Through the media, part of the inner life of Oklahoma City became available to the public. The fascination with the spectacle of the bombing, the drama and pathos of following people's lives and their suffering, the vicarious drama and horror of the stories and images, threatened, attracted, and moved people to imagine themselves as part of an extended bereaved community. Just as work on the memorial task force was an important way for many family members and survivors to engage the bombing, the intense public outpouring of memorial expression was the means of engagement for the wider imagined bereaved community.

4

"A SINGLE CHORD OF HORROR":
THE MEMORIAL VOCABULARY
OF AMERICAN CULTURE

Four days after the bombing, on April 23, 1995, a Canadian social worker wrote a note to "Friends" in Oklahoma City: "In the face of this tragedy we are not two or three. WE are twenty million Canadians and two hundred million Americans entwined into a single cord of horror, disbelief and resolve that this will not happen again. THIS cord is truly strong and will prove unbreakable."

It is clear from reading many of the thousands of letters that poured into the mayor's and governor's offices, often simply addressed to "firefighters in Oklahoma City," "the woman who lost her two grandchildren," "the woman whose baby was carried by the fireman," or often just with a name that someone saw on television, that people took a measure of comfort in feeling themselves a part of an imagined bereaved community.

This sense of connection was clearly expressed in several poems. A woman from Fortuna, California, entitled her poem "Oklahoma City."

> *Grieving for no one I know,*
> *I awaken at 3 a.m.*
> *sobbing;*
> *the air*
> *laden*
> *with the sadness of multitudes.*

Life, like childhood, sacred, to be cherished,
is in an instant
crushed—deliberately.
The deaths linger in the air
like a pall
of black choking smoke
coast to coast
that all of us must breathe
collapsing the lungs of our soul
like thousands of pounds of concrete.

Reverend Mary McAnally, of Tulsa, Oklahoma, was attending the Presbyterian Consultation on Justice and Peace in Chicago, where she watched the memorial service, "Time for Healing." The third and fourth stanza of her poem, "Hope," read:

Hope is a frenetic Chicago O'Hare Airport,
Sunday afternoon, April 23, 1995.
A televised service from Oklahoma City
appears on all the TV monitors.
The President and Governor are introduced.
A choir starts to sing:

"Amazing Grace, how sweet the sound…"
I stand at my seat, alone, and add my voice:
"that saved a wretch like me…"
In ripples moving outward,
busy passengers drop their luggage,
stop in their tracks for a minute and add:
"I once was lost, but now am found…"
Computer terminals are silenced,
red caps and businessmen, commuters and children
sing: "was blind but now I see."
Hope is a busy airport.[1]

Perhaps one of the greatest attractions of a nationwide bereaved community is that it is one of the only ways Americans can imagine themselves as one; being "together" with millions of others through expressions of mourning bypasses or transcends the many ways in which people are divided—by religion, by ideology, by class, by region, by race, by gender. "We were for a moment once again family, outraged and heartbroken," President Clinton said. *U.S. News and World Report* expressed this when it published photographs of all those killed under the headline "An American Family."[2]

People felt connected to those victimized by the bombing for many reasons. Some focused their attention on the horror of the slaughter of children in the day care center. For others, the bombing sparked slumbering memories of traumatic events in their own lives. Letters from veterans of World War II, Korea, and Vietnam, from rape victims, and from those who had lost loved ones in accidents, illness, or acts of violence, bore witness to their own trauma and often offered the sober wisdom that people in Oklahoma City would emerge, but as different people, changed forever.[3]

For example, an artist in Chula Vista, California, wrote Governor Keating about the enduring pain of her infertility. "The years of sadness I experienced resurfaced when I saw the faces of those Oklahoma mothers.... Our grief, though very different, is similar in that it involved the loss of children and a family." She offered to donate a painting, hoping that it could be hung as a memorial or "used as an auctioning piece to raise money toward the efforts to rebuild your city."

Others reflected on their experiences with different disasters. Dr. Ron Anderson, president and chief executive officer of Parkland Memorial Hospital in Dallas, Texas, wrote Governor Keating, "I have assisted in the disaster plan implementation of two large airplane crashes. I understand what the rescue workers in Oklahoma City must be going through better than most.... Unlike their efforts, in Dallas we worked in an open field without the threat of falling debris, and while the dead and injured were all about, we did not have to literally crawl over victims or worry about a second bomb or structural collapse. Further, our evacuations and transport of the injured was over in literally a matter of hours. Still, many of our firefighters, policemen, and emergency physicians who addressed this tragedy on-site and in the care system will never fully put that terrible memory out of their minds."

The Lockerbie, Scotland, Community Council informed Governor Keating that they were "shocked" by news of the "atrocity." The Dumfries and Galloway, Scotland, Regional Council wrote the governor that memories of the terrorist attack on Pan Am 103 were intensified by news of the bombing. "We would wish to send to you and your citizens...a note of hope—we have learned, through our own experiences, that the human will to cope with and learn from such tragedies is strong."

Others were clearly attracted by the prospect of participating—even as distant mourners—in a major national event. By sending a condolence card, writing a poem, donating a memento, creating a sculpture, organizing a fund-raiser, recommending a memorial, composing music, videotaping a tree-planting service, sending money, toys, or clothes, people linked their lives to the event.

There were, of course, unsettling examples of people intruding too far, talking or writing about victims as good friends or lovers or developing "crushes" on family members and rescuers. There are thoughtless letters— people asking the city government in the chaotic days right after the bombing for names, addresses, and phone numbers of all the victims so that they can send their families gifts. And there are arrogant letters—people sending recommendations for a memorial, assuming that *their* proposals will be accepted and expecting the city or state to invite them to Oklahoma City quite soon so that they could put their plans into effect.

The allure of the progressive narrative of civil revitalization transcended Oklahoma City, engendering a nostalgia for the marshaling of national energies, the feeling, for example, of collective effervescence after Pearl Harbor was attacked. Out of the bombing, some hoped, the nation would be energized in ways impossible during "ordinary" times.

During World War II, of course, virulent racism pervaded the home front and the military, and domestic tensions were exacerbated by women moving into the workplace. The cord that held the post-Oklahoma City bombing national bereaved community together was certainly less durable than that of wartime, but many people saw in the Oklahoma Standard civic ideals that needed to be practiced in everyday life, particularly color-blindness. As was said so often after April 19, 1995, all blood ran one color that day, or "there is only one color in Oklahoma City these days—the color of love." It was as if

Martin Luther King's "beloved community" could arise from the response to mass murder.[4]

Not all those touched by the bombing, however, felt themselves equal partners in this community. People from Michigan were uncomfortable with the fact that in 1993 Timothy McVeigh and Terry Nichols lived on James Nichol's farm in Decker, part of the "thumb" area of Michigan. Many were bothered by the accusations that the state was a fertile area for right-wing activity, earning the state the dubious nickname "Militiagan."

Numerous Michigan cities sent official condolences to Oklahoma City, taking pains to distance themselves from the accused. For example, citizens of Grand Rapids, Michigan, sent a petition: "We want you to know that Michigan is filled with decent peace-loving citizens."

Moving letters from schoolchildren in Michigan, particularly from schools in Sanilac County (in which Decker, is located) expressed their "shame" and "devastation," and apologized for the bombing. One angry letter declared, "To think anyone remotely connected with Michigan could have created the blast that caused so much havoc and devastation and took so many lives is abhorrent, repugnant, and repulsive and demands swift, deterring, and lasting action." Some Michigan residents put signs in their windows stating "we're not militia members."[5]

Other communities around the nation felt stigmatized by their affiliation with the perpetrators. Some residents of the small towns in New York State where McVeigh had lived and worked resented the media crush that descended on their towns. Like other communities, they held various fund-raisers to collect relief funds. Bill McVeigh, Timothy's father, was called the "father of baby killer," and "an angry co-worker had spray-painted the slogan across the front of his locker while he was away." Students from Pendleton and Lockport who attended Starpoint, Timothy McVeigh's old school, learned that "they weren't just a bunch of small town folks anymore—they were from McVeigh-land." A track athlete said, "they call us 'the Bombers' or they call us 'the McVeighs.'"[6]

Residents of other communities also felt contamination through association: Kingman, Arizona, the home of accomplice Michael Fortier, where McVeigh lived for a brief time; Junction City, Kansas, where McVeigh rented the infamous Ryder truck that carried the bomb; and Herington, Kansas, where Terry Nichols lived. The Junction City motel room where McVeigh stayed "has been done over with fresh paint, drapes, bedspreads and carpet." As in Michigan, Herington schoolchildren planted trees in remembrance of those killed but were afraid that people would be "mad" at them, and Oklahoma City children wrote them back "we don't hate you." Susan Mueller, a reporter for the *Herington Times*, recalled that Nichols was "someone that was in our stores, in our schools, and in our park." Even though he only lived in Herington six weeks, she remembered, some newspapers characterized him as a "native."[7]

From Quilts to Teddy Bears: The Public Response

Debi Martin, chief of staff for the Oklahoma City City Council since 1988, recalled the frantic days after the bombing. "I remember being at work at 4:30 the next morning, and so many of us in the city worked in a kind of daze. We all just 'did,' but it was as if ordinary life had come to an end. In many ways, the city just shut down." She dealt with the tremendous outpouring from the public. "You cannot imagine the amount of stuff that came to us," she said. "The mail would come on huge dollies full of toys and other gifts. There were dog biscuits for the rescue dogs, clothes, money. We set up telephone banks because we were getting thousands of calls a day." Schoolchildren, sometimes on their own, sometimes in classes, sent drawings of rainbows, the sun with smiling faces, hearts with jagged breaks in them, youthful letters of condolence, "I'm sorry some people got hurt" (or killed), letters with coins.

There were those, Martin said, "who would call and read a poem. It was very, very important to some people that we listen to their poem. It was not enough for them to send it. They wanted us to hear it. You can't imagine the intensity and the volume of response in the early days."[8]

Indeed, judging from the massive collection in the Memorial Foundation's archives, poems were one of the most popular forms of memorial expression: "The Day Oklahoma Cried," "Why?" "We Will Always Remember," "I'm in Heaven," "And the Angels Came," "God's Day Care," "Loss of the Innocents," "A Rescuer's Lament," "Rise Up, Gallant Heartland," "A Time to

Heal," "Heartache in the Heartland," "Let the Angels Close Their Eyes," "Tim's Dance with the Devil," "The Day the Building Came Down." There are poems of comfort, jeremiads warning the nation to turn from its evil ways, poems in which God speaks to parents about their children safely nestled in heaven, poems in which the children assure their families that they are safe in heaven, poems written for individual victims or family members, rescue workers speaking of the horrors they have seen, love poems from family members to the dead, defiant poems expressing the belief that Oklahoma and the nation will never be defeated by terrorism, and poems predicting the eventual triumph of divine justice and retribution for the guilty.

The mayor's office was inundated with messages of consolation and official proclamations from city and state governments, various service organizations, and religious communities. Buena Park, California, mayor Don R. Griffin wrote Mayor Norick that "a tragic disaster of this magnitude affects Americans across the nation, and as fellow elected officials in the municipal service, we are particularly sensitive to the staggering impact to your city government." Some cities had commemorative services or moments of silence in council meetings: flags were flown at half-mast. Manchester, New Hampshire, declared April 19-26, 1995, Oklahoma City Memorial Week, and the city of Whitehall, Ohio, donated a city flag. The mayor of Carmel-by-the-Sea, California, wrote that "the geographic distance between us has vanished . . . blood banks are experiencing a deluge of donors, and churches are offering special services."

Dan Deming, the mayor of Hutchinson, Kansas, informed Norick about an elementary school teacher who helped his fourth grade class make "400 sandwiches, which he then drove last Friday to help feed volunteers working in your city. Several local businesses donated food to this project and a grocery store chain . . . has donated, collected and delivered, by semi-trailer, a variety of supplies." A somber letter from city officials in Houma, Louisiana, told Norick that after experiencing a destructive hurricane in 1993, "we can relate to the feelings of helplessness as a familiar environment changes drastically in just a short period of time. We also know that we are powerless to stop the change or the subsequent loss and suffering."

Richard L. Berkeley, the mayor of Kansas City, wrote as a friend to Mayor Norick, "Having gone through a somewhat similar experience at the Hyatt

Hotel bridge collapse in the '80s please don't hesitate to give me a call if I can be of any help. You will feel the emotional impact for a long time."

The response was not limited to cities in the United States. For example, on May 2, 1995, the mayors of twelve South Korean cities joined the U.S. ambassador to Korea and representatives of the green culture movement to send flowers and cards of condolences to families of those killed.

The bombing evoked a sense of nostalgia for a supposedly peaceful past in a long-lost era. The town of Westerly, Rhode Island, for example, proclaimed May 21, 1995, Good Neighbor Day, declaring that "mankind needs to reflect on simpler times when people were neighborly and respected one another with the hope that we will endeavor to renew this practice."

Blood drives and fund-raising activities took place throughout the nation. On June 16, Donna E. Shalala, secretary of the Department of Health and Human Services, "kicked-off a nationwide summer campaign among federal workers as a memorial to their colleagues who were killed in the bombing." There were innumerable bake sales, bike and track competitions, golf tournaments and concerts—some using music composed specifically for the event—to raise money.[9]

Roman Catholics enrolled those killed in monthly novena masses, for example, those offered at the National Shrine of Our Lady of the Miraculous Medal in Perryville, Missouri. Some individuals took the initiative and planned their own services of mourning. A Connecticut college student wrote to the "people of Oklahoma City" that he had "suggested an hour of silence at my campus."[10]

People envisioned a wide range of commemorative items to be sold to raise funds for families of those killed: figurines, jewelry, teddy bears, decals for car windows, memorial cookbooks, calendars, and Oklahoma City logos. Over 11,000 T-shirts were produced with the statement saying, "Though Our Hearts Are Broken, Our Spirits Soar." Memorial ribbons were popular, a memorial license plate and postage stamp memorializing Rebecca Anderson were proposed, and several cottage industries around the nation (some started by women who had experienced violence in their own lives) sold angel pins to family members and survivors. These became especially popular and often served as a protective device for family members. "I don't leave the house without mine," said one. "For me, it is a visible symbol of remembrance, and it gives me some comfort and hope. Many of us feel this way."[11]

Some Oklahoma companies asked for donations for special memorial projects. In 1998, for example, Kingfisher Lights, a nonprofit organization, created a special Christmas tower sixty-one feet high with a thirty-foot base. "Thousands of lights are used to form the outlines of 171 angels, 168 for each victim and three to represent the unborn children who died that day." It was dedicated November 27, 1998, in Kingfisher, Oklahoma.

Many other organizations and individuals were moved to various forms of memorial expression. Sailors from the Naval Air Wing at Tinker Air Force Base built a memorial bench made of wood from the USS *Constitution*, first launched in 1797, the "oldest commissioned ship in the U.S. Navy." The bench, which sits in the Memorial Foundation's office, is "dedicated to the steadfast spirit of Oklahoma in memory of each life forever changed."[12]

Hallmark Card Company "shut down their production plants to produce the card that is a replica of the very first card ever made by Hallmark." The *Progressive Florist* proudly reported that "florists in Oklahoma and around the nation understood the power the mute flower possessed to deliver the message of love and compassion." Floral arrangements were sent to hospitalized victims, other designs were donated to local churches, over 10,000 bows were sold to raise relief funds, 14,000 roses were distributed at memorial services, others were put on the pillows of the cots of rescue workers, and "massive floral creations" were donated for the April 23 memorial service.[13]

Thousands of individuals donated specialized memorial items either directly or indirectly to family members. A Richfield, Pennsylvania, couple sent the Memorial Foundation 168 china pitchers from their 2,500 piece collection. "We feel," they wrote, "that this is our way of expressing how we feel for the victims of the bombing and their families." A California woman wanted to donate sterling silver coins to families who lost children, and there are many examples of people driving to Oklahoma City to deliver their items to city offices, or, if they had been in direct touch with family members, to their homes.

Many individuals sent quilts to be distributed to family members. The teacher of a fifth grade class in Larchmont, New York, wrote Mayor Norick in December 1995 that her students "felt helpless about the bombing.... Some of their family members, friends, and neighbors had been in the World Trade

Building at the time of the bombings there. They wanted to do something personal. They recalled their fears. . . . They decided to make a quilt for the survivors and the residents of Oklahoma City. The patches in the quilt are from their own clothing. It took months to complete, with the help of parents."

Several quilts were created over the Internet. Barbara Spittler, an artist in Loyalsock Township, Pennsylvania, coordinated the Oklahoma City Tears Quilt Project, communicating with quilters on-line. Small angel quilts were delivered to family members, and a quilt with 217 patches from every state was presented to the city. "Each patch," the *Williamsport Sun Gazette* reported, "has the name and age of someone killed or injured in the bombing. Those who died have purple borders. The injured have blue borders." About the project Spittler said, "Maybe I'm doing some good for someone. Maybe if another bomber is thinking about doing the same thing, he will look at the quilt and see what it did to these families."[14]

Another large quilt was presented to Mayor Norick on September 18, 1995. The Needlework Internet newsgroup had organized the project "within hours of hearing the news [of the bombing]." Two hundred thirty people stitched six-by-six-inch blocks. The quilt, eight feet tall and twenty-one feet long, was shown to the Oklahoma City City Council, but was not displayed until the foundation exhibited it in its downtown offices in 1997. The quilt is a wonderful example of individual memorial design and messages framed in a common form. There are numerous references to scripture, quotes from Lincoln and Shakespeare, in particular the scene in *Hamlet* in which "Ophelia has gone mad with the grief of dealing with the death and pain around her."[15]

Eve De Bona, founder of Palo Alto California's Helias Foundation for Art and Human Rights, also wanted to memorialize the murdered children through quilts. Working with Alyson Stanfield, a curator of art quilts from Oklahoma City, the exhibit *Sewing Comfort out of Grief* opened at the Individual Artists of Oklahoma City Gallery on the first anniversary of the bombing. Twenty quilts were displayed, one for each child and one for children victimized by violence worldwide. The exhibit traveled around the nation, and people often left memorial items in "designated altar areas within the exhibition space."[16]

There were suggestions that the most appropriate memorial response would be a special civic act by Oklahoma City. A representative from the New Hampshire Committee for Peace in Bosnia and Herzegovina wrote Oklahoma's first lady, Cathy Keating, hoping that Oklahoma City would "adopt Sarajevo as a sister city.... The citizens of Oklahoma City have the power now to start a movement in the United States to stop the war in Bosnia. It would be a fitting memorial to those who have lost their lives in Oklahoma City and give meaning to this senseless loss." Others suggested that the public be urged to "sign cards of condolence that would also be pledges of commitment to some act of sharing or community service." A different kind of civic act was envisioned in a letter, urging "all the victim's families adopt a sweet little animal looking for a home."

Memorial Vocabularies and the Murrah Site

Less than twenty-four hours after the bombing, ideas for memorials began pouring into Oklahoma City. Memorialization had already begun, however, at the site itself. Immediately after the bombing, people gathered at the safety perimeter several blocks away, at Sixth and Hudson, and made offerings of "poems, cards, flowers, stuffed animals." National Guard members built a wood frame shelter covered with plastic to protect the offerings, and the site became a "gathering place for families, buses of children, and sightseers." Soon another makeshift shrine appeared in front of the badly damaged YMCA. These spontaneous memorials were the precursors of the now famous chain-link fence, erected after the implosion of the Murrah Building to keep people off the ground and transformed into a "people's memorial" that brought great solace to many family members, rescuers, and survivors.[17]

Rescue workers offered memorial expressions on the site itself, acts of respect for those killed and acts of protest against the horror they had confronted for so many days and nights. Oklahoma City's assistant fire chief Jon Hansen described one such memorial site: "this was our own place filled with the things we'd found, made, or been given. There was a slab painted GOD BLESS THE CHILDREN AND THE INNOCENT. An American flag hung among flowers, teddy bears, a baby's pacifier, poems, personal notes.

Within hours, a spontaneous memorial arose a few blocks from the Murrah Building, at Sixth Street and Hudson. (David Allen, Oklahoma City)

Rescue workers created this memorial amidst the ruins. (Oklahoma City)

Each of the FEMA/USAR teams had gathered at the memorial one last time before returning back home. Now it was our turn."[18]

As the gruesome task of recovery went on, American flags and state flags of rescue teams appeared. ABC News reporter Lynn Sherr reported that an American flag was attached to a grappling hook used in the recovery effort. She told viewers, "That turns out to be the very first flag that was brought out of that federal building and the rescue workers attached it to the grappling hook and every time they go in and pull something out, there's an American flag on it now. That tells you something about the spirit here." Less than a week after the bombing, a floral spray of twenty-nine mums sent by the Alabama Teachers Association was placed near the huge crater made by the bomb.[19]

Discussion about a public memorial began within days of the bombing. Professional artists and their agents, companies that made monuments, and firms that administered design competitions offered their services. A representative for Glenda Goodacre, for example, who designed the Vietnam Women's Memorial, informed the task force that Goodacre brought to her work "the sensitivity of catharsis and healing."

Felix De Weldon, designer of thirty-three monuments in the Washington, D.C., area (including the Marine Corps War Memorial, popularly known as the Iwo Jima memorial, and a twelve-foot bust of Elvis Presley at Graceland), wrote Mayor Norick several weeks after the bombing that he was "inspired" by the reaction of "citizens of Oklahoma, and decent citizens across our nation." Not since 1945, he wrote, "when I first saw Associated Press photographer Joe Rosenthal's photograph of our Marines raising the flag atop Mount Suribachi on a tiny island known as Iwo Jima, have I been this inspired to create a lasting tribute to the spirit of a united people.... I wish now to create one more, and perhaps last, great monument. A monument to help the people of Oklahoma in their healing process and to remind people everywhere of our obligation of civility and decency towards one another.... My monument would be my humble gift to the people of your great city. Any and all costs associated with its creation would be borne by myself."

Interest in creating a memorial was not limited to professionals, however. The bombing moved some people to "visions" of an appropriate memorial.

A woman from California wrote Cathy Keating about her "vision of a special memorial. . . . I remember a park with lush green rolling hills, lots of trees with a picnic area, and a playground." She went on to describe a complex memorial path in the shape of a cross made up of cracked cement from the building, and the names of those killed in a blue granite open book. She concludes her letter, "I had a vision!" Yet another letter to Mayor Norick said, "I started sketching my design after a dream I had one night." "I closed my eyes and saw a statue as clear as day." The statue was of "two giant hands (God's hands)" symbolizing that "God not only holds those that perished, but that he holds each and everyone of us in his hands as well." A landscape architect wrote that while he was not particularly religious, he had received a vision of a memorial and had translated it into blueprints for the city's consideration.

It was not just the immediate shock and horror at the bombing that generated such visions. After watching the one-year anniversary ceremonies, a chief engineer of a hotel in Tempe, Arizona, wrote that "the camera was showing the land that was once the . . . Federal Building. It was at that moment in which I had my first vision of what I now call Angel's Park. So strong was this vision that I immediately grabbed a scratch piece of paper and put down my first impressions of the memorial." He received a second vision later that day at a church service, in which he was given "dimensions, colors, and the symbolism of every part of the memorial. When I returned home, I immediately began to design the memorial, and within 24 hours I had a complete set of elevation, plan, and detail drawings as I had seen in my vision."

Visions of memorials, whether revealed in God's voice, appearing in dreams, or inspired by memorial services, did not come exclusively from outsiders. Calvin Moser, who worked for the Department of Housing and Urban Development (HUD), survived the blast and was involved with the city's memorial task force from the beginning. He got involved, he recalled, "out of respect for my friends who died." Several days after the bombing, having trouble sleeping, he got out of bed and drew a memorial. "It had to do," he said, "with the preservation of an elevator shaft which was still standing. It felt to me like the 'spine' of the building, represented by the elevator shaft, was still intact, and would have been a fitting tribute to our strength. I can't take credit for the drawing. It just came to me over and over, and I just drew it."[20]

Whatever the source of such visions—be they from the divine, from the storehouse of symbols in the collective unconscious, from an individual's conscious engagement with the bombing—it is clear that the impact of the bombing was so strong that it led people to stamp their memorial recommendations with the imprimatur of "vision." It was, perhaps, a way of declaring that "this is not something that I'm just dashing off; this memorial comes from elsewhere through me." Occasionally, a vision so energized people that they would spend hours on the telephone with people in various agencies in Oklahoma City—at the Arts Council, at Oklahoma City Beautiful, at city hall, and eventually with task force members—stumping for their vision. Many individuals were confused or even angry when their suggestion was not met with enthusiasm. How, they wondered, could a memorial idea sent from "above" not be accepted by those so close to the bombing? How could officials in Oklahoma City not appreciate what was obvious, that *their* vision was inevitably destined to be *the* official memorial? This issue would emerge again to bedevil those in charge of the official memorial design competition.[21]

One unique memorial was the naming of a star in memory of those killed. A letter to Mayor Norick expressed the hope that "Star Hope," would

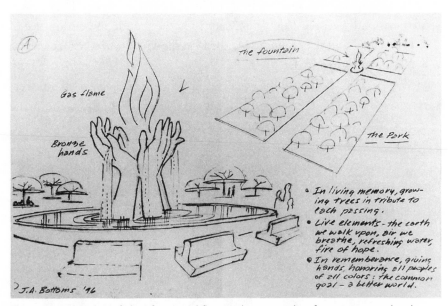

There were a number of ideas for eternal flames—here ascending from statuesque hands. Other elements of familiar memorial vocabulary are present in this design: reflecting pools and trees, for example. (James A. Bottoms)

shine "to remind all the people in Oklahoma City of the love and hope that exists in the hearts of all Americans." The star, he was told, was "registered in the International Star Registry's vault in Switzerland and recorded in the astronomical compendium *Your Place in the Cosmos.*"

Many people thought a monumental structure the most appropriate form of memorial expression. There were recommendations for copper-roofed domes, monumental ribbons, searchlights, commemorative bricks, amphitheaters, murals, reflecting pools, fountains, ponds, crosses, stars of David, obelisks, cenotaphs, a monument in the shape of an open Bible with "all the names who died there etched in the open pages." There was a suggestion to erect the nation's tallest flag pole, since "the biggest blast in the country ought to be remembered" in that manner. There was a recommendation to build an "arch of endurance" made out of "Oklahoma red clay to represent our soil and because it is so beautiful." A resident of Oklahoma City proposed a "light of Liberty statue" based on the Statue of Liberty, with sculpted figures of victims, survivors, family members, and volunteers standing together in the extinguished torch area.

Many people envisioned memorials incorporating hearts. They represented sympathy, tragedy, the widely celebrated strength and endurance of the "heartland," and they represented the love shown by and for rescuers and other volunteers during the crisis.

Hearts also personalized the event. After watching the televised anniversary service in 1996, a woman from Florida wrote that "throughout the

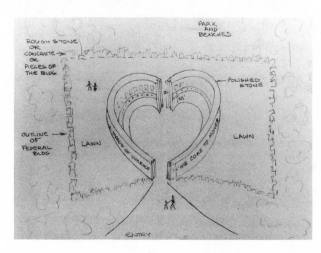

Memorials incorporating hearts were also popular. (Evelynn Leyrer Smith)

morning the word 'Heart' was mentioned innumerable times: 'the heart of the city,' 'the heartland of America,' 'Broken hearts,' 'in a heartbeat 168 people were gone,' 'heart wrenching.' I visualize the memorial being two walls in the shape of a heart.... Through the broken, jagged ends of the heart wall visitors would enter into the peaceful center, sheltered from wind and noise." An inside ledge would contain 168 holes for roses, and "above each rose I would like to see the name of each victim as well as the wonderful photographs printed on permanent metal."

Some envisioned a memorial journey joined by a monument. For example, a letter to Governor Keating recommended a sundial that would cast a shadow at 9:02 A.M., with a "torn calendar at April 1995, or a desk with one side of it whole and tidy, the other side abruptly split down the middle into disarray." Visitors would follow a flower-lined walk and go "underground or into a tunnel or maze of dim lit concrete, and rebar debris ... giving one a feel of what the collapse was like." Different "stations" would provide a history of "the bomb, collapse, and rescue." Finally, the walk would "brighten in color, light, and spirit" as visitors moved "from tragedy ... to rescue and recovery ... sunshine to hope."

Some ideas focused on music. A retired museum exhibit designer in North Carolina envisioned that at sunset "a symbolic sound and light experience would begin with a dim, lighted globe ... rising slowly from the depths of the black-water pool and growing brighter as it breaches the surface at sunset. Sound, perhaps a specially created piece or something [akin] to the '2001' theme, would accompany the ascending symbol of 'enlightenment.'" There were also suggestions for memorial music parks. In one, "people from all parts of the nation [would] come with their acoustical instruments" to play gospel and country and western music in different canopies featuring a plaque inscribed with victims' names.

Shortly after the first anniversary several ideas were submitted for bell towers. A New Jersey resident envisioned one that would strike at 9:02 A.M. every day, and a special consultant for carillons and chimes in Pennsylvania wrote that "statues and/or monuments with names of victims only provide a reminder of the tragedy." A carillon, he argued, would "tend to transform the tragedy into something that is positive and living."

There were suggestions for memorials featuring doves or eagles, symbolizing the ascent of the soul. On the first anniversary, for example, a mourner envisioned a monument of those killed "standing together, holding each other and holding the children, reaching toward the sky with a flock of doves flying behind and above them as if carrying them toward heaven."

Far more popular than doves or eagles, however, was the ubiquitous symbol of angels. It is no surprise, given the recent resurgence of fascination with angels in American culture, that people would turn to this comforting symbol. As already noted, some people took great comfort in the reports circulating shortly after the bombing that guardian angels had been seen at the building, presumably to escort the dead—usually children—to heaven. What prompted some of these reports was the appearance of a flickering, shining light evident to the naked eye in the immediate aftermath of the explosion. For some, this was an unmistakable sign that angels were present. For others, this was a natural occurrence, the result of insulation blasted into tiny pieces and shimmering in the sunlight. A year and a half after the bombing, a woman from California sent Governor Keating a black and white photo-

graph showing a cloudy sky and a letter entitled "Angels! Angels! Angels! Yes, God's Angels Are Watching Over Us." She informed the governor that the photograph was taken by a "young girl 3 days after the Oklahoma City bombing.... In typical child fashion the undeveloped film ended up in a drawer and was not developed for about a year. Upon looking at the pictures...it is plain to those who view it that God's angels do watch over all of us."

Representations of angels became popular memorial forms. The Oklahoma Crime Victims Center placed a Christmas tree decorated with angel ornaments provided by family members or survivors at the state capitol in December 1995. A resident of Colorado wanted to buy a statue of seven angels with trumpets and give it to Oklahoma City. Governor Keating received suggestions for memorial road signs, including one that

Given the popularity of angels in American culture, it is no surprise that there were a great variety of angel memorial ideas. (Teddy Westliene)

cautioned motorists to "Drive Carefully . . . Angels Crossing." A letter to Mayor Norick asked for a memorial inscription that read "Our Lost Little Angels—Gone But Not Forgotten."

Some professional artists also thought of angels as appropriate symbols. Introducing Edwina Sandys's Angel of Hope project to Mayor Norick, Robert A. Heffner III, chairman of a natural gas company in Oklahoma, described her work as "monumental, non-denominational, a shrine that immortalizes those who lost their lives, a celebration of heroes, a symbol of triumph over tragedy, and conceived in a manner which would sustain international importance for our city and state." The Angel of Hope, made of "gleaming stainless steel" seventy to a hundred feet tall, would rise from the rubble. The memorial prospectus exclaimed, "Like the Christ figure on the Sugar Loaf Mountain in Rio de Janeiro, Brazil, ANGEL OF HOPE will join the ranks of 'Wonders of the World.'" [22]

Another popular memorial form was the teddy bear. Long a symbol of security, particularly for children, teddy bears have become increasingly popular in American culture. Historian Elizabeth Lawrence observed that "numerous books, as well as periodicals, on the subject of teddy bears have appeared. Stores entirely devoted to teddy bears have been established throughout the country. Special teddy bear sales, rallies, contests, jamborees, clinics, and exhibitions are often held, and clubs for devotees (known as arctophiles) are active." Teddy bears have become increasingly important in var-

Teddy bears became a popular symbol of mourning and comfort. *Boston Globe* editorial cartoonist Dan Wasserman drew this image the afternoon of April 19. "The image came to me right from the day care center," Wasserman said, "and there was an overwhelming response to it." The cartoon was offered to anyone making a donation to relief efforts, and helped raise over $65,000. (Copyright, 1995, Wasserman. Dist. By Los Angeles Times Syndicate)

ious therapeutic settings: dentists' offices and children's hospitals, for example, and in situations of extreme trauma, "traffic accident victims, runaways...abused and sexually assaulted individuals." The teddy bear became a symbol of grievous loss and necessary solace.[23]

Governor Jim Edgar of Illinois and his wife sent teddy bears to Oklahoma City for the "Time for Healing" service as a symbol of hope. Television

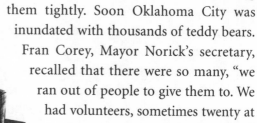

viewers saw many family members clutching them tightly. Soon Oklahoma City was inundated with thousands of teddy bears. Fran Corey, Mayor Norick's secretary, recalled that there were so many, "we ran out of people to give them to. We had volunteers, sometimes twenty at a time, just to sort the bears and other gifts that came in."[24]

There were proposals for teddy bear monuments, teddy bear walls, teddy bear parks, and a zoo memorial with live bear cubs. Dana Cooper, the Murrah Building's day care center director, killed along with her two-year-old son, was remembered by a classmate at the University of Central Oklahoma

There were several suggestions for Teddy Bear monuments or memorial walls. Frank W. Fowler, Oklahoma graphic artist, whose studio was near enough to feel the blast, was prompted to sculpt this design. Together with an eternal flame, this playground-size memorial would be forever dedicated to the children who died April 19, 1995.

who put a teddy bear and wreath at her vacant seat in a course on cognitive development.[25]

The popularity of the Vietnam Veterans Memorial led many people to suggest memorial walls, often with the names of the dead inscribed. Such a wall, a Canadian wrote, "would become a focus of pilgrimage for all time to come, with Oklahoma the Jerusalem of America." Four days after the bombing another Canadian suggested that all the cards and letters received by the city "be saved and displayed as a permanent reminder" on a wall of hope. Governor Keating received a suggestion for a memorial wall made of Oklahoma rose granite, "thought of as strong and sturdy; as is our Oklahoma spirit." The wall would be lined with rosebud trees with heart-shaped leaves and "tiny pink buds for the little children that we lost. Teddy bear bronze statues at either side of the wall or a small statue of a small child hugging a teddy bear, would seem very appropriate."

One early memorial wall appeared in the city of Edmond, Oklahoma, only a few miles from Oklahoma City. Edmond had been seared when a postal employee murdered fourteen coworkers on August 20, 1986, and some people wanted the eighteen Edmond residents killed in the bombing memorialized alongside the Yellow Ribbon Memorial to the postal workers. Instead, Edmond claimed the "first publicly funded monument to the bombing," a bronze plaque with the names of the eighteen Edmond residents who were murdered. The memorial wall was placed in a rock and copper pavilion in a large city park and surrounded by eighteen trees.[26]

Some memorial walls were envisioned as protests against violence. A pastoral counselor in Texas recommended a peace memorial wall that would provide "opportunities for visitors to fashion tokens and symbols of their commitment to peacemaking and incorporate them into the wall." And an artist in West Virginia envisioned a large tiled mosaic wall, made up of a composite of "drawings of the children who were murdered and drawings done by school children of Oklahoma City reflecting their feelings about the bombing."

Numerous suggestions proposed living memorials, many of which would engage the problem of violence. Dr. Robin Meyers, senior minister at Mayflower Congregational Church in Oklahoma City, thought of a museum like the United States Holocaust Memorial Museum that would be a "solemn and beautiful place to come to learn the profound truth of what violence can do, and why violence cannot be allowed to rule a society." There was a call for a national memorial to public service, and a resident of Miami, Florida, proposed the Alfred P. Murrah Federal Building memorial, exhibition, performance, and learning center. This would, he hoped, "give birth to desperately needed solutions for old and new problems and give new life to our frustrated and desperate attempts to settle social unrest."

The power of Lexington Green, where colonial Minutemen were fired upon by British troops on their fateful march to Concord on April 19, 1775, inspired an architectural draftsman from Bellingham, Massachusetts, to send a plan for a peace park that would include a meetinghouse, liberty tree, and Minuteman statue. Others envisioned peace parks with fountains, torches of peace, a heartland peace shrine, a national peace memorial against domestic violence, and a national unity memorial.[27]

Some believed that the most appropriate memorial would be to transform the Murrah area into an execution site, a torture site, or a trophy site, a

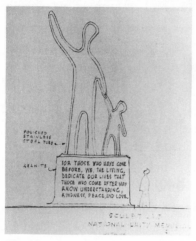

This statue was to be part of a "National Unity Memorial." (Robert Cantrell)

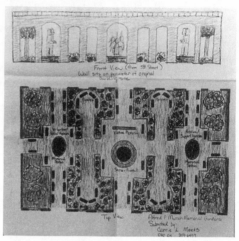

Memorial gardens were also popular, often with detailed instructions about the varieties of flowers and trees to be used. (Carrie Meeks)

place for the display of the remains of the perpetrators. Writing three days after the bombing, a woman suggested that the perpetrators "be hung in front of the Federal Building and left to rot." A grandmother wrote that she would be "happy to burn a toe or leg off day by day without any medication for them." She conceived of a memorial with the perpetrators "strapped to a jagged piece of concrete in the remains of the . . . building." A resident of Princeton, Texas, suggested that the heads of the perpetrators be mounted on the wall of a museum.

Many people envisioned the natural beauty of parks as a fitting memorial, and their letters often included precise instructions regarding types of trees, shrubs, flowers, and soil, each with specific symbolic meaning. An Edmond, Oklahoma, resident wrote to Cathy Keating a week after the bombing, proposing a children at play park, in which "bushes and flowering plants would encircle certain portions of the park to attract butterflies. . . . In Greek mythology the butterfly represents the soul leaving the body. Thinking of all the butterflies, it would almost be like the souls of those killed would be there with us."

A year and a half after the bombing, a representative of a group specializing in the creation of memorial gardens envisioned a "landscape returning to life through the cheerful innocence of birds and a special habitat created for them." Visitors would "smell honeysuckle or lemon verbena filling the air.

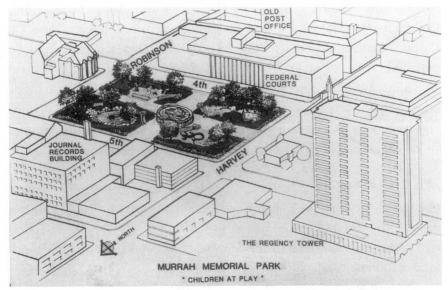

Many people envisioned cheerful parks designed especially for children. (Otto A. Marinick, Dallas, Texas, and Susan Marinick)

... Lilting songs of mockingbirds, cardinals and finches will fill the air and reclaim the land on which the garden resides to ... be filled with life anew." Another letter spoke of a "healing garden," with flowers "from winter's winter jasmine, pansies, and nandina to spring's jonquils, lilacs, and iris to summer's wildflowers, garden flowers, and shrubs to fall's mums, asters, and sunflowers."[28]

The enduring memorial tradition of tree plantings received impetus from the widely publicized meeting between President and Mrs. Clinton and the children of federal workers at the White House on April 22, 1995, only three days after the bombing, when a little girl said that trees should be planted for the victims, and the president and first lady responded by planting dogwoods on White House grounds. Trees were planted by city governments, schools, churches, civic organizations, hospitals, senior citizen centers, day care centers, nature centers, YMCAs, and thousands of individuals around the world. They planted apple, aromia, ash, cherry, crabapple, white and pink dogwood, linden, magnolia, maple, oak, pear, redbud, redwood, and weeping willow. People planted them on various anniversaries of the bombing: the first week, the first month, annually. They planted them at 9:02 A.M., on Memorial Day, on Arbor Day. Trees were planted for individual victims, for the children, for survivors, and for rescuers and rescue dogs. On the one month anniversary, for example, St. Paul, Minnesota city employees passed out 168 tree seedlings on the steps of the federal building.

Thousands of trees were planted in Israel. The mayor of Yehud, Israel, wrote Mayor Norick three days after the bombing, informing him that the Oklahoma City Garden had been dedicated with Foreign Minister Shimon Peres taking part. On December 19, 1995, Mayor Norick led a delegation to Jerusalem for the dedication of a lot donated by the Israeli government that could accommodate 10,000 trees. Inspired by the exhortation in Leviticus to plant trees, the Women's Zionist Organization of America planted 500 trees in Israel in memory of those killed. "As Jewish Americans, we know all too well the horror and grief engendered by terrorists who think nothing of callously murdering and maiming innocent civilians."[29]

Children throughout the nation planted trees as part of school memorial activities and as the centerpiece of family or neighborhood memorial services. For example, a woman in Quincy, Massachusetts, wrote Governor Keating about her niece and her niece's best friend, who "decided that they wanted to plant a tree, as suggested by the young girl at the President's talk. Within twenty-four hours they had organized the other neighborhood children, prepared readings and cleaned up the site where the tree was to be planted. . . . About ten neighborhood children, their parents and friends attended the dedication."

In West Virginia, Governor Gaston Caperton encouraged citizens to plant trees, and in Oklahoma, several thousand redbuds were planted along Turner Turnpike between Tulsa and Oklahoma City. A memorial grove was planted at the Oklahoma Department of Agriculture Building in the shape of a heart. "The hearty bur oak symbolizes the tenacity of the Oklahoma spirit. Its branches, like outstretched arms, embrace the memory of the adult victims, children, rescuers and volunteers. Redbuds, which burst forth purple flowers each spring, remind us of life's renewal with the birth of each child. The white blossoms of a lone whitebud hint of innocence lost." On November 19, 1995, on the grounds of the Oklahoma Capitol State Park, a memorial grove with one linden tree for each adult killed and one prairie fire crabapple tree for each child murdered was dedicated as a gift of "hope and healing" from the citizens of Iowa.

Many letters about tree-plantings read like family letters, often with photographs of individual families or schoolchildren in the act of planting. Occasionally a videotape of a tree planting ceremony would be included. Some towns, like Cedar Hills, Utah, enclosed personal letters from townspeople. "I hope," wrote the mayor, Martha Spoor, "that you can feel their sincerity and love."

It is now commonplace to take notice of the popularity of memorialization in American culture, and there are certainly many reasons for this intense interest. The Vietnam Veterans Memorial was transformed from a memorial designed for the public through a traditional design process into a

The memorial grove on the grounds of the State Capitol, a gift of "hope and healing" from the state of Iowa. (David Allen, Oklahoma City)

There were a great number of memorial ideas focusing on the murdered children.
(Contributor unknown)

memorial by the people, through the offerings left at the wall. It was not enough for people to just look at the wall or to be satisfied with public interpretations of what the wall "meant." People needed to touch the wall, trace the names of loved ones on the wall, leave offerings at the wall. With the Vietnam Veterans Memorial as a model, individuals did not hesitate to shape the meaning of a memorial through their own actions and energies.

Also, in a period of intense culture wars, memorialization emerged as an effective, highly visible way to make an enduring statement. For ethnic groups wishing to publicize grievances past or present, memorialization offered a physical and ideological presence in the culture that had previously been denied. For example, a planned Indian memorial at the Little Bighorn will forever alter the nature of that site, emplacing Native American memory as never before. Museum exhibits at the Smithsonian Institution, be they about the incarceration of Americans of Japanese ancestry during World War II, about the difference between the chivalrous war in the air and the horror of the trenches in World War I, or an ill-fated exhibition about the end of World War II and the use of atomic weapons, engendered widespread interest in the representation of American history in various memorial venues: not only museums but living history activities, historical reenactments, and traditional monuments.

Adding to popular enthusiasm for memorialization was the tremendous attention given to the opening of the United States Holocaust Memorial Museum, and its intention to be a storytelling museum. Its stated purpose was to bring about the civic transformation of those who visited, and it popularized the idea that memorial forms—museums, learning centers, archives, reflective space—could serve as memorial environments in which the various components could fulfill different and related tasks: expressions of remembrance (often mourning); education (learning the story of an event and its historical context); living education (outreach programs designed to energize students to learn the lessons of an event); and research (another form of living memorial, a hope that, for example, delving into the mysteries of the Holocaust or the dark terrain of domestic terrorism would offer clues to combat recognized evils, and ensure that those murdered did not die meaningless deaths).[30]

Numerous memorials came to mind as people envisioned an appropriate model for Oklahoma City: the Vietnam Veterans Memorial and the Holocaust Museum, of course, but also the Marine Corps War Memorial; the Soldiers National Cemetery at Gettysburg; the cemeteries at Normandy; a garden in a cemetery in Lockerbie, Scotland; the Lexington Green; Pearl Harbor; the Kaiser Wilhelm Cathedral; the Berlin Wall; the ruins of a church in Munich; the Peace Dome in Hiroshima; Dealey Plaza, site of the assassination of President John F. Kennedy; the Lorraine Motel in Memphis, site of the assassination of Martin Luther King, Jr.; the Smithsonian Institution; the Statue of Liberty; the Eiffel Tower; the Western Wall in Jerusalem.

People wanted the memorial to remember the event and mourn the dead; serve as a warning about the dangers of terrorism; send a message that terrorism had not won; serve the local community as a place for music, for reflection in a natural environment, or as a forum for discussion of issues and events; and serve the national community as a place in which terrorism would be studied and resisted. This is what people expected of memorials at the end of the twentieth century.[31]

The Ambivalent Symbol of the Murrah Building

One of the enduring images of the Oklahoma City bombing was the mortally wounded Murrah Building. Aerial photographs made it seem as if a gigantic ice cream scoop had carved out part of the building, creating a grotesque architectural shape. The damage revealed its insides—its guts—with dangling rebar, massive cement slabs hanging dangerously, and other building materials creating a dense thicket of rubble inside and outside, where floors had "pancaked" together.

The future of the wounded building was argued immediately. And it was the Murrah Building—the target of the terrorists—that attracted almost all the attention. There was little public interest in the fate of two mortally wounded buildings across the street that were eventually torn down: the Water Resources Board Building, where two were killed, or the Athenian Building, where one was killed. Many spoke of the site as "sacred ground." Rebuilding there, conducting business as usual, would defile the site in the eyes of many. Rebuild, said others, for a new building would signal defiance of terrorism. Leave as is, some argued, and the ruins would be an evocative reminder of loss, and of the enduring dangers of violence.

Within a few days of the bombing, discussion began in the federal government about what to do with the building. When search efforts ended the first week of May 1995, a committee in the House of Representatives passed a resolution giving the General Services Administration (GSA) sixty days to assess the "need for acquiring, constructing, or reconstructing a federal building in Oklahoma City." Appearing on *Good Morning America* one month after the bombing, Governor Keating called the building an "eyesore" and said "it's important to get the building out of there.... It's a memory that most people in this community would like to see gone.... Those jagged, broken walls, those huge pieces of marble that are still hanging out ready to break away, that's a symbol of destruction and terror that people here would much rather put behind them and they will." Keating informed viewers that he hoped for a "memorial park even larger than the building site itself."[32]

Many people saw the building as a symbol of evil, contaminating the city's skyline. "For me," said Phillip Thompson, whose mother's remains were recovered after the building's implosion, "it was like a tomb, and for many of us, it just couldn't stay. It would drain you every day." Pam Whicher thought that the building, like her husband, was dead. "It symbolized to me the broken bodies of those that died inside it."[33]

Richard Williams and Dot Hill of GSA, who had worked in the building, and Jim Loftis, who worked as an architectural designer of the building, had different feelings. Dot Hill had been in the GSA break room, which she characterized as "sort of like a bomb shelter, and it saved my life." She hated to look at the terminally wounded building because it had become much more than just a workplace—it was a place in which friendships were born and grew, and people shared joys and sorrows. "Right after the bombing," she said, "I felt like I needed to give the building a hug."[34]

Richard Williams began working at the building in August 1976, when it was only three-fourths complete. He eventually became assistant building manager. "I knew the building very well," he said, "like the back of my hand." Williams knew almost everyone in the building and played softball with the credit union staff. "In many respects, we were truly a large family. I spent a big part of my life—almost nineteen years—with these people. Some of us had very strong feelings about that building, and it was difficult to see it come down, even after what had happened."[35]

Jim Loftis recalled the challenge of architectural design in the construction of the Murrah Building. "Like most architects," he said, "I have a certain amount of cerebral ownership of building projects, and I imagine that I have the usual conviction among architects that everything I design will outlast me." He arrived at the site shortly after the bomb exploded, hoping that his knowledge of the building's design would be helpful. "I didn't ever give up on the building," he recalled. "I saw it as a wounded building, and I was in the minority." Loftis never thought of the building as evil; in fact, he thought it extraordinary that the building had not completely collapsed from the strength of the bomb. "I saw it as I would a faithful dog or horse that had saved lives and it should have been praised as a hero and should have been salvaged if possible."[36]

Members of the extended bereaved community also had strong feelings about the Murrah Building. Some felt that if a federal building was to be erected, it should be elsewhere in the city. The Murrah site, some argued, should be preserved for memorial functions. An Oklahoma City couple went further, writing Senator Don Nickles (R-Okla.) that no federal building be erected in Oklahoma City. For them, "a new building [on the same site] would always be 'haunted,' and a federal building elsewhere in the city would be too tempting for the violent fringe."[37]

Many people, however, believed that the act of rebuilding would be a significant act of protest against terrorists and would also help the city recover. A "MEMORIAL FEDERAL BUILDING," one person wrote, "would symbolize our determination to be steadfast and not be swayed by terrorism, and honor those career employees and citizens who died there." A resident of Santa Barbara, California, whose mother's house was destroyed in a 1977 fire, said, "I was not whole again until the house was rebuilt and stood again on the same spot.... Please rethink your plans to build another memorial park." A new building would, she thought, convey victory over terrorism; those murdered would "rest better because the building they worked in—that housed their darling children—was back up again where it belongs."

Other suggestions called for rebuilding with a granite memorial inscribed with names of victims, rebuilding with a new day care center or with a memorial park surrounding the building. A survivor of the bombing said that the "plaza and the parking garage is all that remains of the area that was a part of my daily routine for 10 years.... I would like to suggest that individual name plates for each of the people that lost their lives be displayed in individual parking spaces in the parking garage."

Some thought about other memorial sites in their recommendations for the Murrah Building. A resident of Lawton, Oklahoma, wrote the Keatings about his emotional visit to Dachau, the Nazi concentration camp on the outskirts of Munich, Germany, and how a replica of the Murrah Building would be similarly evocative. In June 1997, a resident of Virginia sent a drawing of a memorial idea in which a model of the building would hold replicas of the heads of those killed, "correct in detail... formed onto the recessed part of the damaged structure and peering out with a serious expression, similar to Mt. Rushmore." Another thought of how quickly the superstructure was removed from the USS *Arizona* after the attack on Pearl Harbor and cautioned that the building should not be torn down too soon.

There were numerous suggestions that the ruins of the Murrah Building become the memorial, for, as one Oklahoma City resident wrote, they were a "most powerful metaphor for the sense of community that exists here because of the bomb." Others observed that the site "already attracted large crowds," and "the visual images ingrained in Americans through television coverage are too strong to ignore." A professor of graphic design at the University of Central Oklahoma characterized the building as an "icon" and thought that it should be left standing because "we need to connect, to touch the reality of the tragedy.... The structure could be retained, cleaned up, reinforced, sealed, and lighted during the night.... Removing this icon will leave a wound in our national psyche."

It was a source of deep sorrow for many that Judge Murrah's name would now be forever linked to this horrific act. An editorial in the *Tulsa World* several weeks after the bombing thought Oklahoma City would gain strength through rebuilding: "think what it would mean to the Murrah descendants to see a thing of beauty, rather than evil, associated with the name." A former law clerk to Judge Murrah wrote Senator Nickles, urging that Murrah's name "continue to be honored by gracing some federal building in Oklahoma City," so that "the name of this great Oklahoman is not lost due to the tragic events that recently occurred in Oklahoma City."[38]

At 7:01 A.M., on May 23, 1995, the remains of the Alfred P. Murrah Building were imploded. It crumpled in a cloud of dust in approximately seven seconds. Hundreds of people witnessed the implosion, and some family members and survivors gathered with Mayor Norick to watch from the twelfth floor of the badly damaged Regency Towers apartment building. Many others, however, had made a conscious decision to stay away. Some feared their reaction to another explosion. And city officials and mental

On May 23, 1995, the Murrah Building was imploded. (David Allen, Oklahoma City)

health professionals feared that the implosion could have adverse psychological effects on people working downtown. Gwen Allen, director of Project Heartland, said that "some people feel the site is like a battlefield or a shrine, and changing it will upset them.... But others with jobs downtown believe that having the building gone will make it easier for them to go to work."[39]

Garner Stoll, Oklahoma City's planning director, recalled that "most people were ready for the building to come down. Looking at it you could easily believe there was a hell." The building may well have been imploded at an earlier date, but for the objections of Timothy McVeigh's attorney, Stephen Jones. For him, the building was a site of evidence, and he filed a motion to prevent the government from proceeding with the implosion until he had been given an opportunity to examine the site. "By the time we were allowed in, just a few days before implosion," he recalls, "the building was sanitized."[40]

Survivor Richard Williams was ambivalent about the implosion. Still recovering from his injuries, he watched it on television and went to the site later that day. "I looked at that three-story pile of rubble and said my good-byes to the building. We in GSA lost a building that had meant something to us. I felt safe there, but out of ignorance, I didn't realize how dangerous the building was."

From the first moments, rescue and recovery workers risked their lives working in a highly unstable building. Jerry Ennis of Boldt Construction, whose employees had labored hard to shore up the building, rolled his eyes at the very mention of arguments that the ruins, or even some of the ruins, be used as a memorial. "I was flabbergasted," he said. "The idea that this terminally damaged building could be left up was ridiculous."[41]

Soon after the implosion, the site was cleared, and a grassy area surrounded by a chain-link fence marked where the building once stood. Not yet demolished were the ruins of the Water Resources Building or the Athenian Building, and the devastation from the bombing was apparent to those who visited the site. Even though the Murrah Building was no longer standing, however, Murrah rubble was transformed into a sacred relic and commercial commodity.

From Rubble to Relic: The Transformation of Murrah Debris

There were numerous suggestions that Murrah rubble be a crucial part of any memorial. For example, someone was "struck by the vision of two workers attaching a large steel cable around a huge reinforced concrete monolith, which was to be lifted from the rubble.... That monolith should be salvaged, and stored until the site of the bombing has been rebuilt, or rededicated. At that time, the monolith should be stood on end and set in concrete, as it stood in the rubble. At the foot ... should be a bronze plaque, bearing the event, the date, and the names of those confirmed murdered in the massacre."

Several persons suggested making the Murrah rubble part of a memorial mound. One recommended that the building be taken down and the pile of debris covered by each state sending "a truck load or so of top soil; then landscape the resulting hill-park with shrubs and trees native to Oklahoma." Governor and Mrs. Keating received an idea from a former federal worker who thought of Germany's "lovely memorial" hills made of debris from World War II in Munich, Germany. She thought that Oklahoma City should place the ruins of the Murrah Building at a "strategic location so that people coming into our city could view a lasting symbol." Inspired by many sleepless nights, she wrote a poem that began, "Let's build us a mountain for all the world to see, made by human hands of the Murrah Building debris."[42]

From Arkansas came a suggestion that a new building, made up of the material memory of the bombing, "the mangled tricycle, wagon, and file cabinets ... flags of volunteer organizations, U.S. flag, photos, videos," would be a "very real and grim reminder." Mayor Norick received a similar letter from Texas, suggesting that the "twisted and broken toys of the children's day care center" not be discarded with the "rest of the rubble" but used to make a monument.

Pieces of Murrah granite and marble were transformed from ordinary material into sacred artifact, infused with a unique power that brought the bearer of the relic the prestige of possessing material from the event, which was itself an enduring material reminder of such an event.

The transformation of ordinary matter into sacred relic is commonplace at national historic sites. For example, soon after the Alamo fell in 1836, tourists hauled away small pieces of the old mission. The first Alamo monument was made from such rubble and carried by wagon around Texas, with people being charged to see it. At Gettysburg, those interested in the preservation of the battlefield feared for the survival of the famous "copse of trees," reportedly General Robert E. Lee's objective when he launched the dramatic Pickett-Pettigrew charge on the third day of the battle, because people were carving walking sticks out of the trees. Scrap from the USS *Arizona* was sometimes looked upon with reverence, bricks from the Warsaw Ghetto wall or items from Nazi concentration and death camps can often be found in the offices of those who work in institutions of Holocaust remembrance. And after the Chicago Fire of 1871, "there was an active trade in souvenirs...such as charred chunks of noted buildings or twisted clusters of plates or spoons welded together...and one resourceful entrepreneur opened a saloon that was supposedly constructed entirely out of materials salvaged from the fire."[43]

The horror of the Oklahoma City bombing sparked a hunger for relics. A collectibles expert predicted that "henceforth, no major museum in Oklahoma will be without something from the bombing. People will save newspapers and photos and pins and medals and chunks of concrete.... Collectors will pay a few bucks for anything signed by victims, like canceled checks. And they will pay a bit more for anything connected to a bomber, especially if it's in the assassin's handwriting and describes the building or has some political content."[44]

Murrah rubble was a convenient commodity because there was so much of it. The *Daily Oklahoman* reported that for several days in late May "trucks hauled nearly 800 tons of debris from the site...and plan to haul more than 1,200 tons today." Even though some of this was from other buildings and destroyed automobiles, a great deal of it was Murrah rubble. Some of it became evidence for the trial, some was taken to a landfill, and some was taken to the area around the office of Midwest Wrecking, an Oklahoma City company that worked for two weeks beginning the night of the bombing to remove debris. Ben Kates, Midwest Wrecking's president, recalled that "we hauled some of the rubble to our location for family members and survivors. Some still come out, even in 1999. In the first three months, it was incredible. There were people out here all the time."[45]

Some wanted to sell Murrah rubble to raise money for bombing relief efforts. Governor Keating received a suggestion that "debris could be loaded on trucks from the site of the demolition and taken to different cities so that all Oklahomans would have an opportunity to donate." Others recommended selling pieces of the rubble with a certificate to prove authenticity.

There were numerous suggestions that Murrah granite be used either in a memorial or as a memorial. It had lined the building's walls and floors, and

Granite from the Murrah Building was used in several memorials, including this one at the new Federal Employees Credit Union in Oklahoma City, designed by Sunni Mercer. In the "Pool of Tears," the fountain "mourns continuously as water spills over the fallen Murrah granite."

the pavers on the plaza were granite. A letter to Mayor Norick asked that he consider "using granite for benches or plaques. Maybe a big chunk of granite could be salvaged and all the names of the victims be engraved on it as a 'jagged' memorial to the victims." Others envisioned memorial gardens with slabs of Murrah granite, and it was the material of choice for those who recommended memorial walls.

It was also preferred material for those who wanted to possess a piece of the building. "There were buckets of granite at the site after the implosion and people could just come by and pick it up," said Richard Williams. "Trophy shops were inundated with pieces of granite from the building. Government agencies all over the nation who lost people in the bombing have a piece of Murrah granite as a memorial. Once we decided that granite would be used in the memorial we stopped giving it away."

Robert A. Heffner, who was pushing the merits of the Angel of Hope memorial, whose base would be made of Murrah rubble, was concerned about the unregulated distribution of Murrah rubble. He wrote Mayor Norick that the city, not the federal government, should regulate its distribution. "I think that no matter what eventually goes into that spot, Oklahoma City should have control over the debris.... Apparently, the GSA had once thought that people would want pieces of this building, just as they did pieces of the Berlin Wall. I think that in itself expresses such a significant interest that it strengthens the conclusion that rubble should be used for the base of whatever monument might be erected on that tragic spot."[46]

It was difficult, however, to control the distribution of Murrah rubble. In addition to its presence in state and federal agency waiting rooms and offices, or in special Murrah memorial rooms or walls, thousands of businesses and individuals throughout Oklahoma City and beyond possessed Murrah rubble. For example, pieces were given to three Kansas City area schools that had held fund-raisers for students who lost their parents, and the principal of John Adams Elementary School in Oklahoma City wrote Congressman Frank Lucas that she had helped coordinate with U.S. marshals the "breaking up, hauling, and delivering granite from the building to all the local schools (84 in our district alone), as well as Fire Departments, Police Stations, Ambulance Services, and a plethora of other service agencies."[47]

I have had my own struggles over being in possession of Murrah granite. As Richard Williams and I became friends, one night after dinner he gave me a box that held a small piece of Murrah granite. It was clearly an act of friendship, one that I appreciated. I had no thoughts of saying "no, I do not want to possess anything that was a part of something so horrible," but I felt uncomfortable. Was I in some way also guilty of being too fascinated with horror? Was there a danger that I would show this to colleagues and friends as if to say, "Gee, look what I have." I feared losing a kind of moral integrity if fascination with the rubble ever led me to diminished feeling for all that was lost in that building. I was uncomfortable too because such materials have a powerful presence. I recalled my visit to a warehouse in Maryland when I was writing my book on the making of the United States Holocaust Memorial Museum, and how artifacts large and small—part of a women's barrack from Auschwitz-Birkenau, cans of Zyklon-B gas—exuded a malevolent presence. I had similar feelings when I worked in the Memorial Foundation's archives in Oklahoma City. On shelves in a large room that I had to walk through were personal objects from the building not yet claimed: shoes still dusty from the rubble, a woman's purse, clothes. I always walked on the other side of the room because it seemed inappropriate for me, an "outsider," to come too close to those charged objects. I decided to keep the granite in the spirit in which Richard Williams offered it, but I have never taken it out of the box.

An American Icon: The Fireman and the Baby

There are certain images that both capture the essence of an event and transcend the event, expressing through their eloquence what seem to be eternal human feelings, principles, truths. In recent times, we think of images such as the superstructure of the USS *Arizona,* smoldering in Pearl Harbor, the flag raising on Mount Surabachi during the battle of Iwo Jima, President Kennedy lurching forward after having been struck with an assassin's bullet, and the ghastly image of his head being blown apart with the second bullet. We think of the mushroom cloud over Hiroshima, which came to symbolize modern apocalyptic consciousness. We remember Kim Phuc, the naked Vietnamese girl running down the road after being burned with napalm during an American/South Vietnamese air strike, a photograph that seemed to capture so powerfully what was for many the moral bankruptcy of the war in Vietnam.[48]

Oklahoma City has added the image of the fireman and the baby to this list of cultural icons. It appeared in newspapers and magazines around the world. It captured the horror of the murder of innocent children. It captured the tenderness of rescuers. It offered the aesthetic opposite to images of a mother or father protecting a child through loving embrace. There was no protection for these dead infants and young children. All rescuers could do

Amateur photographer Charles H. Porter, IV captured the dramatic moment when Oklahoma City policeman John Avera handed Baylee Almon to Oklahoma City fireman Chris Fields. The photograph of Fields cradling the child captured the horror of the bombing and appeared in newspapers and magazines around the world. (Copyright 1995, Corbis-Sygma, photographed by Charles H. Porter IV)

was gently hold their dying or dead bodies, and be marked permanently by the encounter. And yet there was a special tenderness in the images of police sergeant John Avera carrying Baylee Almon to fireman Chris Fields, and Fields holding Baylee before handing her to a member of an emergency services team who put her in an ambulance. Cindy Alexander, a paramedic who was at the building shortly after the bombing and then coordinated critical incident stress management services for rescuers, spoke movingly about this. "Look at the way that they both cradle Baylee," she said. "Those are fathers carrying the body of this tiny girl."[49]

I will never forget stories told to me about the murdered children. Ginny Moser worked in a dentist's office in Edmond, Oklahoma, and drove to the site to look for her husband, Calvin. After finding him alive, she told someone that she knew CPR and was put to work carrying dead and dying children in the triage center in the plaza area. To this day, it is difficult for her to talk about her experiences. She didn't seek counseling for over a year. "I didn't think I deserved it, I didn't want to take away the money from someone who might need it worse than I did." She described to me a nightmare she continues to have: "I'm looking for Cal and stepping over bodies and hearing babies crying."[50]

I heard from several people the story of a crane operator who had to clear rubble for several days in order to reach a dead child pinned upright, its eyes open, seemingly staring at the man. The image of the fireman and the baby seemed to capture all these horrific stories and linked together the lives of Aren Almon-Kok, Baylee's mother, Avera, Fields, photographers Lester LaRue and Charles Porter IV. More than any other image from the bombing, the photograph of the fireman and the baby sparked a response from people around the world.

Sergeant Avera recalled going into the Murrah Building and helping two injured women. Then he and another officer "heard a baby crying." The other officer found an infant and, said Avera, "I picked up my baby and started out of the building through the parking garage. I could not find any life signs. I thought the left leg and arm were broken. It was too dark to do any more than try and immobilize the baby . . . until I could get out of the building . . . I carried my baby to the first firefighter I saw. He pointed to the ambulance parked in the intersection. I . . . was met at the front of the vehicle by a firefighter [Chris Fields] with his arms outstretched to me. I told him I had a critical baby and wanted him to care for it.... I handed the baby to the firefighter and immediately turned around and reentered the building through the parking garage."[51]

Avera found out about the famous photographs the next day. "The first time I saw them I was doing an interview on camera, and I lost it." He did not know immediately whether Baylee Almon had survived. "Some media person told me the next day that she was alive, but right before meeting Aren Almon I was informed that she was dead. That drive to her family's house was the longest drive of my life. I was terrified that she was angry at me for not saving her baby."[52]

Avera still lives with the anguish of this moment. "You know in your mind that you did everything that you could, but you always wonder if you could have done more." He did not return to the site for four years, when the Memorial Foundation invited him to walk through the Journal Record Building, undergoing renovation to house the foundation's Memorial Center. "I received lots of mail, and answered about 90 percent of it. I still get recognized, still get letters telling me that babies are named after me." Avera, who had an uncle killed in the bombing, still has not been able to dispose of the bloody clothes, hat, and boots that he wore that morning. His experience convinced him that there should be legislation that would allow every policeman, fireman, rescue worker, anyone who dealt with the dead, to receive intensive counseling away from home with no penalty at work. "I want to work on this, to make it easier on others who have this kind of ordeal."

Chris Fields's fire company was one of the first to arrive at the scene. "I remember seeing Sergeant Avera," Fields said, "and he told me 'I have a critical infant here.' I knew she was already dead, and I held her for a couple of minutes before handing her to the EMSA unit. I went back to the station at about 10:30 that evening; by 11:00 another officer called and asked if I had carried a baby out of the building. He had received a fax from a British newspaper wanting my name. There were not many firemen with a five on their helmet and a mustache who held a dead infant that morning. That was the beginning of some really intense attention from the media."[53]

This horrible drama was captured on film by both Lester LaRue, then an employee of Oklahoma Natural Gas, whose photograph appeared on the cover of *Newsweek* on May 15, 1995, and amateur photographer Charles Porter IV. LaRue was immediately involved in controversy with his employer, who argued that since the photograph was taken on company time, LaRue had to hand over any profit from the photograph so that the funds could be donated to charity. He refused, claiming that the photograph was rightfully his. He was fired and sued the company unsuccessfully.[54]

Porter's photographs—of Avera handing Baylee Almon to Chris Fields and of Fields cradling Baylee—were taken from the same angle at the same time. Porter worked as a lending specialist at a downtown bank. After the explosion, he ran to the site and began taking photographs. "I was just walking, taking pictures, as if I was on autopilot. For two or three weeks, I couldn't have told you in what order I took these. I didn't remember any of them."[55]

Later on the morning of April 19, Porter had his film developed. "I remember flipping through them, felt relieved that they were in focus, and showed them to some elderly women in the store. They began crying, and then I looked carefully at them." He took them to the local Associated Press office and was treated "dismissively." But "they scanned some frames into their computer. I was so innocent about all of this. The AP folks asked me what I wanted for one-time use and I said 'I don't know.'" He was promised a check, went home, and only began to realize what was to come when the *London Times* called early on the afternoon of April 19. "They asked me, 'How do you feel knowing that one of your photographs will be on the cover of every newspaper in the world tomorrow?'"[56]

Fierce jockeying for position took place between *Time* and *Newsweek*. "I reached an agreement with *Time*, then *Newsweek* said they would double the offer, but I told them I had given my word. *Life* called and I told them the same thing, but since they were a monthly, I could reach an agreement with them as well. The next day I went to work, saw the photo in every paper, and then the phone never stopped ringing, I remember Tom Brokaw was the first. I did a lot of interviews, and my favorite was about a week after the bombing, when a Canadian Catholic priest asked me what the photograph made me think of. I told him that for me it captured the emotion of compassion, for in the photograph Chris Fields has taken his gloves off. But it is also a terribly tragic image."

Porter won both the Pulitzer Prize and the British Picture Editors' Award, the first American and first amateur to receive the latter award. He also won an award from the International Association of Firefighters for, he recalled, "depicting the true act of what a fireman is and does." "It was tough when the phone calls stopped coming," he said. "I talked again with my pastor, who was so helpful in the early days, and he reminded me 'you're not that important,' and I've tried to remember that."

The Associated Press arranged a meeting between Porter and Aren Almon-Kok on Friday, April 21, at her family's home. "I apologized to her. She gave me a hug and thanked me. I asked her 'why,' and she told me when she saw the photograph that she knew it was Baylee, that at least she knew far earlier than many others." Chris Fields and Sergeant Avera met Aren Almon-Kok the day before, Thursday, April 20. "It was personal for me," Fields recalled, "and it was also part of my job. We met at her grandparent's home in Midwest City, a television station filmed it, and I remember a lot of crying and hugging."

Aren Almon-Kok and Chris Fields remain close friends. Charles Porter, however, recalled that there was some tension with her when pirated commercial use of his photograph began appearing. "I think Aren was angry with me when she saw some T-shirts with the photograph on it, but I always tried to make the stores stop selling them whenever I saw them. I turned down lots of marketing ideas that people proposed: coins, a statue that would sell for $9.95, shirts, and lots of other things people dreamed up." Porter obviously regretted whatever rift developed and recalled with some emotion Baylee's funeral and his continued link with her. "I don't think many people know that I drive by the cemetery every day, and every so often I'll stop at her grave if no one is there."

Chris Fields has his own collection of Baylee Almon memorabilia— including a belt buckle and key chain. The commercialization of the image of the fireman and the baby is a disquieting reminder of how virtually nothing is beyond the boundaries of consumer culture. Fields and Almon-Kok joined Oklahoma Natural Gas in their suit against LaRue because he allegedly authorized commercial usage of his contested photograph. They were unsuccessful in legal efforts to control commercial ventures using Baylee's image. "Our feeling," said state senator Brooks Douglass, who repre-

consumer public culture : memory [handwritten margin note]

sented Almon-Kok and Fields, "was that not all the uses were legitimate, and that Aren particularly should have had some control over the use of that powerful image of her daughter."[57]

Almon-Kok and Fields entered into an agreement with the Feed the Children organization, which had been active in postbombing relief efforts. For a short time the organization advertised an eighteen-inch bronze statue for $1,495 or a "bronze-tone cast" for $300, with most of the funds earmarked for relief. It was entitled "Innocence Lost," and the brochure informed potential buyers that the statue "stands as a reminder of the unimaginable evil that lurks in the hearts of some and the unquenchable courage of those who overcome evil with acts of love."[58]

While Almon-Kok and Fields sought to limit the use of the famous image to commemorative projects they thought helpful in fund-raising for family members and survivors, other commercial use went on without their knowledge. For example, Globalnet Communications in Gulfport, Mississippi, advertised a Baylee Almon phone card that "will *memorialize* the tragedy . . . in a way that no other depiction ever could."

Addressing concerns regarding inappropriate commercialization of this image, Globalnet declared that actual use of the card would be a memorial act, as each time people used the card, *"they will be reminded of this despicable waste of life and actually hear the salutation: 'Thank you for supporting the Oklahoma City Disaster relief fund.'"* Following this impassioned call to commercial memorializing, Globalnet offered suggestions for recharging the card, which, readers were told, would increase bombing relief funds. Those who needed extra incentive were assured that "immediate media attention could generate a frenzy of demand all over the world for this card as a *'collectible!'*"[59]

An Oklahoma company, Advantage Marketing Systems, also produced a phone card bearing the image of the fireman and baby for relief efforts. Fields recalled, "We were told that we could cooperate with the company or not, but either way the card would be done." "We decided to cooperate, not because we liked the idea, but for Aren especially, it was important to tone down the image. The company agreed to take most of the blood off Baylee and put her one-year-old birthday photo in a corner of the card." (Baylee Almon turned one-year-old the day before the bombing.) Almon-Kok and

Fields were also offered the opportunity to make "mutual comment" on the phone card to the public: "this picture...has come to symbolize the tragedy and the heartbreak of the Oklahoma City bombing. Since a portion of the proceeds from this phone card will go to the survivors...by purchasing the phone card you are expressing your support for victims of the tragedy and providing some tangible assistance to them."[60]

For Aren Almon-Kok, it was important to have Baylee's birthday photograph in public. It showed her alive, not a lifeless body in the arms of Chris Fields. "After the famous photographs," she recalled, "I had a hard time remembering her alive."[61]

Aren Almon-Kok and Baylee Almon, April 18, 1995, Baylee's one-year birthday. (Courtesy of Aren Almon-Kok and the Oklahoma City National Memorial Foundation, photograph by G. Jill Evans)

The image of the fireman and the baby thrust all of these people into the public eye, but none so much as Aren Almon-Kok. All of the deaths from the bombing were "public deaths," belonging in some usually unarticulated way to a larger bereaved community, and Baylee Almon's death was the most public of them all. This, of course, thrust Aren Almon-Kok into intense media attention within hours of learning of the death of her child. "I wasn't the only one to lose a child, and all of us who lost loved ones suffered terribly. But I had to look at the photograph of my child every day, in newspapers, magazines, on T-shirts and figurines." She recalled with sadness, disgust, and justifiable anger, coming upon a street vendor selling statues of the fireman and the baby, telling him that this was her baby, and he proceeded to invite her to buy a raffle ticket to win a statue. "I had to live her death all over again day after day."

Her life was one of enduring interest for the media. *People Weekly*, for example, covered her wedding on April 5, 1997, informing readers that she laid her bridal bouquet on Baylee's grave. There was a great deal of national publicity when she gave birth to her daughter Bella on January 28, 1998. "I remember that the media was buzzing around before I went into labor," she recalled, "and the hospital wouldn't let my nieces and nephews into the room to see her, but somehow some cameras made it into intensive care. I received a lot of calls to appear on various shows, and I did agree to appear on the *Today* show."[62]

I first met Aren Almon-Kok in the small delicatessen she ran for several years, Miss Baylee's Deli, located on the ground floor of the Regency Towers apartment building, only a block from the Murrah Building. She and Baylee had lived there and, like all other residents, she had to move out for months because the building was so badly damaged. We talked while her daughter Bella scooted around the deli. As with so many other family members and survivors, I felt a familiar guilt asking her to go back once again into a painful and intimate story for someone she did not know. And, as with so many other family members and survivors, I watched the event take over her face as she traveled into a familiar and horrible site within, evident on her face through deliberate speech, carefully chosen words, and eyes filled with tears in the course of conversation.

"No one really thought about the effect that photograph had on me," she recalled. "Some parents who had lost other children were hurtful because they thought that their loss was going to be forgotten, and only Baylee remembered by the public. They seemed to forget that it wasn't my fault that the photograph was taken." More than many others, she had to deal with the burden of recognition immediately after the bombing. "People would come up to me in the grocery store and ask me if I was 'that' person, and when I went to buy burial clothes for Baylee, I was stopped by a couple who wanted to have their picture taken with me."

Aren Almon-Kok has not been active in official memorial efforts, although she did have a collection can for the memorial in the deli. "One reason I was hesitant to become active was that I didn't want people to say 'well, she just got her way because of Baylee.'"

The burden of having to share Baylee's death with the whole world made her fearful of projecting the wrong image in public. "In the midst of this intense grief," she said, "my life belonged to everyone else. I was scared of going out in public for a very long time because I kept thinking 'I shouldn't smile or laugh because people might think I don't care enough about Baylee.'"

Thrust into the public eye immediately, Aren Almon-Kok and Chris Fields appeared together on several television shows. For her, it was an opportunity to talk about Baylee's short life and remind people that there was a life beyond the body everyone saw in the photograph. Chris Fields found some of the interviews therapeutic. "It forced me to talk about a lot of stuff that might have remained buried." Their appearances generated an enormous public response, beginning, of course, with gossip. "I tried to make sure that when I received an interview offer," Fields said, "I contacted Aren and we often went together. What really brought us together initially was trying to stop the use of the photograph, but we became good friends as we went through so much. Like Aren, I am married with a family, and it hurt when gossip started that we were having an affair. We still do see each other socially as couples."

Fields received lots of condolence mail, "often addressed to the 'fireman in the photo,'" received requests for the photograph, got "lots of patches, shorts, hats, from other fireman," had to deal with autograph seekers, and was asked to attend as guest of honor the annual volunteer firefighter day in Pamlico, North Carolina. He smiled as he told me that he also received two wedding proposals.

In her home, Aren Almon-Kok has four huge plastic containers of mail and a study filled with Baylee Almon memorabilia. There are letters—many handwritten, some two or three pages, some from other mothers who had lost children to disease, accident, or violence, some unsigned, some just signed, for example, "from a caring family in Minnesota." Schoolchildren sent drawings of rainbows, other letters offered reassurance or offered to help "in any way we can." Some sent money. One couple offered their condominium in Florida for when it got "too tough to take." One woman sent various skin-care products, informing her that "part of your road to recovery will be to relax. What better way than to have all the 'stuff' for a good long bath and some skin care."[63]

A family from Florida promised to visit Baylee's grave. Aren Almon-Kok's grade-school classmates wrote letters to her, which arrived two days after the bombing. Numerous women wrote that they either had named or would name their baby Baylee. Other mothers of newborns wrote "every time I look at her I think of you and Baylee." A father and daughter sent a photograph of the "Baylee tree" they had planted, and a Pittsburgh, Pennsylvania, Web site carried messages. One attributed protective powers to the memory of Baylee Almon. "When I picked up the *Newsweek* magazine and saw Baylee Almon, I burst into tears. Pictures of her the day before the bombing showed a happy baby, celebrating the first year of her life. I instantly became attached to her, and I have a picture of her in a Minnie Mouse jumper smiling happily at nine-months-old. She brings happiness into every day of my life and protects me from danger. I love her very much. Seeing her lovely smile is all I need to get through this horrible tragedy. I know she is in heaven now."[64]

Aren Almon-Kok responded to each of the thousands of letters she received, and she developed an enduring relationship with a special education class at Grandview Elementary School in Dothan, Alabama. The children saved money to plant a tree in memory of Baylee Almon. The *Dothan Eagle* reported that "whether it's picking weeds or decorating it for the different holiday seasons, the children have taken the tree under their care and made it part of their family." Almon-Kok corresponded with the class for over a year and visited Dothan in July 1996 with her fiancé. They visited Baylee's tree and released a balloon for each of the nineteen children murdered. In 1998, the Boys and Girls Club of Dothan joined the class in planting three more trees on Baylee's birthday.[65]

One of the most moving letters Almon-Kok received was written on the first anniversary of the bombing by a nurse in Oklahoma City. "You have conducted yourself in a dignified manner all this year, even in the face of some horrible events. Even as young as you are, you have presented yourself in a mature way, one that Baylee would be proud of. I will be celebrating Baylee's short life on her birthday and mourning her death the next day. I'm sure I will not be the only Oklahoman thinking of you on those days."

Almon-Kok also received mountains of memorial materials: angel pins, angels holding babies, poems, a gold Baylee Almon necklace, pendants, cotton crosses, a replica of a brick that was laid in memory of Baylee Almon at the Atlanta Olympic games, wreaths, a large pink heart, and numerous paintings of the fireman and the baby.[66]

In June 1995, Almon-Kok and Fields attended the unveiling of a drawing created by a student in a life drawing class at the University of Oklahoma. Gregory Blaksley donated the pastel to St. Anthony Hospital, where Baylee

The photograph inspired numerous art works, some depicting a sleeping, clean Baylee in the arms of Chris Fields. (Contributor Unknown)

Some artists found consolation in their vision of Baylee Almon moving from the arms of Chris Fields to the arms of Jesus Christ, accompanied by angels. (Eva Marie Ippolito)

Dick Locher's editorial cartoon in the *Chicago Tribune* depicted Chris Fields handing Baylee into God's waiting hands. (Tribune Media Services, Inc. All Rights Reserved. Reprinted with permission)

Almon was pronounced dead, and it was placed in the lobby. In another painting, Rosie Lara, an amateur artist and homemaker from Arlington, Texas, transformed the famous image, placing Baylee in the arms of Jesus. "In the days following the disaster, I discovered that Jesus had been there amid all the chaos and destruction," she said. "It was his face in the firefighter holding that precious baby." A family-produced press kit included information on her presenting a copy of the painting to Chris Fields. The original painting was displayed in the Governor's Blue Room in the Oklahoma state capitol. The *Dallas Morning News* reported that "Mrs. Lara also hopes to find a sponsor who will help her make copies to present to the families of the victims and to display in churches. She says such displays might help others see what she saw: a vision of Jesus among the bombed ruins."[67]

Interestingly, some of the paintings I am familiar with—in Aren Almon-Kok's home, in her deli, and in the archive—transform the battered and bloody body of Baylee into the peacefully sleeping Baylee. Sometimes, as in a painting in Miss Baylee's Deli, she is adorned with angel's wings. Often she rests clean, as if emerging from a bath in the arms of Chris Fields.

The power of the image of the fireman and the baby made it the single most popular memorial idea. Within several weeks of the bombing, Governor Keating said that people wanted a "very substantial bronze statue of the firefighter carrying the child." It was, he said, "the metaphor for the heroism and the decency and the integrity of those who served in this tragic enterprise." A letter to the governor recommending such a statue stated that "this picture will last as long as the flag raising on Iwo Jima, invasion at Normandy or any other of WWII, Korea, or Vietnam."[68]

There were proposals for larger-than-life bronze statues, and a Florida company offered to donate $30,000 toward such a statue. Eric Fischl, a New York artist, had created a statue of an adult male and child in 1992, and after he saw the photograph of Baylee Almon he donated the statue to the Oklahoma City Art Museum, where it was unveiled in April 1996. The renowned sculptor Felix De Weldon, who indicated his desire to donate his expertise to create a memorial in Oklahoma City, envisioned a statue of the fireman and the baby for his memorial gift. The Minnesota Jaycees proposed a stone of life memorial, with the famous image on a large center stone slab. Some proposals wanted a fireman and baby statue surrounded with rescuers, often holding hands. One person, mistaken in her recollection that Baylee lived, wrote "I believe the statue of the child being rescued is certainly appropriate. Since so many dogs worked tirelessly in the rescue efforts, would you consider adding a dog possibly carrying a child's tennis shoe?" A Wisconsin woodcarver wrote Mayor Norick for help in finding a proper home for a woodcarving of the fireman and the baby, "Why the Innocent?" that she had created and entered in various competitions. "The response from the public was astounding," she said, "and it has taken first place awards throughout."

In 1996, Sam Butcher, creator of Precious Moments, was inspired by the image of the fireman and the baby to create two six-foot statues based on the

Noted Oklahoma Indian artist Cliff Doyeto featured the image of the fireman and the baby in his commemorative painting. (Cliff Doyeto)

artistic design of the Precious Moments figurines. One was placed in the gallery of the Precious Moments Chapel Center in Carthage, Missouri. He hoped the other would be placed in a memorial park on the site of the bombing. Butcher's assistant, Larrene Hagaman, recalled leading a tour in the Precious Moments chapel while recovery efforts in Oklahoma City were still under way. The chapel features large paintings of Biblical scenes, including "Hallelujah Square," a 504-square-foot painting in which heaven is viewed through the eyes of children. "I told the group that I couldn't help thinking of the children who were killed when I looked at the paintings," she said. "A visitor pointed out that they had recovered the bodies of sixteen children so far, and he noticed that there were sixteen children in the painting standing around Jesus. Not long after we learned there were nineteen children killed. It was then I realized that there were three additional children climbing the stairs to join the others. Knowing that the painting had been done seven years earlier it sent chills down my spine. Sometime later I told this story to some family members and survivors from Oklahoma City who had come to visit the chapel in a bus. It was an unforgettable time of sharing."

Sam Butcher had planned to make a smaller commemorative figurine as well and donate the proceeds to relief efforts. But he decided not to proceed after he learned of Aren Almon-Kok's discomfort at so many commemorative representations of the image. "People still beg us to make the figurine," Hagaman said, "and they constantly ask, 'where is the tribute to the bombing?'"[69]

There was some sentiment in Oklahoma City to place one of Butcher's statues at a new playground dedicated in October 1995 to the murdered children in Oklahoma City at Lake Hefner. Aware of Almon-Kok's strong objections to having her daughter's death become part of the memorial landscape of the city, however, the Memorial Foundation's former executive director, Sydney Dobson, wrote Governor Keating in October 1996 that they could "not support this image for public display. . . . No matter the form . . . this particular image is too painful."

Samuel J. Butcher, artist and creator of Precious Moments®, with the statue he created in remembrance of the children. (Samuel J. Butcher)

For one former secret service agent, the image of the fireman and the baby would have been a part of the ritual execution of the perpetrators. "At the moment the death sentence is carried out," he wrote Governor Keating, "the last thing [the murderers] should see is the picture of the fireman and the baby. Let that be their last image of this earth." Geographical connection with the perpetrators so shamed an art professor at the University of Michigan that he offered to produce a life-size sculpture of the fireman and the baby as an expression of penance. "At the fireman's feet is a skeleton representing evil and death. The fireman is pushing the skeleton away from the child trying to save her life."

There was also significant public ambivalence about a Baylee Almon statue. The *Daily Oklahoman* declared on May 10, 1995, "officials should avoid the tendency to micro-manage memorial plans. They do no honor to those murdered by arguing over who should be honored and how. Police Chief Sam Gonzales is already playing this game with his objection to a memorial that stresses a statue of the fireman carrying Baylee Almon. Gonzales wants more emphasis on the role played by police." Occasionally a letter would object to the statue because it offered a "display of grief and horror,[and] we truly will have given in to the terrorists who perpetrated this crime."

Beyond official memorial proposals, however, there were plans for Baylee Almon statues in Oklahoma City. Some statues were just sent, unsolicited, to the city. "I remember one huge statue that must have weighed a ton or more," Aren Almon-Kok recalled. "Someone just brought it on a flatbed truck and left it in front of city hall. They wanted it placed in a park. I had to go the mayor and governor and tell them I didn't want any statue of Baylee erected."[70]

Kari Watkins, the Memorial Foundation's executive director, recalled a concern that many submissions for the official memorial design competition, which was announced on November 15, 1996, would contain some version of the fireman and the baby. "There were many reasons why we didn't want this," Watkins recalled. "Certainly Aren's feelings were important. I introduced myself to her on the first anniversary and told her that the foundation would work hard not to perpetuate the image." Indeed, in the design competition booklet, participants are specifically requested "not to depict

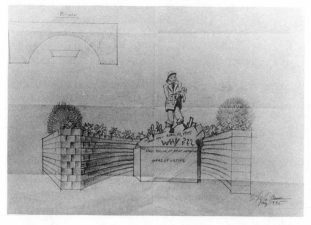

Percy Ossmann's interpretation of the fireman and the baby posed the question so many struggled with, "Why?" (Designed and submitted by Percy W. Ossmann)

Oklahoma artist Una Jean Carter offered a strikingly different interpretation of the fireman and the baby in "He Conquered Death." (Una Jean Carter: artondisplay.com)

A skeleton representing death attempts to pull Baylee Almon from Chris Fields's arms. (Denis Lee)

physical representation of any known person, living or dead, in their Design Entry." While this instruction helped rule out other potentially problematic images (e.g., statues of Jesus), it was unofficially known as the "Baylee Almon clause." In spite of this, Watkins said, "One of the five finalists did include a small sketch of the fireman and the baby. I called Bob Johnson, told him that 'we have a problem,' because this design could have won! We informed Aren about this, and the judges of the competition were told that this particular segment of the submission would not be acceptable should this design win. It did not."[71]

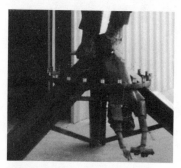

Shipped from Virginia, this 11-foot, 1500-pound scrap-iron statue might have found a home in an Oklahoma City park, except for the objection of Aren Almon-Kok. Note that the fireman is standing on the body of a prone terrorist, still holding an explosive device in a hand. (Oklahoma City National Memorial Foundation, photographs by Jane Thomas and G. Jill Evans)

By the fifth anniversary of the bombing, Aren Almon-Kok's active grief led her to become the national spokesperson for the Protecting People First Foundation, dedicated to "raising awareness about the deadly effects of flying glass caused by terrorist attack or natural disaster." (The force of the explosion turned glass into lethal projectiles in Oklahoma City.) Supported by Chris Fields, Almon-Kok presents a Safety Award, that bears the image of the fireman and baby to organizations that "protect their employees and customers from flying glass hazards." Tes-

Several memorial ideas incorporated both Chris Fields and Baylee Almon and Murrah ruins. (Michael Weber)

tifying before the House Subcommittee on Public Buildings, appearing on various news and talk shows, Almon-Kok said, "I want to create a new

Baylee Almon's chair, Oklahoma City National Memorial. (David Allen, Oklahoma City)

national understanding of that image and in the process ensure that some good comes out of the tragic death of my daughter and 167 other victims."[72]

The Murrah Fence and the Survivor Tree: A People's Memorial

I first visited Oklahoma City in the spring of 1997 at the invitation of Toby Thompson, who was active in the Memorial Foundation's activities and whose brother was killed in the bombing. We went to the site shortly after I arrived, and I was stunned by the desolate feel of the area. The Athenian and Water Resources Buildings had been torn down, but the gutted remains of the Journal Record Building and the boarded-up ruins of the six-story YMCA, lifted off its foundations by the bomb, were still standing. Next to the Journal Record Building stood the "Survivor Tree," scrawny and charred but still alive, even though automobiles exploded around it when the bomb went off. It became a symbol of endurance so important to family members and survivors that they insisted significant sections remain as part of the permanent memorial.

We walked slowly around the chain-link fence that contained the site. From the night of April 19, when the police perimeter was twenty square blocks the fence location changed as debris was cleared and the building was imploded. Finally the site was no longer considered an active crime scene. By the time I visited, a fence surrounded the one-square-block area that contained the Murrah parking garage and plaza and the grassy area where the Murrah Building had stood. As already noted, spontaneous memorialization began shortly after the bombing, and the fence soon became a memorial site. (On October 26, 1998, the day after ground was broken for the memorial, a fence-moving ceremony took place, with portions of the fence preserved along the edge of the memorial ground so that people could continue to leave items.) It was hard for me to "read" the fence on this first visit. I saw a bewildering collection of items, from profoundly moving personal letters to those killed to tasteless kitsch, for example, two smiley faces printed with the message, "Think of the good times that will happen in the future!"

Like many others, I immediately thought of the Vietnam Veterans Memorial as a "model" for the fence in Oklahoma City. They are both memorial sites where "the public"—person by person—has made the site its own through a gift, an offering, a desire to leave something of oneself. Some of the offerings are items—wreaths, teddy bears, condolence cards—that make up mainstream material memorial culture. Others are items with uniquely personal meanings, left by those who have personal attachments to the dead. Through memorial offerings at both places the living communicate with the dead, and the living make statements to one another about the meaning of the event and people they are so actively remembering.[73]

There are significant differences, however. The Vietnam Veterans Memorial was created through a formal design competition, and despite the tumultuous history of its coming into being, it was built to be a memorial. The fence in Oklahoma City was initially constructed to do what fences do— restrict access—first to a crime scene, then to a hazardous site, and then to a space that became, for some, "sacred ground." One family member said, "The fence was a perimeter of a site too horrible to get close to. It protected

The fence protecting the grassy area where the Murrah Building once stood quickly became an important memorial site. (David Allen, Oklahoma City)

us from further physical harm and even symbolic harm in that it held us back from getting nearer to something incomprehensible."

The fence surrounding the Murrah site was spontaneously transformed into a memorial by the acts of tens of thousands of individuals. The fence shared as much with various ethnic funerary traditions in which people left personal items on grave sites or even in coffins as it did with the Vietnam Veterans Memorial. It shared something with a tradition prevalent in Catholic memorialization: marking sites of death with a cross. "These wood, metal, and cement crosses," wrote Martha Cooper and Joseph Sciorra, "manifest the belief that the souls of those who die unexpectedly and fail to receive the Last Rites of the Catholic Church are suffering in purgatory's purifying flames. The marker serves then as a lasting reminder for passersby to pray for the person's soul and thus speed its eventual arrival into heaven." Such practices have always been popular in areas of the United States influenced by Latino culture, and they have now spread as various groups adopt this centuries-old custom. "Roadside crosses are showing up from the Mormon heartland to the Mississippi Delta," one newspaper reported in 1996.[74]

There are always hundreds of small crosses hanging on the Murrah fence. A few crosses are fashioned from crochet or cross-stitch, but most are made of egg cartons, Christmas paper wrapping tubes, metal, plastic, cardboard, match sticks, and plain sticks tied together.[75]

Often shorn of specific theological content, spontaneous shrines to victims of violence serve as sites of mourning, sites of protest against the conditions of violence that contributed to the death, and sites of public commemorative ceremonies. Cooper and Sciorra note that outdoor memorial murals for those murdered in New York City "create new public spaces for community ceremony. Life is celebrated at the walls with parties marking anniversaries and birthdays." The fence in Oklahoma City draws something from each of these traditions: like the Vietnam Veterans Memorial, it is a memorial site transformed by the diverse motives and materials people bring; like roadside shrines, it marks a particular site where life unexpectedly ended and, consequently, transformed an ordinary space into a "charged" site; like the increasingly popular tradition of spontaneous memorials to victims of violence, it serves a variety of purposes, which we can begin to understand by thinking about the things people carried to the fence.[76]

Jane Thomas, curator of the Memorial Foundation, and a group of volunteers have painstakingly collected, cleaned, preserved and catalogued what has been left at the fence. It consists of wonderfully eclectic material, a cacophony of clashing tastes, from the most traditionally religious to the most embarrassingly bizarre and superficial. (What can be said about a brochure from the Fort Sill Museum, with a photo of a large mounted gun being fired and a caption: "The French 75. A new gun for a new century," or about a poem to Benny Goodman and Malcolm X that ends, "Jesus is Lord! He must increase, I decrease.") "I remember being asked why the foundation needed a curator to collect 30,000 teddy bears," Thomas said. "As people connected with the foundation began to visit, they began to realize the extent of our collection." [77]

Thomas thinks that much of the material left at the fence reflects impulse offering. "I have been at the site many times and watched people take in the place. They are shocked, they are overwhelmed by the magnitude, and they decide to leave something. They don't expect to see so much from others, and they want to participate. I have seen people take off their shirts, women take off earrings and bracelets. They want to leave a piece of themselves, perhaps to show respect, often with a message."

People often leave items they can write on, and it is the message, not the material, that counts. They write on hats, shirts, scarves, military jackets, Boy Scout uniforms, pillow cases, towels and washcloths (sometimes taken from nearby hotels), cardboard, pieces of boxes, loose-leaf paper, amusement park passes, sports tickets, luggage tags (with a message in the address area), paper plates, church bulletins, part of a torn wing from a styrofoam toy glider, a dollar bill, a school schedule, the back of a book of invoices.

People leave items that tell where they came from: key chains and driver's licenses, flags and maps from various countries, student and business identification badges, and thousands of business cards. Some leave items that are even more personal, various pieces of jewelry, for example. Occasionally, they leave things that highlight the ethnicity or nationality of those killed. For example, a Mexican flag at the fence carried a message: "Because three Mexicans were murdered when the Murrah Federal Building was destroyed, I bring this Mexican flag in their honor."

Some, in contrast to those who make impulse offerings, come to the fence planning to leave something, and this has increased since it became public knowledge that materials left on the fence were being collected by the Memorial Foundation's archives. But distinguishing impulse offerings from planned ones may be impossible. How can it be determined that someone planned to bring something to the fence in the hopes that it would be collected and become part of the history of the memorialization of the bombing?

"I think of planned offerings," Thomas said, "as people saying, 'I'm going to the fence and I want to leave something special.'" School groups, musical and theater groups, sports teams, visiting church groups, fraternities and sororities, for example, left huge signed cards, signed T-shirts, medals, pom-poms from cheerleader squads, group letters, poems, drawings. The aware-ness that this material was being saved, as well as the hope that their offerings would be included in the collection, is evident in the many framed or lami-nated poems or letters, sometimes including an address to write for copies and sometimes copyrighted.

There are items that could fit into either category: toys of all kinds, sets of coloring books, a massive collection of beanie babies, numerous baby items: clothes, rattles, pacifiers, diapers, baby blankets. There are golf clubs, fishing rods, ceramic figurines, paintings, poems.

Unlike the Vietnam Veterans Memorial, a huge number of religious items have been left at the Murrah fence. Scriptural messages of reassurance, of solace, of joy in the world the Lord has made, or the illusory power of death, rest next to printed prayer cards: some to various saints—Saint Anne and Saint Jude, for example; a card with an "ancient prayer to the Virgin"; inspi-rational messages; and popular devotional wisdom. (The Serenity prayer, "The Cross in My Pocket," and "Footprints" show up regularly; the children's prayer "Now I Lay Me Down to Sleep" also appears.) People bring literature that they think will help those who grieve at the site: an article on healing from *Sesame Street Magazine* and an advertisement for a book by Ed Hearn, a former professional baseball player who overcame serious illnesses, enti-tled *Conquering Life's Curves.* There is an occasional Star of David, an occa-sional Buddhist prayer, an occasional Native American version of the Twenty-third Psalm, an occasional quote from the twelve steps of Alcoholics Anonymous. Bibles (mostly New Testaments), rosaries, What Would Jesus

Do? bracelets, drawings of praying hands, cards explaining the role of guardian angels, angel drawings, pins, and ribbons are also popular.

In addition to being a site of public mourning, the fence clearly represents to many who visit it a site for the continuing cosmic battle between good and evil. A prayer card of Saint Michael the archangel asks that God "be our protection against the wickedness and snares of the Devil. . . . By the Power of God, thrust into hell Satan and all evil spirits who wander through the world for the ruin of souls." Another message included a list of "frustrations leading to roots of bitterness" and a declaration, "Satan, we nail them up here—No More!" And there is a scorecard of the battle that took place on the site:

APRIL 19, 1995
THE FINAL OUTCOME
HEAVEN 168
HELL 2

For evangelicals, the sudden death of so many served as a warning sign to all those yet unsaved; consequently, the site is a fruitful place to harvest lost souls. Numerous prayer cards exhort readers to turn to Christ before it is too late, and prayers for the revival of America appear regularly.

The fence is also a public forum. All who visit are free to share their interpretations of what this event and site mean. There are messages calling people to work for nonviolent solutions to social problems, a brochure for abortion recovery assistance, occasional written statements about ongoing conspiracies concerning the bombing, and occasional bizarre advice to the visiting public, for example, a typed announcement alerting visitors to go to the nearest fire or police station to get information on "cyberkinetic death methods," since "cybercops have caused the death of many," including, the letter implied, those in the Murrah Building. The fence is also a forum for memorial site testimonials, poems and letters about the significance and power of the fence itself. For some people it is not enough, apparently, for the fence to "speak" to visitors. Rather, visitors must first be educated about the fence so that they can truly appreciate it.[78]

The transformative power of the fence was dramatized in an episode of the CBS Series *Promised Land*, in which the Greene family travels about the nation in an Airstream trailer. Martha Williamson, producer of *Touched by an Angel*, conceived of this episode after the April 23 memorial service, when citizens nationwide were urged to ring bells in remembrance. "I stood out on the porch and rang a bell, and I heard bells up and down the street." She said of this episode, "we're going to ring a bell every Tuesday night and make people feel good about America."[79]

The fence episode begins with grandmother Greene and her grandchildren Josh and Dinah driving to Oklahoma City. Josh is unenthusiastic about the trip, and asks his grandmother, "Why do you want to go?" She responds, "Because I've forgotten and that's not right. What happened there in the middle of the country, really happened to all of us." When they arrive, the camera gives the audience a "tour" of the Oklahoma City skyline and then moves slowly down the fence. The three visitors approach the fence on foot, with Josh bored beyond words, saying, "I just can't get worked up about it." As the grandmother's anger grows, a National Park Service ranger meets them, talks about the significance of the fence, and offers them a tour of a short exhibition of the bombing in a small room in the Murrah parking garage. As the action develops, the audience can clearly see Josh begin to change. He runs to the Survivor Tree, exclaiming, "I feel them" (the presence of those killed). His grandmother advises him to "take the feeling with you, wherever you go. We owe it to them, and to ourselves."[80]

For many family members and survivors, the fence is also domestic memorial space, a place in which the boundary between this world and the next disappears, a place for prayer, eulogy, and testimonial. Many family members leave offerings at the section of the fence nearest the place in which their loved one died. They claim an area of the fence that becomes their memorial area. "Many parents," Jane Thomas observed, "put things on the fence in the same place." The archive's policy is to leave items "directly relating to victims" on the fence unless families indicate otherwise.[81]

Family members and survivors leave offerings that are personal yet public. They leave love letters to a dead spouse, to children, sisters or brothers, parents or friends. They leave written eulogies enclosed in large wreaths with photographs and items that represent a person's life. There are heartbreaking personal letters on the fence: "Dear Mamma, I'm writing to you to tell you good-bye. I have to try and get on with my life.... I have to face the fact that you're dead and you won't be coming home ever again. I love you mom. Good-bye."

Some family members leave challenging letters to visitors. Deborah Ferrell-Lynn, whose cousin Susan was murdered, informed visitors that Susan would want her death to "stand for something." She then offers a challenge: "How will you change because of this place and the people who died in years to come? Or will you ask, 'How can I stop the pain, the suffering, the tears?'"

The fence is also a gathering place for family members and survivors on special occasions. Shortly before Christmas 1995, approximately 150 relatives gathered at the site to decorate a Christmas tree. Some family members have had small birthday parties at the fence; others come regularly on certain holidays. Twenty-four-year-old Scott Williams was killed making a delivery to the Murrah Building when the bomb exploded. He was a baseball coach and his team would come to the fence after a game and leave a ball in his honor. Rescue workers come to the site and leave messages that communicate how much the event lives on in them. An emergency nurse left a hard hat at the fence on the third anniversary with a message, "Why couldn't I do more? I'm so sorry." A message from another nurse read, "I was here two years ago—helping. My heart still aches."

"Sometimes," Thomas recalled, "we get a pair of gloves on the fence, standard contractor gloves that I am sure were worn on the site during rescue and recovery efforts, and I know that many rescue workers come back after other disasters. They've left their team's patch, a shirt, a hard hat, and work boots. Sometimes I will find a baby's shoes, and wonder if they belonged to one of the murdered children. Family members have come regularly to place hats a daughter wore on the fence. We find lipstick and other personal items that I suspect were brought by family members."[82]

People have transformed the Survivor Tree into a "people's memorial" as well. Sydney Dobson, former executive director of the Memorial Foundation, commented in July 1997 that "each day, more and more people are sticking items into the bark, or hammering things into the bark or tying something on the tree, or more recently, taking a piece of the bark home as a memento."[83]

Standing just across Fifth Street from the Murrah Building, the tree became a symbol of resilience and endurance. Bud Welch, whose daughter Julie was killed, took notice of the tree after the bombing because Julie always parked near it. On his way to a meeting of family members and survivors one evening, he saw a bulldozer grading a ledge between the two parking lots near the tree, arousing fears that the tree might be destroyed. He told family members, "This is the only living thing left. It's a real survivor."[84]

This particular tree, an American elm (or slippery elm) was indeed a hardy survivor. According to Mark Bays, the urban forestry coordinator for the Oklahoma State Department of Agriculture, the tree was not planted intentionally but was a "volunteer," growing from a seed that settled on the spot. "We have a photograph from the 1940s," Bays said, "that shows the tree on the edge of someone's property line." "The tree," Bays pointed out, "was not dealt a great hand to begin with." It survived being surrounded by asphalt up to its trunk. It survived several waves of Dutch elm disease in Oklahoma City; it survived the blast from the bomb and fires from exploding cars around it; and it survived massive debris hurled into it from the force of the blast. It lost all its leaves after the bombing, and it was not until Welch took notice that there was interest in preserving the tree.[85]

It soon became a sacred object. Volunteers and a tree service company donated their time to take care of it. Applying for a grant to document the life of the tree, the Oklahoma Vegetation Management Association summarized the preservation activity. "The asphalt parking lot surrounding the tree has been removed allowing vital oxygen and water to the root system. Dead, broken and burned limbs have been removed to help reduce the spread of decay. Parasitic mistletoe has been removed. Frequent inspections are made to monitor disease and pest infestation which may require treatment. Soil and plant tissue samples have been taken to analyze for possible nutrient deficiencies. Seed from the Survivor Tree has been collected, first-post bombing generation seedlings were given to survivors, victims's families and others as a symbol of life." The tree was vaccinated against Dutch elm disease, and a local television station brought its viewers footage of the tree being sprayed to protect it against an insect infestation.[86]

Mark Bays recalled that "many people wanted seedlings for memorial gardens and arboretums" and expressed hope that eventually "thousands of seedlings can be distributed to the general public." On August 13, 1997, during the presentation of the winning memorial design at the White House, family member Toby Thompson presented a seedling to President Clinton. The president called it a "great gift to the American people" and promised it would be planted "alongside the dogwood" [planted shortly after the bombing]. The seedling comes, the president said, "from what is a true tree of life, and that tree will always remind us of the city, the people who bent but did not break." Seedlings—the offspring of the tree—will not do, however, when the tree dies, so cuttings have been taken to create clones. Housed in a nursery, another tree of the exact genetic material will eventually replace the Survivor Tree.[87]

Like the fence, the Survivor Tree became a gathering place for family members and survivors on important occasions. On the evening of June 2, 1997, shortly after Timothy McVeigh was found guilty, Murrah survivor Dr. Paul Heath, a psychologist with the Department of Veterans Affairs and president of the Oklahoma City Murrah Building Survivors Association, organized a ceremony attended by several hundred people. They were given plastic bottles of water, symbolizing the grief brought on by the bombing. Heath

A ceremony at the Survivor Tree on June 2, 1997, the day of the McVeigh verdict. (Oklahoma City National Memorial Foundation)

said, "we're going to pour out our grief, enough to symbolize the grief that we've resolved." People poured water on the roots of the tree. Others kept some water to pour out when Terry Nichols was convicted, December 23, 1997.[88]

This incredible public memorial energy was already at work within weeks of the bombing by July 1995, when Oklahoma City's mayor asked attorney Robert Johnson to organize a memorial task force to submit recommendations for a permanent memorial. The process was turbulent and painful, and it led family members, survivors, indeed all involved, far beyond their initial expectation of selecting an appropriate memorial design. It is to that fascinating story that I now turn.

Note: sources for this chapter include written material—letters, poems, official proclamations of condolence, and so on—in the Memorial Foundation archives, catalogued in several major collections. Much other material, however, was uncatalogued when I had access to it. Since my research notes will be made a part of the archives, I have decided to simplify the text and not offer endnotes for each letter I quote from, each item from the fence I speak about. The major sources for this chapter are Governor's Collection 9501/27, Youth and Adult; Miscellaneous File: Trees in Israel, minimemorials, Survivor Tree, Site History, Newsletters (3 boxes); 1003 Memorial Ideas, 4 boxes: (1) Alaska-Louisiana; (2) Maine-Newcastle, OK; (3) Norman, OK-Oregon; (4) Pennsylvania-Wyoming, D.C., International; 1095 Memorial Ideas f/OKC Beautiful; Memorial—Surveys 64-3198; Paper Items (36 boxes): 56/18212—YMCA Memorial and 126/2986, Susan Thiessing Collection; Mayor's Office Documents, 9663/74; 10/759 Mayor's Cards and Letters, Youth, Individual, and Adult; 931 Governor's Cards and Letters—Youth; 9501/927 Large Cards—Governor's Collection, Youth; 15c United Way; 112/2340 Cards and Letters Youth, Jack Poe Collection; 9618 Iowa Trees; 9658/864 Contractors Info. on Recovery; 9610/759 Internet Quilts; 9663/734 Mayor's Office Documents, two boxes, in same collection two boxes proclamations, one oversize box; uncatalogued materials from Sydney Dobson, Kari Ferguson (Watkins), and Sunni Mercer.

5

"WE COME HERE TO REMEMBER":
CREATING THE MEMORIAL IN
OKLAHOMA CITY

As we have seen, intense interest in a memorial to those killed in the bombing was evident within a few days after the bombing as suggestions from around the world poured into the mayor's and governor's offices. There was widespread concern, however, that an influential person or group would successfully make a case for a memorial that would represent the triumph of personal taste over community conviction. Jackie Jones, then the executive director of the Arts Council of Oklahoma, recalled that "many of us were scared that any memorial process would be short-circuited, that it was going to get away from us quickly in the first few weeks after the bombing."

Resentment also began to build among family members who heard rumors that the "powers that be" in the city had already decided on a memorial design. John and Sandy Cole, godparents of two murdered children, Aaron and Elijah Coverdale, remember other family members saying, "Well, this has all been decided anyway." Hearing that the same firms which were responsible for the downtown improvement program, MAPS, were going to build the memorial, Kathleen Treanor, whose young daughter and in-laws had been murdered, called the Coles and several other family members and held a press conference at the Murrah site, calling for the inclusion of family members in the memorial process. Treanor became cochair of several memorial task force committees and volunteered to produce a newsletter.[1]

There was good reason for concern. Individuals offered to pay for the memorial, as long as they were given freedom to choose a design, and there were exorbitant offers of bombing relief donations in return for the privilege of building a memorial. People used their influence—financial, social, or even the status of a family member—to champion their favorite memorial idea.

A concerned Mayor Norick believed that "we couldn't have all these different memorial agendas; the city needed to take control of this." Several weeks after the bombing, he asked Robert Johnson, a well-known Oklahoma City attorney in the firm of Crowe & Dunlevy, to organize and direct a memorial process that would be representative of the community. Johnson was very active in the community, chairing Arts Festival committees, serving on the board of directors of the American Red Cross and the Arts Council of Oklahoma City, for example, and he was willing to serve as volunteer chairman of what became the Oklahoma City Murrah Federal Building Memorial Task Force.

Johnson selected a dozen people who could help identify different constituencies to include in memorial planning: "We thought of people from different parts of the area, those who would represent racial, religious, city, state, and federal government, those who could represent rescue and recovery people," he recalled. They faced a daunting task: in the midst of a city reeling from the impact of the bombing, they had to create a process that would include those seared by the loss of loved ones, a process that would lead to a memorial that might offer some solace to this bereaved community. From the beginning, Johnson realized that the credibility of the project rested on the privileged place of the voices of family members and survivors, and this commitment became the bedrock on which the entire process rested.[2]

From June 10 to June 13, 1995, Johnson and several other task force members attended the National Assembly of Local Art Agencies convention in San Jose, California, "Contemporary Culture: The Interaction Between Art and the World Surrounding Us." They learned, in Johnson's words, that "the common thread of troubled projects is a lack of community input and participation, a resentment at not being allowed to be heard." Jimmy Goodman, a colleague of Johnson's at Crowe & Dunlevy and a member of the memorial task force, said of the San Jose trip, "We had no blueprint, nor did anyone else, of how to begin a memorial in the midst of such a broadly devastating event and absolutely raw time. We came back with two commitments, first, to have any chance of success we would need to let family members and survivors have a primary voice, and then we would recognize widening circles of impact. Secondly, the process, if handled properly, would be more important than the final result. These have always been the guiding principles, and I think they have served us well."[3]

The task force took shape in July 1995, only three months after the bombing. It was charged with ensuring an inclusive planning process. The task force would gather "extensive input from families, survivors, and the public about what visitors to the memorial should think, feel, or experience; develop a mission statement for the memorial; carry out a design-solicitation process based upon objectives in the mission statement, and recommend to the Mayor and Oklahoma City City Council a plan for design, construction, administration and maintenance of the memorial, including citizen oversight during the construction."[4]

There were ten operating committees, an advisory committee of 160 people, a coordinating committee, and a volunteer executive director. Family members and survivors were encouraged to serve on any committee, in addition to their own. The executive director was Rowland Denman, president of an Oklahoma City business, who was very active in the community, serving, for example, as the president and treasurer of the Oklahoma County Mental Health Association. During his tenure as president of that body, he was deeply involved in organizing volunteer mental health work after fourteen postal employees were murdered by a coworker on August 20, 1986, in nearby Edmond, Oklahoma.

Denman began with a post office box and phone in his office. "Bob Johnson's firm helped with some of the office work, but we didn't have much support at the beginning," Denman said. "Some family members volunteered to help out, but it was too soon for them; they couldn't be around this all day. About 80 percent of my time was spent on the telephone with people from all over the world. They wanted to tell you how much they wanted to help, and many of them were quite emotional."[5]

Denman asked Phyllis Stough to direct the day-to-day work. She had worked in political campaign offices and had done community volunteer work. "I didn't realize the scope of this project when I said yes," Stough said. "I think we all grew into this slowly." She laughed as she characterized the early days as a "mom and pop operation," and went on to say that "it was important that we were all volunteers. I'm not sure how a professional staff would have been received by family members and survivors in those early months." She recalled especially the importance of Denman's empathy. "Rowland was the heart of this in the early days," she said. "He remembered the stories of family members and survivors and he remembered their names, and this was very important."[6]

Bob Johnson, Rowland Denman, and others found out early on just how volatile and difficult this process would be. On July 17, 1995, between fifty and seventy-five members of the Victims Families/Survivors Liaison subcommittee met for the first time at the First Christian Church, the site of the Family Assistance Center during the recovery effort. "This was a real mistake," said Johnson. "We thought that since this is where families gathered after the bombing to await official word of the recovery of remains, it would be a familiar place to begin this memorial work. Instead we quickly sensed that this was a horrible place for them, and the absolutely wrong place to meet. These were people who had been directed through the whole event, 'wait here, go here, we'll tell you when we have some news,' and they were not going to take anymore direction from anyone else, especially 'outsiders' who they thought were going to tell them how the immeasurable pain of their loss would be memorialized in public."[7]

Denman also remembered this meeting well. "It was really us and them," he said. "There was real anger that those of us who were serving as volunteers and were perceived as having some power in the city were going to try and shove a memorial down their throats. They asked, 'why were you selected?' They didn't believe that we were really concerned, or at least didn't believe that we were able to understand the depths of their grief and their need to make this memorial with their own energies." Denman smiled as he recalled being labeled as "one of the coats and ties" at the meeting. "I really regretted dressing up that evening!"

Clearly concerned that this struck me as evidence of mean-spiritedness or that I would blame these angry people, Denman emphasized the need to understand all this in the context of the time. "I hope you don't read this too harshly," he said, "because many of these people were speaking out of their deep anger at what had happened, speaking out of their grief, and I know that they regret having said some harsh things, if they even remember. Sometimes," he said, "you just have to listen and understand."

Phillip Thompson, whose mother's remains were recovered at the time of the building's implosion, and Toby Thompson (no relation to Phillip), whose brother was murdered, chaired the meeting, representing family members. Phillip Thompson recalled the "incredible pain bottled up in that meeting." Many people already had strong ideas about a memorial. "Everyone wanted the memorial to be something different: statues of children, memorialization of the unborn [three of the murdered women were pregnant], statues to rescuers, names on a wall, a statue of Christ or angels, and so on. I remember looking at Toby and thinking 'my God, what have we gotten into.'"[8]

Thinking back to this time after several years, Phillip Thompson spoke of how his family had helped him move through the initial anger at his mother's murder. But

> it was clear at this meeting that many had no way yet of handling this. We set up monthly meetings, small groups with facilitators, we talked about our feelings at length. I recall being asked at that first meeting "why were you chosen to be a leader in this?" I told my story, and that I had said to the mayor, "if there is anything I can do to help, please call on me." When I said that I didn't want the memorial just to be a personal thing for mom, but it had to be something more, some people got angry, but after telling my story, the hostility toward Toby and me lessened. They began to trust us when I also said at the meeting, "I have concerns, family members need to be involved, it can't be done for us, or without us." These first few months together were wrenching. We were all thrown together in the worst of circumstances. Many people had never worked in a group or talked in public at all. And here we all were in this situation. Sometimes the discussions were so ugly we had to step back and pay attention to how we were dealing with each other. We all had to learn to listen, we all had to learn not to argue about emotions. After this meeting, we knew we had a tiger by the tail.

It would take time for trust to be nurtured by the hard work of individuals demonstrating the integrity of the process. Mayor Norick made it clear at the meeting that this task force was to be in charge of the memorial process. But fault lines based on divergent personal experiences during the bombing ran deep, not just between the "suits and ties" and others but also between family members and the few survivors who ventured to early meetings. Survivors often felt—and on some occasions were made to feel—that they really didn't belong in the deliberations because they were still alive. This often exacerbated the guilt that many survivors felt already, just for having survived. GSA's Dot Hill, for example, spoke of "carrying around the thought that God wanted me to die that day and Satan pulled me out so that I would be sentenced to live." She was haunted by the memory of her daughter's rape when she was living in a different city, and how God seemed to be punishing her by hurting loved ones. In her mind, then, "the bomb was my fault. I moved up here and Satan punished me by doing this to those around me." She felt too guilty to work with family members at all in these early days, finally feeling more "comfortable" when she attended the last two weeks of the McVeigh trial and the Nichols sentencing, and spoke at the Fortier sentencing.[9]

LeAnn Jenkins, director of the Oklahoma Federal Executive Board, whose task it is to increase efficiency between federal agencies and serve as an advocate for federal employees, served on the family and survivor committee, and she remembers the range of survivor feelings in the early days. "Some were guilty, thinking 'I'd trade my life for the babies.' Some simply felt as if they didn't belong, and some were angry that they were treated as if their feelings of grief and loss for so many close friends didn't count, but they didn't want to say anything for fear of inflaming the situation."[10]

Amy Petty, who worked in the Federal Employees Credit Union in the Murrah Building, is an example of a survivor who never felt comfortable on the task force. When the bomb exploded, she fell through three floors and was trapped for six hours. "It was completely black and I thought perhaps I had died. I heard moaning and other unpleasant sounds, and I worried that I was in hell." By the time she left the hospital, the task force was under way. She said, "I guess I would have felt as if I was barging in. I was a survivor, and I just couldn't have felt comfortable disagreeing with family members of friends who died. My focus became to get back to work, to get up and help the place get running to help people." (She served as chairperson of the memorial committee at the Federal Employee's Credit Union's new building. "This and my own memorial garden have been my way of remembering my friends," she said.)[11]

A few survivors participated from the beginning. HUD's Calvin Moser was a member of the original task force. "I got involved out of respect for my friends who died." Polly Nichols, badly wounded in the Journal-Record Building, recalled that "the process worked because we allowed the process to work its way out." "I have a real need," she said, "that the world know that it was not just those in the Murrah Building who were affected. Even though no one died in the Journal Record Building, there have been a lot of broken lives from that morning." And GSA's Richard Williams was involved with numerous memorial task force projects after recovering from his injuries.[12]

Over time, family members and survivors came to appreciate the experiences of others. Survivors consented to privileging the voices of family members, and family members acknowledged that survivors, many of whom had lost close friends and an important part of their world, were, as one survivor said, valid members of the "trauma club." Family members also came to see, LeAnn Jenkins pointed out, "that the survivors were often sources of information about their loved one's lives."

There were fault lines between family members as well. Many resented the few who sought solace through the media, often perceived as speaking inappropriately for all family members. There was some resentment at suggestions that the memorial privilege the children. Everyone who died, one family member said, was someone's child. And, inevitably, there were strong disagreements about what the memorial should look like. Wisely, Robert Johnson and others recognized that beginning the memorial process with arguments over physical design would likely become a quagmire and end with some faction "winning" but no consensus on a memorial, only more hurt. They decided to focus on a more immediate and central concern, the development of a mission statement that would serve as the group's constitution, a document that would provide enduring orientation for the memorial process.

Toward the Mission Statement: Memorial Feel and Function

The task force's design solicitation committee was charged with recommending a design selection process for the memorial. It learned, however, that it was an "absolute necessity" for the task force to have a "clear mission statement before attempting to engage in design solicitation."[13]

To that end, the task force began a process of gathering information on what visitors to the memorial should "think, feel or experience," not on what a memorial should look like. This information, it was hoped, would serve as the basis for the creation of a mission statement. This process was carried out in meetings of family members and survivors, through public meetings in the greater Oklahoma City area, through meetings with specific groups of memorial constituents ("groups of people who, by virtue of their experience with the bombing...had a particular perspective to share"), and through a public memorial survey that appeared in Oklahoma City and Tulsa newspapers, at post offices, libraries, and on an Internet home page with local, national, and international access.[14]

Robert Johnson characterized these focused discussions with family members and survivors as "difficult sessions." He was mindful that there was no way to plan what someone might think or feel at a memorial, but, he said, this focus accomplished several things. "It redirected people's energies away from design arguments, and it got people to talk about their own feelings without being on the spot, without feeling threatened. When people said, 'I want a visitor to experience loss,'" he remarked, "they were often saying 'I suffered a great loss.' People had a great need to let others know that those who died were innocent people doing their work. We didn't ask people in our meetings 'how do you feel.' Perhaps they would have said, 'that's private.' But we got them to talk with each other through this process."

It was draining work. Emotions were raw, voices were sometimes raised, and people returned to stories of their loved ones over and over again. For some task force volunteers, especially those who were used to organizational efficiency, adjusting to a rhythm of mourning that was intertwined with memorial planning was difficult. "I learned how to listen and I learned great patience with the process," Johnson said.

Public input mirrored family/survivor desires about the feel and function of a memorial: a focus on the stories of individuals murdered, a place to honor rescuers, a serene place for reflection, a place for children, and a place for visitors to learn about the event and be inspired to work for nonviolent solutions to conflict. There was widespread hope that visitors would "leave the memorial personally inspired to live their lives in some meaningful way differently than they had intended before their visit."[15]

Fewer people than expected attended the seven public meetings—eighty-four in all—there were approximately five hundred responses, including those from twenty foreign countries on the Internet, and there were approximately 5,000 memorial survey responses. Despite low turnout at the public meetings, Jimmy Goodman remains convinced of their importance. "Some family members who were not yet involved discovered what we were doing, and also found out about various services that were available for them. These meetings were about more than gathering ideas for the memorial. They played an important role in creating a larger family/survivor community."

The memorial surveys revealed strong and widely divergent feelings about who and what the memorial should honor: "Don't overemphasize the kids that got killed"; "don't forget state workers"; "a memorial for Waco's children"; "do nothing which will perpetuate the memory of those found guilty"; "honor the rescue workers and rescue dogs"; "express the horror of the event so that it will never happen again"; "promote healing"; "memorialize only victims"; "memorialize only victims and survivors"; "make sure all victims are included from surrounding buildings"; "we need to know it was Americans who did this crime"; "celebrate the ethnic diversity of the Oklahoma workplace"; "include information on militia groups"; "should be inclusive religiously"; "a nation turning to Jesus Christ in times of affliction."

Inevitably, some people expressed their design ideas. Many of these echoed those examined in the last chapter, but a few new ideas surfaced in the surveys. There were proposals for a "time capsule to be opened in 50/100 years after the bombing," a desire to "see an actual photo of the convicted's head on a pole," a "panorama, like [a] Civil War cyclorama," a "clenched fist holding a flag with the word 'why?' inscribed below it."

An assistant U.S. attorney hoped that the plaza on the south side of the Murrah Building could be rebuilt "as it was before the blast. This is the only part . . . which can be preserved as it was when it was enjoyed by the people who worked there. . . . It was one of the pathways of everyday life before it was turned into a place of horror by the bomb." (In 1997 the plaza was restored to its original appearance, with seals for each of the seventeen federal and three nonfederal agencies that had been housed there.) Another hoped that a memorial would "acknowledge that a neighborhood . . . was destroyed and completely forgotten. Five hundred-plus persons homeless for six months and no one ever mentioned this or cared. How soon people forget." The return address was, "forgotten, angry, and homeless."[16]

Beginning in spring 1996, a committee met to write a mission statement designed to be a "cornerstone . . . in shaping the meaning and guiding the design and development of the memorial." It would represent, Robert Johnson said, "a remarkable community consensus document which evolved under the most difficult circumstances."[17]

The mission statement declared that "few events in the past quarter century have rocked Americans' perception of themselves and their institutions, and brought together the people of our nation with greater intensity" than the bombing. It observed that the devastating impact of the bombing has been shared with "a community, a nation, and the world."

The document set forth priorities that were significant challenges for those who would compete to design the memorial. In addition to resolutions from family members and survivors requesting the inclusion of an information center in any memorial complex—an idea that would evolve into the Memorial Center—and the insistence that any memorial include the Survivor Tree, the document called for a memorial site that would stretch from the Murrah Building across Fifth Street to the Journal Record Building. It noted that family members and survivors wanted the memorial located on the vacant site where the Murrah Building stood, and the site "must incorporate the names of those who died (noting in some way, if the family desires, each victim who was carrying an unborn child)." It was also required that names of survivors be incorporated in the site, "but in a manner separate, distinct, and apart from the tribute to and presentation of the names of those who died." And the document presented a variety of themes to be embodied in the memorial: remembrance, peace, spirituality and hope, cherished children, comfort, recognition, and learning.

John Cole, godfather to the Coverdale boys, served on the mission statement subcommittee and remembered "analyzing every word. We wanted it to be timeless, to set the pace for what came after." Beth Shortt, director of Leadership Oklahoma City, served on the task force and, given her experience working with small groups in business and government, was asked to facilitate the mission statement process. The most difficult part, she recalled, was constructing the preamble: "We come here to remember those who were killed, those who survived and those changed forever. May all who leave here know the impact of violence. May this memorial offer comfort, strength, peace, hope and serenity." This was, she said, "the kind of statement you put over your door. It was important for us all to strike the right chord with this. We focused on words, voted on concepts."[18]

The first sentence, she observed, is worded in the first person plural. "We chose this because of its inclusiveness and its personalness. No matter who comes, they are assumed to come in order to remember, and they are one with all those who came before and will come in the future. . . . Those who were killed—passive, past tense. Individuals. Those who survived—active, past tense. Individuals. Those changed forever—active and not necessarily completed, not limited to individuals—families, organizations, governments. An attempt to convey a sense of timelessness, that those [who] are still alive continue to change, and those who visit this memorial in the future may be changed."

A good example of the power of one word to include or exclude is the word "killed." Had the group used the word "murdered," certainly appropriate for 167 of the victims, it would have excluded nurse Rebecca Anderson, who rushed into the building, sustained a fatal head injury from falling debris, and died several days later. Some wanted to remember those whose lives were "lost." Others strongly objected that these lives were not misplaced but killed in an act of malice. Karen Luke, who served as vice chair of the task force and eventually chair of the Memorial Foundation, recalled a family member objecting to use of the word "hope," saying to the committee, "I'll never have hope again."

The phrase "impact of violence" was also contentious. Some committee members wanted the statement to proclaim the "futility" of violence. However, "we did not know the intent of the attacker," Shortt observed. "Words such as 'futility' imply that the attacker had a purpose which was not fulfilled. We do not know this. If the attacker intended to commit mass murder, he . . . achieved that goal. No one wants this memorial in any way to glorify violence. . . . But we do not want to minimize the heartbreak, unfairness, and callousness of this evil act." The word "impact," she observed, allowed various feelings: "to be heartbroken at the losses, to be angry at the selfishness and unjustness, to be proud of the reaction of those affected."

A draft was presented by family members and survivors to the advisory committee on March 26, 1996, and adopted by unanimous vote. Robert Johnson characterized this meeting as "extraordinary an experience as I've gone through. Less than a year after the bombing, so many people who had suffered such grievous loss came together to produce a memorial vision. It was a source of comfort for many of them. They knew what would come, their grief would be expressed in an enduring manner, and the mission statement, which has guided all our work, insured that the memorial would not be alien to their experience."

Who Owns the Process?

As work on the mission statement proceeded, the design solicitation committee wrestled with other issues. Should someone be commissioned to create the memorial? Should there be a design competition? If so, who would run the competition? Members of the committee talked with Michael Berenbaum, former director of the Research Institute at the United States Holocaust Memorial Museum and former project director at that museum. He emphasized the importance of having a clear purpose in mind before the design competition got under way. What, he asked, are you memorializing: "loss, violence, coming together?" Throughout the fall and winter months of 1995 the design solicitation committee learned about how other memorial projects, including the Vietnam Veterans Memorial and the Korean War Memorial, had dealt with the design process. They learned that "design competition is the preferred approach . . . the solicitation process is a complex one . . . an experienced professional adviser should be retained." After discussion with Charles Atherton, Secretary of the Commission of Fine Arts in Washington, D.C., the committee recommended that the task force "engage on a trial basis" Paul Spreiregen, an architect who lived and worked in the nation's capital as a design consultant. Spreiregen, a fellow of the American Institute of Architects, had a long and distinguished career designing, for example, the Maryland Vietnam Veterans Memorial, a plan for the Boston Government Center, and the historic Virginia town of Warrenton. He had served as an adviser to a number of design competitions, including the Vietnam Veterans Memorial in Washington, D.C. Certainly, a figure of Spreiregen's status offered credibility to the design process and virtually assured that numerous "name" architects and designers would enter the competition. For this bereaved community, which so much wanted a "world-class" memorial (the phrase is used quite often), Spreiregen represented an important step toward that goal.

Spreiregen delivered a forty-four-page "Operational Plan for a National, Open, Design Competition," on January 10, 1996. However, on January 18, 1996, Robert Johnson advised Spreiregen in a lengthy and detailed letter that "after considerable thought and painful deliberations, we have concluded that while you have an admirable reputation as a design competition adviser, we do not universally share the same philosophical approach to the design selection process as it relates to community involvement."

This letter represented what several family members called "a moment of truth," a "defining moment," for the volunteer leadership's commitment to the principle of family and survivor involvement in every step along this arduous process. Spreiregen's plan assumed that the jurors who would evaluate the memorial designs would be professionals and that their judgments would be privileged above all. Johnson, however, had conveyed to Spreiregen the importance of "thorough and meaningful participation by those directly affected," including participation in the design selection process. To this end, Spreiregen wrote that "jury members will meet with the working committees, kin, survivors, and officials. This affords an opportunity for the jurors to obtain a first hand impression from the people they are serving."[19]

For Spreiregen, these conversations were to be advisory only, and he strongly recommended to the design solicitation committee that an all-professional jury select the design. On January 10, after several hours of meetings in Johnson's office, it seemed a compromise was reached in which some family members and survivors would join professionals in a two-stage process of evaluating and selecting the design. An evaluation panel made up of six "professionals" would be joined by three members of the family and survivor group. This panel would choose five finalists, and a selection committee made up of fifteen people, eight of whom were family members and survivors, would make the final choice. (This two-stage process was the model that the task force used.) After a meeting of the family/survivor group that evening, however, Spreiregen reiterated his belief that including family members and survivors was problematic and the design would suffer. "It was not worth the price," Johnson said. "When I told family members that we would adhere to the commitment we had with them, they stood and gave us an ovation."

Through the months of 1995 people had moved from the angry confrontations of early meetings to at least wary accommodation based on the need to work together to create a memorial. Committees were at work collecting memorial information and devotional material from the fence, and thinking about fund-raising possibilities, but none of this demanded a dramatic, clear-cut decision on commitment to the principle of an inclusive process. Would the leaders of the task force choose to listen to an experienced and prestigious consultant? They knew better than anyone, after all, that including family members and survivors in every decision made for a ponderous and volatile process. Would they compromise by including family members and survivors in an advisory capacity but reserve final selection of a design for a professional jury? Would they risk the embarrassment of, in effect, "firing" Spreiregen and perhaps risking negative publicity? Johnson demonstrated that they were willing to risk such repercussions rather than "sell out." As we will see, there were many contentious issues that would test the creativity and patience of the task force, but there was, after this decision, a reservoir of trust that would prove invaluable.

In a parting-shot editorial in the journal *Competitions,* Spreiregen observed that "one is left with the impression that an outside opinion [in Oklahoma City] is only grudgingly tolerated." He said that the organizers of the Vietnam Veterans Memorial competition decided to leave veterans off the jury because professionals would be likely to defer to them. And after generals became involved in the Korean War Memorial process, "ensuing results have been disappointing." The Oklahoma City memorial, he argued, was not for those closest to the tragedy who, he erroneously believed, "will have dealt with their trauma" by the time it is completed. Rather, it symbolized the rebirth of a community, "a true sign of optimism and belief in the future." He reiterated his skepticism about the process. "The design community which will participate in this competition—if they choose under the present circumstances to do so—needs to be reassured that their entries will be subject to a reasonable selection process. Personally, I don't go to an accountant to have my appendix removed."[20]

After a brief and intensive search, the task force chose a team of competition advisers, Don Stastny and Paul Morris from Portland, Oregon, and Helene Fried, a public art consultant from San Francisco. Beth Tolbert, former chairperson of the Assembly of State Arts Councils and twice chairperson of the Oklahoma City Festival of the Arts, had developed the procedures for the first public art competition sponsored by Oklahoma City. With Jackie Jones, she cochaired the design competition committee and felt strongly that these three advisers contributed greatly to the success of the competition. "After we decided not to retain Spreiregen," she said, "it was crucial for us to work with experienced people who would appreciate the unique challenge we faced. We were fortunate to find them."[21]

The new advisers were aware of the conflict with Spreiregen. As Don Stastny recalled, "We knew from the beginning that ownership of this project had to be local. We were always mindful of including family members and survivors in meaningful ways, and during the work of the evaluation committee [that pared down the hundreds of formal submissions to a few] and the selection committee [that chose the design] everybody's voice was respected. The process worked very well."[22]

The task force itself underwent important changes over the summer and early fall of 1996. There had been criticism that the name "Murrah Federal Building Task Force" excluded the one person killed in the Athenian Building, two killed in the Water Resources Building, and one person killed on the street, as well as those who survived in other buildings, some grievously wounded. It also sounded, Jackie Jones noted, like "a memorial to a building." On September 1, 1996, the name was changed to the "Oklahoma City Memorial Foundation." Also on that date, the first two paid staff were hired, an executive director and an assistant.[23]

The task force had to deal with several issues before any design competition began. Could Fifth Street, the one-way street that ran in front of the Murrah Building, be permanently closed so that the memorial could expand from the Murrah site to the Journal Record Building without an open street bisecting the memorial? Also, given the mission statement's requirement that the names of survivors appear on the memorial site, who was a survivor? How would the task force identify whose names would appear, particularly since the mission statement invited an inclusive interpretation of a survivor by speaking expansively of those "changed forever." Conceivably, almost anyone could translate their anguish over the bombing into some form of "survivordom." Given the cultural prestige of the category of "survivor," there was a clear danger that the allure of being so anointed could tempt some to claim such status inappropriately, thereby trivializing the wrenching experiences of others.[24]

Sacred Ground: The Closing of Fifth Street

The task force envisioned a memorial zone that "includes the Murrah Building block, the south half of the Journal Record Building block, including the Oklahoma Water Resources Board Building and Athenian Building, and Fifth Street between the two blocks." Focusing specifically on Fifth Street, the task force noted that "this area is considered 'sacred ground'—because people died not only in the buildings but on the street as well. It is a hallowed place deserving of the respect and solemnity associated with great loss."[25]

For many members of the task force, especially family members and survivors, this portion of Fifth Street had also been "changed forever," transformed by the cataclysmic events that transpired on its surface. It deserved, in their minds, the same status as a battlefield, where great suffering and death was commemorated in numerous ways, among them a commitment to physical preservation of a historic landscape and extreme sensitivity to acts of defilement, such as commercial intrusion.

Before the bombing, Fifth Street was a busy one-way street that had been designed to transport traffic between several major expressways. Many area businesspeople and residents expected the street to be reopened after final debris removal took place, but the city waited for the memorial task force to make its recommendation. In spring 1996, the city purchased property immediately north of Fifth Street because, city planning director Garner Stoll informed area residents, "the task force believes that additional space is needed for memorial-related purposes with or without the closure of Fifth Street."

When the task force made it clear in spring 1996 that they intended to ask the city to permanently close the street, many area businesses and residents vigorously disagreed. Many businesspeople were concerned that the disruptions they had already suffered would only grow worse from permanent closure. The owner of a paint and body shop wrote the city council that "the benefit of a token commemoration is overwhelmingly outweighed by the benefits of reopening the street. We hope that you will recognize this and do Oklahoma City a favor by giving us back our link to life." Others argued that public safety was involved, wondering if the nearby fire station would be "greatly inconvenienced in getting its vehicles and fire equipment in an easterly direction."

Some objections to the closing rested on strongly held convictions about the purpose of memorialization. Altering the cityscape of Oklahoma City by closing Fifth Street would, one petitioner wrote city councilwoman Ann Simank, grant the bombers a victory. Opening the street, on the other hand, would help put the bombing in its "appropriate place." A couple from the badly damaged Regency Towers apartment building linked the street's opening with the city's healing from the wounds of the bombing and a return to normalcy. "For a long time we have awaited the reopening of Fifth Street and wished that this would not become a tourist attraction. However, the city is helping to ruin these wishes." Opening the street, they believed, would "remove what is an obvious and constant reminder of that tragedy."[26]

Others objected to calling the street "sacred ground." Characterizing the claim as "absolutely ridiculous," one angry letter writer declared that "every lake, highway, street, and structure where someone has been killed, would have to be designated 'sacred ground.' We do not need a constant reminder that it did happen."

These arguments, especially the one that goes "don't immerse yourself in tragedy, move on with life and you'll recover," were greeted with incredulity and some anger by many family members and survivors. It was as incomprehensible to them that Fifth Street would be opened as it was that a floating Burger King would appear next to the USS *Arizona* Memorial in Pearl Harbor. Governor Keating wrote the traffic commission that he was "not aware of a traffic artery running right beside the Wailing Wall in Jerusalem, the Tomb of the Unknown Soldier... or George Washington's tomb at Mt. Vernon. This site is already a shrine.... You do not run vehicles across sacred ground."

Others called attention to the events that, in their view, transformed the street. Ernestine Clark, who served as cochair of the task force's survivor definition committee and worked as director of development at the city's downtown library only a few blocks from the site, wrote Mayor Norick, "Fifth Street will never be normal again. What happened here was not a pothole, a bad wreck or a broken gas line disturbing the street temporarily. This was a grinding, horrible disaster of indescribable terror and loss. Fifth Street cannot be treated like any other street.... I've spent the last fifteen months finding new ways to get around Fifth; others can too."

Michael Reyes, whose father, Antonio Reyes, was killed, combined concern with public safety with a heartfelt question about appropriate behavior at a memorial. He wrote the planning commission that a busy street would be quite dangerous once a memorial opened, particularly since visitors would want to cross Fifth Street to visit the Survivor Tree. "On the personal side," he wrote, "my father and many others died in the 'pancake' area which was partially on Fifth Street. How many people would drive over the site of their deaths? And how many of these drivers would be appalled if they learned that they had driven over this sacred ground?"

Sally Ferrell, whose daughter Susan was murdered in the bombing, also asked the mayor, city council, and planning commission to think about the importance of maintaining the integrity of the site. It must be "preserved and protected," she wrote, because "the street is where days of heroic rescue took place, where families stood amidst wreckage to look up at the towering gutted building and cry in shock and despair. The bombing and its actual site must not be forgotten, nor traveled over daily by everyday traffic. There is much to be gained by having a sense of place, an awareness of the meaning of historic sites.... It was the street that was used for placing and detonating the explosion that carried out instant mass slaughter. It was the street that served the killers well."

Failure to close the street, others said, would not only defile sacred ground but also dishonor the dead who died across the street from the Murrah Building. Sydney Dobson, then executive director of Oklahoma City Beautiful (and subsequently executive director of the Memorial Foundation), wrote councilwoman Simank, "This section of the street is as much a part of sacred ground as the Murrah Federal Building footprint. To leave it open to traffic will send the message that those who were killed and injured across the street were not important. The fact that leaving the street open would destroy the aesthetics of the memorial is secondary to remembering those who were killed and injured."

Others argued that it was essential to close the street if the memorial was to be a place of "reverence and serenity." Still others believed that reopening Fifth Street would communicate to the rest of the world that Oklahoma did not know how to memorialize the event appropriately. Toby Thompson wrote the planning commission, "It would be a tragedy if Oklahoma City reopened Fifth Street, thus creating the only 'drive-thru' national memorial in the country. I want Oklahoma City to be remembered for the valiant face we placed on catastrophe, not our collective inability to recognize the significance of this event to our city and the nation."

The summer months found the task force concerned about the vocal opposition to the closing of the street, and they asked the city's Traffic and Transportation Commission to delay a meeting on the issue originally scheduled for July 15, 1996, so that they could convince people in the area that the street needed to be closed. After a meeting at St. Anthony Hospital on July 15 attended by over a hundred people, Robert Johnson formed a task force subcommittee made up of people on both sides of the issue. Members walked the area, talked with people, listened to their concerns, and discussed various alternative traffic routes. Kari Watkins, who was hired by the foundation in spring 1996 as director of communications and became executive director following Dobson's resignation, recalled joining Rowland Denman, Karen Luke, Robert Johnson, and family members and survivors "knocking on every door on Fourth, Fifth, and Sixth streets. I saw people's minds change as we talked with them. Some were adamantly opposed to the closing until they stopped to think about what it would mean to have people driving over a place where people died, and where we wanted to build a memorial."

The intensive community work resulted in the subcommittee's Oklahoma City Memorial Fifth Street Proposed Plan, which urged the city to close Fifth Street. "We believe" the committee said, that "the City's proposed plan will direct the proper traffic around the Memorial site and allow for easy access to the nearby interstates, businesses and residential areas."[27]

On August 1, 1996, the city's traffic commission split 4-4 on the issue, but on August 13, the city council approved a resolution beginning the process to close the street. The city's planning commission took up the issue at a September 12 meeting. In his opening statement, Robert Johnson reminded commissioners that the Memorial Foundation "must resolve the Fifth Street problem before we move forward." He noted that the foundation's hard work over the summer months had garnered support from almost all the businesspeople and residents of the area. He was convinced that the memorial would help revitalize the area, and he put the issue into a larger context when he concluded that "how we respond to the Fifth Street issue will tell the world what the Oklahoma Standard really is."

Only one person spoke against closure, noting that Dealy Plaza, the site of the assassination of President John F. Kennedy, is a memorial with an open street running through it, and she mentioned polls showing "overwhelming" support for keeping Fifth Street open. Fourteen people, almost all family members and survivors, offered emotional pleas to close the street. Jannie Coverdale, grandmother of the murdered boys Aaron and Elijah, implored the commission, "I'm here asking for one block, just one block in memory of 168 lives." Surprisingly, given the thoroughness of Robert Johnson's presentation and the emotional appeals of family members and survivors, the commission voted only 5-3 in favor of closure. After this meeting, however, the ultimate decision was not in doubt, and on October 22, 1996, a city ordinance permanently closed Fifth Street.

Memorial Hierarchies: Survivor Definition

It is never enough for a bereaved community just to "remember." It must strive for exactitude in what is being remembered, who is being remembered, and the forms through which remembrance is expressed. Such memorial precision is a way of paying what people understand as their debt to the dead. Conversely, failure to accomplish this, to mischaracterize the significance of an event, to blur lines between different groups, or to commemorate in inappropriate ways is often perceived as an act of defilement, a polluting of memory. The construction of accurate memorial hierarchies is a volatile and important task, for the stakes are very high.[28]

It is important to many in the town of Lexington, Massachusetts, for example, that the encounter between British troops and colonial Minutemen on the Lexington Green be understood as a "battle" and not a "massacre." In the early nineteenth century, many residents took great umbrage when citizens of Concord, Massachusetts, called the encounter at Concord Bridge the first battle of the American Revolution. The argument is not trivial. Those killed in a massacre are not usually perceived as active fighters, giving their lives in battle for cause and country. We speak of massacre victims but battle heroes.

A similar controversy has simmered for a number of years over proper classification of the violent encounter at the Washita near Cheyenne, Oklahoma, between the Seventh Cavalry under the command of Lt. Col. George A. Custer and the village of Southern Cheyenne Peace Chief Black Kettle. Custer's dawn attack on November 27, 1868, was immediately controversial, and many labeled it a "massacre."

Custer remains a potent and polarizing symbol in American culture, and different American communities have a vested interest in winning the struggle over naming the Washita encounter. Custerphiles do not wish to see their hero tarnished by the term "massacre," and Native Americans, for whom Custer has become a convenient symbol of the injustices of the Indian Wars, find it in their interest to so name the conflict.[29]

Memorial exactitude bedeviled attempts to define the Holocaust in the negotiations between the President's Commission on the Holocaust, chaired by survivor and Nobel laureate Elie Wiesel, and the Carter administration.

Wiesel insisted on the primacy of Jewish victims, but the Carter administration insisted on linking Jews and "others" more closely. For Wiesel and many others, any blurring of the centrality of Jews in the Holocaust was a step toward the murder of memory. Wiesel saw it as his sacred responsibility to ensure that this did not happen.

Throughout the creation of the museum, an enduring tension involved negotiating the boundaries of the Holocaust: Who belonged as victims and how should they be represented? Should the Holocaust be compared with any other event, or should its uniqueness be proclaimed?

The elevation of those killed in Oklahoma City to the hierarchical status of culturally meaningful public deaths reminded some that there were victims of everyday violence who remained largely forgotten, their deaths counting only as byproducts of everyday American violence. Their lives and deaths were consigned to oblivion by the vagaries of what registered as culturally meaningful death. Intense public mourning for the children murdered in Oklahoma City, for example, provided an opportunity for some to call for a "remembrance" of these forgotten child victims through increased efforts to end domestic abuse in the United States and child slavery in various countries.[30]

Marian Wright Edelman, for example, informed readers that in a day and a half, "gun violence kills as many children as the 13 [sic] who were killed" in the bombing. An editorial in the *Phoenix Gazette* observed that a federal report on child abuse released one week after the bombing revealed that "at least 2,000 children a year are killed as a result of domestic violence and abuse, and another 140,000 are seriously injured—the vast majority of them under four." Why, the editorialist wondered, was there so much indifference to this epidemic of violence, and, if Timothy McVeigh and Terry Nichols were characterized as "cowards, psychopaths, vermin and wackos," what characterization fit "those who would kill, maim and wreak havoc on their own children?"[31]

In addition to those who did not even appear on the hierarchy of public deaths, there were highly publicized deaths of those ranked as "unworthy" victims, specifically the children killed in the Waco debacle. Any widespread empathy toward these children was short-circuited by various distancing mechanisms: antipathy toward a religious group believed to have violated cultural codes of what "normal" religion was about (hence the "cult" label), which in turn led to a perception that the Waco dead were "not like us." An FBI agent went so far as to say that the Branch Davidian mothers did not love their children, or they would not have put them in harm's way. How could the public be expected to care for children supposedly unloved by their own parents? The inability to penetrate the dehumanizing stereotype of a "cult" member and the lack of empathy for children of a "cult" accounted for the lack of public lamentation. An exception was an editorial in the *Denver Rocky Mountain News:* "No flags at half-mast. No special words from the president and first lady, who assume that children are upset by the deaths of youngsters in Oklahoma City, but not upset at roughly the same number of children incinerated on the Texas plains. To the alienated, the message is clear: Children killed in a government raid are not worth mourning."[32]

The shared grief of Holocaust survivors or family members and survivors in Oklahoma City does not obliterate hierarchies. In fact, the deeply felt need to get the story of what happened to whom, and who was affected in what ways, to get it all "just right," makes hierarchies even more important. These relationships are often at work in subtle ways. I have already mentioned examples of survivors not feeling "worthy" of being considered equal to family members in meetings, let alone disagreeing with one regarding the memorial process. One survivor offered this mapping of memorial hierarchies in Oklahoma City: family members who lost more than one person; those who lost small children; those who lost a direct relation; those severely wounded; those suffering "indirect loss" (cousin, aunt, for example); those suffering lighter injuries, those who survived.

Survivors also had unspoken hierarchies: those injured in the Murrah Building; those who came out of the building without physical injuries; those injured in other buildings and hospitalized; those injured in other buildings who received medical treatment and were released; those uninjured in other buildings; those in damaged buildings in the area. Some Oklahoma state employees who worked in the Water Resources Building across the street from the Murrah Building resented the fact that, in their view, Governor Keating ignored the death of two state workers in Water Resources by focusing his attention on the hundreds of federal employees murdered in the Murrah Building.[33]

Placement of the names of the dead in memorials is often a volatile issue. For example, the names of those who died on the USS *Arizona* are engraved in a shrine room at the memorial in Pearl Harbor. There has been some resentment on the part of those who had loved ones die on other ships or mainland locations (e.g., Hickam Field) that their sacrifices did not "count" quite as much since their names were not publicly memorialized in an enduring manner. To offer a memorial corrective, the *Remembrance Exhibit*, which included plaques with the names of all civilians and military figures who died in the attack, was dedicated at the National Park Service's visitor center during the fiftieth anniversary ceremonies in 1991.

The overwhelming number of names engraved on the Vietnam Veterans Memorial brought home to many the cost in American lives of the war. People look for names, they read the names, they touch names, they trace names. Names transform numbers of dead into individuals, and clearly the increasingly popular fashion of listing names on memorials is an act of protest against the anonymity of mass death. Sometimes the introduction of names of the dead recovers the forgotten history of a community. In the 1960s, the names of Tejanos (Mexican-Texans) who fought with Alamo defenders against the Mexican army were added to the commemorative reading of Alamo dead during anniversary ceremonies.

In Oklahoma City the mission statement called for the names of those killed to be incorporated on the site, perhaps on the memorial itself. Survivors were also to be remembered through the presentation of names in a manner "separate, distinct, and apart" from commemoration of the dead, but still within the sacred environment of what came to be called the Murrah "footprint," the area where the building once stood. This spatial separation was quite important for family members. As Jeannine Gist, mother of Karen Gist Carr, who was murdered in the bombing, told me, "Those who died aren't here to tell us what they want for a memorial. The survivors are."[34]

At first, some family members were uneasy with the idea of any representation of survivors' names on the Murrah footprint, but the mission statement made it clear that this was to be the case. And, as the committee began its work and survivors began to tell their stories, the appreciation for their ordeal grew. In the chaotic moments right after the explosion, before professional rescue and recovery operations began, they went back into the building to search desperately for their wounded friends and coworkers. "Many of us," one survivor said, "went to more funerals in several weeks than most people do in a lifetime, and we often had to choose between funerals of friends, there were so many."

Once it was decided that survivors' names would appear on the Murrah footprint, the task force had to decide, Who is a survivor? The mission statement did not define survivor, but it did identify survivors as a "group distinctly different from victims and others affected by the bombing." (It spoke of the memorial focusing on victims and survivors, helping visitors understand victims and survivors "as individuals," through personal stories and photographs.)[35]

Beth Shortt, who served as facilitator of the mission statement subcommittee, also worked with the survivor definition subcommittee. "We knew when we worked on the mission statement that the term 'survivor' would become an issue," she said, "but we left it for another time." Several members of the survivor definition group spoke of how crucial Shortt was to the process. Ernestine Clark, the committee's cochair, recalled, "I had watched Beth in action in other meetings and had witnessed over and again her incredible strengths as a tactful but strong leader, incisive thinker and 'group processor'.... Beth would see to it that one person would not dominate, that all would participate, and that hard decisions would be led through a process that honored both feelings and logical decisions." Shortt recalled the difficulty of this particular process. "It felt like it took forever. We wrote the mission statement rather quickly. This was much more difficult."[36]

The committee began their work on July 17, 1996, met weekly until October, monthly until February 1997, and then occasionally for several months. "In our work," Shortt said, "we used two examples, the Holocaust and the TWA 800 plane crash. We asked 'who is a survivor?' What about family members of the plane crash? What about liberators of the camps? What about the children of people in the camps? We learned to be careful of unintentionally degrading the memory of those we considered actual survivors. I continually reminded the committee that we had to draw a line, and people needed to know on which side of the line they were placed, whether or not, to put it bluntly, they were going to be on a wall."[37]

The committee believed it important to identify and commemorate survivors because they were an "invaluable link between the dead and the loved ones left behind, and they are a link between the event and those who seek to understand the event now and in the future." This living link would, it was hoped, provide a "priceless gift" for family members, who could talk with "someone who was actually there," and a gift for survivors as well, for the telling of stories could be "healing."[38]

The committee had to correct the misperception that their work was intended to define survivors for the purposes of financial benefits. They had to wade through studies of where the dead and wounded were located, where the most severe damage occurred. And they had to struggle with two major issues. First, where was the perimeter of the "zone of danger" within which one's experience would be harrowing enough to warrant the label "survivor"? And, second, how could they gauge the impact of the bombing on those who were not in this zone but were emotionally injured enough to qualify as a survivor?

American courts have struggled with similar issues in their attempts to decide if bystanders suffer a "compensable injury" if they witness an event that causes emotional distress. "The common law," Thomas Uhl wrote in the *Brooklyn Law Review*, "has long recognized that mental distress is a compensable injury. In the last fifty years, courts have established that the intentional infliction of emotional distress is a valid cause of action." Since the New York Court of Appeals in 1896 faced the question of "physical distress caused by shock," Uhl noted, "courts developed a test that established the accident area as the limiting device."[39]

Courts envisioned a "zone of danger," within which anyone, related to the victim or not, could sue for recompense for emotional distress. The key was physical proximity to danger, not an emotional bond with the victim. An arbitrary zone raised difficult issues, however. A mother outside the zone who witnessed the death of her child would not be seen as emotionally distressed as a bystander within the zone with no attachment to the child. In 1968 the California Supreme Court, faced with just this scenario in *Dillon v. Legg*, introduced other factors for consideration, "1) whether plaintiff was located near the scene of the accident as contrasted with one who was a distance away from it. 2) Whether the shock resulted from a direct emotional impact upon plaintiff from the sensory and contemporaneous observance of the accident, as contrasted with learning of the accident from others after its occurrence. 3) Whether plaintiff and the victim were closely related, as contrasted with an absence of any relationship or the presence of only a distant relationship."[40]

In a related case in California in 1989, *Thing v. La Chusa,* the State Supreme Court ruled that a mother who did not witness her child being struck by a car but arrived soon after could not seek damages. The Court of Appeals reversed the decision. One of the justices raised the issue of the importance of "sensory perception of the impact" and asked questions raised by the same court twenty-five years earlier, "How soon is 'fairly contemporaneous?' Is the shock any less immediate if the mother does not know of the accident until the injured child is brought home.... Could it be argued that the emotional distress is even more traumatic... for parents... who fail to witness the accident and later blame themselves for allowing it to occur?" "We are," Justice Kaufman lamented, "no closer to answers today than we were then."

Without arbitrary limits set by the zone of danger, however, and once "it is admitted that temporal and spatial limitations bear no rational relation to the likelihood of psychic injury," Justice Kaufman warned that "it becomes impossible to define... any 'sensible or just stopping point.' By what humane and principle standard," Kaufman asked, "might a court decide, as a matter of law, that witnessing the bloody and chaotic aftermath of an accident involving a loved one is compensable if viewed within 1 minute of impact but noncompensable after 15? or 30? Is the shock of standing by while others undertake frantic efforts to save the life of one's child any less real... when it occurs in an ambulance or emergency room rather than at the 'scene?'"[41]

The survivor definition subcommittee did not face the burden of making law, but for commemorative purposes, committee members faced the challenge of establishing arbitrary yet defensible boundaries. How far, they asked, should a zone of danger extend? Police lines could not frame this zone, since they were changing during rescue and recovery operations. Should the zone include the Regency Towers apartment, whose residents were forced from their homes for six months? What about badly damaged buildings nearby? What about buildings not so badly damaged but whose owners had suffered great financial loss? What about people in downtown buildings who had experienced shattered glass, the chaotic fright of the first few hours, and who fled from a second bomb scare? One committee member felt strongly that the term "survivor" should be restricted to those who came out of the Murrah Building, since they were the primary targets of the bombing. "We tried to define the area that was most devastated, the targeted area. Locating survivors within this area is an ongoing one," recalled Richard Williams, a cochair of the committee.[42]

The committee used the terms "inner circle, outer circle, primary, secondary, in the blast zone" to try to define the area. "We began with a limited zone," said Shortt, "two blocks in radius around the Murrah Building, and then it grew bigger. We found out quickly that people felt left out. Even some memorial board members told us 'I lost property, I was underinsured, I lost a lot and should be a survivor.'"

The committee carefully expanded the perimeter, but, of course, it was never satisfactory because some were going to feel dispossessed by being just on the other side of whatever line was drawn. "Occasionally," Shortt recalled, "some committee members felt we could never solve it, and that we should just include all of downtown. I reminded them that such a decision would trivialize the horrific experiences of so many grievously wounded people that came out of the Murrah and other buildings."[43]

Just as courts have had to struggle with claims for emotional distress from those not at the scene of an accident or crime but linked by bonds of affection to victims, the committee also had to decide the status of various "witnesses," those who "felt the blast, heard the blast, had concrete particles on them, [had] ceiling [fall] on their head." Over months of painstaking work, boundaries expanded and contracted as the committee agonized over these issues.[44]

One of the most wrenching issues was evaluating the status of those who worked in the Murrah and other buildings in the immediate area but were not at the site on April 19. Clearly, these people did not meet zone of danger criteria, but were they eligible for survivor status in a zone of distress? "These were the most difficult conversations," Shortt recalled. "What should we do about those who were not in the Murrah Building for one reason or another, but lost so many friends? We didn't hear from a lot of these folks during our work. More often we heard, 'I was there, but I'm not really a survivor.'" Committee member LeAnn Jenkins said, "We were talking about whether to include co-workers and friends, those who just happened to be sick, to be at a doctor's appointment, to be on a work assignment, and it was painful because we all knew how much they had lost as well."

As a way out of this dilemma, the committee established a primary zone of danger and a secondary zone of distress. Those in the zone of danger, who might have become, as Richard Williams said, "the 169th victim," could, if they wanted, have their name engraved on the survivor wall of the memorial. (Some survivors, particularly those from law enforcement agencies, did not want their names to appear anywhere.)

The zone of danger was flexible, however, if certain criteria were met. All people, in any location, who "suffered an injury which caused them to be held for care at a hospital (not 'treated and released'), regardless of their physical location at 9:02 A.M., and who do not object to being included, are to be identified on the site of the Murrah Building and in the Memorial Center." All persons in the larger zone of distress, whether present or not at 9:02 A.M. on April 19, 1995, were eligible to have their names listed in the Memorial Center. Consequently, those who worked in the Murrah Building but were not there would be represented only in the Memorial Center. Their names would not appear on the wall.[45]

The boundaries of the larger zone of danger remained contentious. A federal employee who worked in the U.S. Courthouse just south of the Murrah Building wrote the committee, arguing that the courthouse and the old post office nearby "were within the 'perimeter' established for security/investigation purposes after the bombing, and every federal employee in these buildings felt as if they, too, were the targets of terrorism; hence, we certainly felt like survivors. . . . The Murrah Building was, in all respects, 'connected' with our two buildings. It contained our babies, our bank, and many people whom we worked with and socialized with everyday."[46]

Several people in the area whose businesses were just outside the secondary zone voiced strong opposition to their exclusion, claiming that damages inflicted on their businesses qualified them for this secondary zone. In September 1997 the committee recommended to the board of directors that the boundaries be accepted as drawn. But, given the difficulty of establishing the secondary boundary, "after the Memorial Center is opened anyone may self submit for survivor status. A committee will be formed to review applications." Should any applications meet one or more survivor definition criteria, the applicant would "be included among any listing or representation of survivors within the Memorial Complex."[47]

The decision to allow people to self-select for survivor status is an ingenious way of maintaining boundaries of danger and distress and allowing individual "cases" to be evaluated. Certainly, the lure of memorial prestige could entice some to "buy in" to the perceived status of survivorhood. It is apparently a price worth paying (evaluating each claim) to complete a process done, said Robert Johnson, with "integrity and generosity."

From Design Competition to Memorial Selection

The design competition for the memorial was announced to the public on November 15, 1996. The competition booklet provided participants with the mission statement, informed them that "the wishes of the Families/Survivors Liaison Subcommittee are to be given the greatest weight in the Memorial planning and development process," provided the survivor definition, and informed participants of the themes to be embodied in the memorial.

Competitors were invited to visit the site in January 1997 and to view a special exhibit on the events of April 19, 1995, in an area in the underground Murrah parking garage. This powerful exhibit was planned by the foundation's archives and design solicitation committees, and in particular Oklahoma artist Sunni Mercer and Tom Toperzer, for many years the director and chief curator of the Fred Jones, Jr. Museum of Art at the University of Oklahoma. Both were very active in the foundation's work. Toperzer served on the board of directors and several committees, and Mercer, former executive director for the Oklahoma Visual Arts Coalition, had attended the San Jose conference, served on numerous committees, and directed the memorial center from 1999 to 2000.[48]

"We wanted designers to taste and smell the event," Mercer said. "We wanted to convey that in addition to the horror there was the remarkable ability of people to move beyond petty indifference and respond." Toperzer recalled that "we did the whole thing, from assignment to completion in less than two weeks. The space became our canvas, and we got something out of our system by doing it." Planned as a private exhibit for design competitors, it took on, Mercer noted, "a life of its own." Through word of mouth and newspaper stories, thousands of people have visited this exhibit.[49]

Entering a small, darkened room, wall-size murals of the devastated Murrah Building and the surrounding area locate people in the middle of Fifth Street. They encounter a pile of rubble: broken granite, glass, a damaged file cabinet, dangling rebar, ceiling tile, and a crumpled notebook from a desk. Standing in this small dark space in the presence of Murrah debris, visitors hear an audiotape of a meeting in the Water Resources Building that began at 9:00 A.M. on April 19, 1995, and captured the sound of the blast. Immediately, nine television monitors convey the utter chaos of the moment, assaulting exhibit visitors with a nine-minute cacophony of aerial and street level scenes of the immediate aftermath of the bombing. Some visitors will even recognize a fleeting glimpse of Aren Almon-Kok crying out, "My daughter's in there." The voice of President Clinton offers a bridge to the rest of the exhibit, "May God's grace be with them. Meanwhile, we will be about our work."

A narrow hallway offers a color mural of a rescue worker and her dog, and a wall of letters from children written to rescue workers. A second room holds a neatly prepared cot with a message from children and candy on the pillow (symbolizing the Oklahoma Standard), helmets of rescue workers, and paper cranes hanging from the ceiling. Brief text tells the story of twelve-year-old Sadako Sasaki, who died in 1955 of leukemia caused by radiation poisoning from the atomic bomb dropped on Hiroshima. In Japanese folk belief, the folding of a thousand paper cranes is thought to help cure illness. Sadako died thirty-six cranes short of a thousand, and "her classmates made up the difference.... The children founded the Folded Crane Club and continue to fold cranes to commemorate more young radiation deaths." Folding paper cranes as an expression of mourning has spread beyond commemoration of victims of the atomic bomb, and after the Oklahoma City bombing, schoolchildren folded cranes "in increments of 1,000 and sent them . . . to protect and heal."[50]

The exhibit ends with color photographs of the Murrah implosion, a wall with 168 vertical lines to represent the dead, a mural of early commemorative objects in the Murrah rubble, and, in front of that on the floor, commemorative items from the archive. In addition to family members, survivors and rescuers, foreign dignitaries, representatives of law enforcement agencies, school groups, foreign students, even an AAU baseball team have visited the exhibition. Some visitors have placed wreaths in the exhibit space and offered a prayer, turning a "museum" visit into a commemorative occasion.

Many design teams, of course, did not travel to Oklahoma City to "taste" the bombing through the garage exhibition. At the competition's closing date, 624 memorial designs were submitted from every state (144 were from Oklahoma) and twenty-four countries. JoAnne Riley, Memorial Center coordinator during the design process, remembered "hundreds" of design boards arriving on the deadline. "We got everything including the kitchen sink," she recalled. (Indeed, an Italian submission never arrived, but a sink from Italy did.) During the design competition, people who continued to have "visions" of the memorial kept calling her. "I told them that they could send their idea even if they didn't meet design competition regulations, and their vision would become part of the archive."51

The design boards went on public display in the Oklahoma Hardware Building in a renovated area of Oklahoma City known as Bricktown on March 20, 1997. Survivor Calvin Moser proposed hanging the design boards on a fence in the building because, he said, "the fence had become so important to so many. That is where people came to leave something of themselves. I thought it only fitting that these people who entered the competition and gave of themselves have their ideas displayed in the same way."

More than 15,000 people viewed the design boards, and Riley recalled vividly the first evening, when only family members and survivors viewed the display. "This was one of the first times I didn't see a lot of people crying," she said. "They weren't looking at 168 faces or a bombed-out building or the fireman and the baby. They were looking at the tangible creative caring of people, and I think many of them were stunned at the volume, overwhelmed by how much people cared."

Many of the designs used predictable elements of the memorial vocabulary envisioned by so many people in early memorial ideas. There were, however, several unusual submissions. One, entitled "Tragedy of Disengaged Soil," stated that "our present infrastructure distances us from soil, community and the prospect of peace and sustainability." Noting the tragedy of the Dust Bowl of the 1930s, the designers observed that "on more than one occasion it has turned firm soil into rootless dust." Sixty years later that same infrastructure "has given us the landscapes that makes terrorism a possibility. On April 19, 1995, it unleashed the worst. It gave us the detached fertilizer that did not nurture the life of soil, but destroyed life. . . . Urban dust made by fertilizer is the ultimate tragedy of disengaged soil."

This memorial plan served as a corrective, "inviting visitors to engage soil . . . so as to renew life, cultivate the city, and change the world." There would be a place for children to learn about soil, a grass plain near the Survivor Tree to serve as a public forum, a garden for visitors to plant "tokens of remembrance," a well at the Murrah footprint, which "sustains the life of the site," and a soil room containing the names of victims. A wheat field "to be cared for by seasonal seeding, tending, and harvesting . . . by the children of Oklahoma City will be witness to our ability to care and to use fertilizer to nurture life rather than turn it into dust as was done on this ground."

In March 1997, thousands of people had the opportunity to view all the entries in the design competition. (Oklahoma City National Memorial Foundation, photograph by G. Jill Evans)

One design led into a "descent into earth," an underground victim's sanctuary from which visitors ascended to the survivor's garden. Another envisioned a "suspended sculptural garden enclosed in glass shells" signifying the
"fragility of life." An ambitious design envisioned "Towers of Triumph," the
tallest of which would rise eighty-four feet and would shine a xenon beacon
for one hundred miles. Although most designs focused on the more soothing themes expressed in the mission statement, one called for a "Panic Pavilion," within which the "havoc ridden interior of torn steel, collapsing slabs"
would evoke the "experiences and emotions of the survivors and victims
trapped in the wreckage." Some designers thought it important to locate
commemorative activity in vessels with Oklahoma roots. A proposal for
memorial domes, for example, was "inspired by the prehistorical burial
mounds of eastern Oklahoma." Each dome would contain a chamber of
remembrance for victims, survivors, and rescuers.

Designs dealt in a wide variety of ways with the most sensitive issue: how
to memorialize the 168 victims. They were represented by individual
columns, by photographs "taken, if possible, from a family album," by a "victim pedestal," with 168 chiming rods. There were plans for 168 garden plots
or 168 "abstract plant forms of prairie grasses native to Oklahoma," with a
tendril sewn around each stem that included the name of a victim.

One entry envisioned a memorial pavilion with 168 bronze chairs.
Another suggested bronze bells for each victim that "would toll individually
in random order." Yet another proposed 168 slit openings in a granite wall.
The sun's rays would be perpendicular to each opening only once each day,
"individually illuminating the memory of each victim." There were designs
for a lighthouse with 168 stars, a tower with 168 musical strings, a field with
168 markers, weeping willows for each victim to be planted by survivors,
bubbling fountains for each victim, engraved stones, doves, windmills, 168
water jets accompanied by a life-sized bronze portrait of those killed, a great
mobile of wind chimes, "each dangling by a thread as did 168 lives that day,"
and a sculpture of 168 stainless steel petals, each with a DNA symbol. They
would appear closed "in bud-like form," representing serenity, soon to be
shattered by a "great explosion of water and flame . . . as [the] water tur-
bulence subsides, the 'flower' sculpture slowly opens, transforming the

explosive violence into a symbol of hope reaching out towards each victims' namestone."

The nine-member evaluation panel met on March 25-26, 1997, selecting five designs for a "short list." The decision, their report said, "was based on much discussion, professional and personal examination, and collaborative rigor among all nine members of the Panel. . . . The common thread

Members of the evaluation panel that selected the five finalists in the design competition joined foundation members. Standing: L-R: Cheryl Vaught, Kari Watkins, Richard Williams, Toby Thompson, Bob Johnson, Bill Moggridge, Robert Campbell, Juane Quick-To-See Smith, Richard Haag, Jackie Jones, Yvonne Maloan. Seated: Sydney Dobson, Adele Santos, Polly Nichols, Michaele Pride-Wells, Karen Luke. On Floor: Don Stastny, Beth Tolbert, Helene Fried, JoAnn Pearce. (Oklahoma City National Memorial Foundation)

throughout is that each of the selected entries creates a 'place' of remembrance that is timeless, not just an icon whose meaning and importance diminishes as memories fade."[52]

"Members of the panel were looking for ideas that really stuck out," Stastny said. "You could tell immediately which were professional submis-

sions, and I worried that a potentially great idea might be lost because its presentation was not as professional-looking as some others. It was interesting
that some of the ideas that grabbed people were not done by professionals."

Panel members looked at every board, and Stastny worried about "board
fatigue." "We asked them to look for design excellence, for those twenty that
were worthy of further discussion," he said. "We cut down fairly easily to about
eighty, then we put together everyone's top twenty, and already we had a
strong consensus." The next day, the panel revisited those "cut," to see if there
were any worthy of inclusion, then made further selections. "In our meetings,
seating was integrated—family members and survivors sat among the professionals—and everyone talked about every board," Stastny recalled. "The professionals," he said, "made a real contribution, not only for their expertise but
because they told the family members and survivors, 'you're not burdened
with picking a winner, but the best of a range of designs.' This helped the panel
focus on what they believed was the best of any particular idea." After several
stages of discussion and selection, the panel picked the final five designs. "Even
then," said Stastny, "we went back and looked for interesting designs that we
had not chosen. It became clear that the panel picked good, strong concepts,
any one of which would have been an extraordinary memorial."

The five finalists were introduced at the Murrah site during the second
anniversary ceremony on April 19, 1997. They had several months to prepare
their designs for the scrutiny of the selection committee. They had to
respond to concerns raised by the evaluation panel, submit four design
boards and a three-dimensional model of their design concept, all of which
was thought necessary to help "increase the layperson's comprehension of
the concept."[53]

James Rossant and Richard Scherr of New York City proposed "The Barn
Raising," featuring a leaning sixty-foot wall of gray granite which, they said,
"refers initially to the horrific event of the explosion by symbolizing destabi-
lization, the fracturing of civilized norms, and more literally, the destruction
of a building."

The wall, however, was meant also to symbolize rebirth through the
"mythic American institution" of a barn raising. It was a "wall which rises
again, a reversal of the original act." An irregular reflecting pool in front of
the wall, evocative of the outline of the Murrah footprint, "implies that the

explosion caused subterranean water, a healing substance, to seep through the ground to the surface offering hope and renewed life for those who were killed." Irregular bronze supports for the wall symbolized those who came to help. Beneath these supports would appear survivor names, and on the other side of the wall the names of victims, with the opening words of the mission statement above. The children's area contained a glass panel with an image of a fireman and baby, ignoring design guidelines.

Susan Herrington and Mark Stankard of Iowa State University proposed "Footfalls Echo the Memory," a complex memorial environment that included an "Answering Wood" near the Survivor Tree, where "quotes from the survivors appear etched on the surface of the walks." A lawn covering what had been Fifth Street would commemorate the rescue effort. Visitors would then ascend on Oklahoma red granite and sod footfalls—providing a place to "pause, sit, gather and commune"—over the Murrah footprint to the "Echo Wall," glass panels etched with victims' names. Impressed between the glass layers would be an object selected by family members symbolizing those killed. A stainless steel grate parallel to the wall covered a fissure

One of the five final designs from James Rossant and Richard Scherr, "The Barn Raising." (David Allen, Oklahoma City)

Another finalist from Susan Herrington and Mark Stankard, "Footfalls Echo the Memory." (David Allen, Oklahoma City)

A third design chosen as a finalist was submitted by J. Kyle Casper and Brian Branstetter, "Celebration of Life." (David Allen, Oklahoma City)

extending downward through which visitors would "hear the echoing of remnant sounds and feel the inert dampness of the void below."

J. Kyle Casper and Brian Branstetter of Dallas, Texas, proposed "Celebration of Life," the heart of which was an enclosed victim's memorial that served as a "sanctuary" between a memorial lawn and a remembrance court on the Murrah footprint. The victims' memorial contained personal memorial blocks for those killed. "At 12 noon on each victim's birth date, sunlight penetrates the opening of the Memorial walls and illuminates the personal memorial," each of which would be inscribed with the person's name, birth date and "personal messages from friends and family" and would hold "personal devotional belongings."

Hanno Weber, Kathleen Hess, and Michael Maher of Chicago, Illinois, proposed a commemorative circular wall within which visitors would enter a circumambulating path framed by 168 trees, "accompanying the surviving elm and creating a diadem of sentinels as the perennial custodians of hallowed ground." A lawn would occupy the space inside the commemorative wall, a segment of which would be a "peaceful meadow for reflection" on the

The design of Hanno Weber, Kathleen Hess, and Michael Maher was also chosen as a finalist. (David Allen, Oklahoma City)

Murrah footprint. Water would trickle into a well located at the epicenter of the explosion, and the names of those killed would appear on a nearby wall.

The selection committee met to select the winning design on June 23-24, 1997. Before they met, however, the nine-member evaluation panel returned to offer their comments on the refined designs, and family members and survivors were asked to view the designs and respond. The fifteen-member selection committee, made up of eight family members and survivors, four

Members of the selection committee that chose the final design join foundation members. Standing: Ignacio Bunster-Ossa, Luke Corbett, Jeannine Gist, Paul Heath, Cheryl Scroggins, Calvin Moser, Kimberly Ritchie, Phillip Thompson, Kari Watkins, John Cole, Douglas Hollis, Richard Williams, Tom Hall, Lars Lerup, Mayor Ron Norick, Bob Johnson, Karen Luke. Kneeling: Bud Welch, Helene Fried, David Lopez, Laurie Beckelman, Dan Stastny, Crystal Radcliff. (Oklahoma City National Memorial Foundation)

design professionals, and three community leaders, reviewed this material before visiting the site and the garage exhibit.[54]

There was both praise and substantive criticism of each of the aforementioned designs. Despite the fact that the raised wall was a visible landmark, "with [the] possibility to serve as [an] image or icon of the city," the Survivor Tree was not well integrated into the design, the fierce Oklahoma wind might threaten the wall's stability, the names of victims and survivors were too close to one another, and "the basic question was whether it would be symbolically understood or would it require interpretation?" One family member noted, for example, that the wall and its supporting poles conjured up a troubling image, "I see ... the poles holding the wall in place just before the Murrah Building imploded."

Many people were intrigued by the "footfalls" design. Family members, in particular, liked the space for devotional material near the glass panels. Others were impressed with the "audible element" of the fissure. There was concern about the location of survivor names, however. Most importantly, "the proliferation of 'wall memorials' since the Vietnam Memorial is an issue in this design."

People were also impressed with Casper and Branstetter's victim memorial design. They were "intrigued by the strong focus of shafts of sunlight illuminating the stainless steel personal memorials," and the "aesthetic simplicity" of the buffalo grass on the footprint. There was concern that "one strong idea may limit the desire for return visits" and concern about the "workability of the concept on days when direct sunshine was not evident.... Would families that came for that special moment of illumination be disappointed through some loss of ideal climatic condition?" Some family members and survivors also thought the interior space would be claustrophobic, and one commented on the square block memorial: "It looks like a tomb. It is cold and impersonal."

There was also appreciation for the "timeless and enduring symbol" of the commemorative circle design and admiration for the "strong internal spatial experience" and the "wonderful dialogue between water and the survivor tree." Some members of the selection committee wondered, however, if the form was too universal for this memorial and whether the "size and scale feels monumental and might find a better home in a world capital." Concern also centered on the presence of the well located near the bomb crater, an "uncomfortable reminder of the bomb for many of the families' and survivors' representatives."[55]

On June 24, the selection committee took a secret ballot and voted unanimously for a design created by the husband-wife team of Hans and Torrey Butzer, with the assistance of a German colleague, Sven Berg. The Butzers had both graduated from the University of Texas at Austin, and their design partnership had taken them to Berlin, Germany, where they lived and

Representatives from the Memorial Foundation who went to Washington, D.C., to present the design to President Clinton, August 1997. Back Row: L-R: Cheryl Vaught, Kari Watkins, Hans Butzer, Bob Johnson, Toby Thompson, George Hosendorf, Richard Williams, Phillip Thompson. Front Row: L-R: Kathleen Treanor, Torrey Butzer, Judy Kelley, Gennie Johnson, Bud Welch, Polly Nichols, Brenda McDaniel. Kneeling: Mike Treanor. (Oklahoma City National Memorial Foundation)

Hans and Torrey Butzer, creators of the winning memorial design. (David Allen, Oklahoma City)

worked. They entered the design competition quite late, having only seen the announcement in late January 1997, leaving them six weeks to submit a design. Unlike many of the design teams, they had no opportunity to visit the site. Torrey Butzer, who was born in Oklahoma, observed that this was not necessarily a hindrance. "We got to start with a cleaner slate," she said. "We were somewhat removed, we didn't live with all the media images, and by virtue of geography we were somewhat less emotionally involved. The first thing we did was build a model of the site."[56]

Hans Butzer recalls their early conversations about the need to "limit" their aesthetic vision. "We had to think about what this event meant, and how we wanted to embody that meaning in design. We needed to isolate what happened, isolate the meaning of the event." This project was unlike any other they had worked on. "We are used to designing extremely functional buildings which have a very limited emotional content, and suddenly, we were presented with something where pain and healing were at the heart of the design." They agreed that their design needed to be about individuals and should be an intimate, quiet place.

The Butzers wanted to "freeze the time of the bombing in space" by creating what seemed to be a large outdoor room. They envisioned large "gates of time" at the east and west edge of the site, one marked "9:01" and the other "9:03." The gates marked the line "where the city's edge stops and the memorial site starts." "Inside," Hans Butzer said, "we would do this with doors, but even doors shut one out, and these gates both frame and take the site completely out of ordinary space, but they also allow the site to interact with ordinary space, the world where people have to deal with the impact of the bombing." The two primary memorial zones—the Survivor Tree and the Journal Record Building (which would house the Memorial Center) to the north and the Murrah footprint to the south—were to be "mediated" by a long reflecting pool that spanned what had been Fifth Street. The pool, the Butzers hoped, would be a site to help promote "healing" and "provide a peaceful background to our thoughts." As visitors gazed into it, the water would reveal "the faces of those changed forever."

The Survivor Tree is an important "power point" within the memorial environment. The Butzer's design created a level ground plane along the Fifth Street site, and the Survivor Tree, resting on a promontory and surrounded by cascading terraces, became even more visible. The design also created memorial space to honor rescuers. Learning of the many people who rushed to help in the chaotic moments after the bombing, the Butzers recall that "we began to imagine an army of helpers, rushing in from all directions to the site. We have translated this army of helpers into an army of fruit trees, marching forth from the streets' edge to surround the survivor tree. We saw fruit trees as symbolic in their bearing of fruit representing the fruits of labor, as well as the continuation of the life-cycle.... The harvesting of fruit in the fall would be the focus of an annual celebration, honoring those who helped, as well as those who survived."[57]

Near this orchard was a place for children, who had written letters by the thousands to rescuers, to continue to write on chalkboards. These letters would be "temporary, as rain and time will wash them away, only to make room for new ones."

The south side of the memorial site presented designers with formidable challenges: a proper location for survivors' names, and, of course, memorial representation of those killed. On one end of the Murrah footprint stood several remaining walls of the Murrah Building, and here would appear survivors' names, in what the Butzers called a "side chapel."

Every designer had to struggle with an appropriate memorial to those killed, surely the most sensitive and challenging design task. While those responsible for selecting a memorial design were impressed with the Butzer's plan, clearly one of its most powerful "selling points" was the idea of 168 empty chairs on the Murrah footprint. Hans Butzer characterized this as a "very simple yet powerful portrayal of someone not being there. The image of 168 empty chairs clustered on the grassy slope...seemed so quietly overwhelming.... Like an empty chair at a dinner table, we are always aware of the presence of a loved one's absence. These chairs will provide family members with a special place where they can stand near, or even sit and think about their loved one. They may choose to leave a token of remembrance on the chair, as is done with the fence today."

At a meeting with family members and survivors, Hans Butzer said that the empty chairs were personally meaningful as well. He told them of his grandfather ("one of my few heroes"), who used to take him to a small lake in western Germany. "He would sit on one of the park benches...as I rowed

The Oklahoma City National Memorial, viewed from the Journal Record Building.
(David Allen, Oklahoma City)

a boat around the lake. Each time I return to this lake since his passing thirteen years ago, I see my grandfather sitting there on one of the benches quietly watching me."[58]

The chairs have a bronze back and glass base, and they are etched with the name of each person killed. The base of each chair is lit in the evening hours ("beacons of hope"). They appear in nine rows, evocative of the floors of the Murrah Building. "This grid," Hans Butzer explained, "is then filled with chairs according to where the most damage was done to the building... . The row of five chairs on the west end of the grassy slope acknowledge the five victims who were not in the Murrah Building at the time of the bombing."[59]

Members of the evaluation panel were mightily impressed with the chairs. They were a "powerful and original symbol of loss, the 'presence of absence,'" they were "individually human scaled, while collectively monumental," and members of the selection committee agreed. The entire design, members said, embodied the mission statement, and the "symbolism of the lit empty chairs makes us aware not only of our loss, but also sends beacons of light for peace."

As in every other part of this process, the final design bears the imprint of family members and survivors. Some felt the original plan for chairs of stone and glass too evocative of a tombstone, and straight-backed chairs too severe. Consequently, chairs are made of bronze and glass, and chair backs are somewhat curved. Some family members questioned the Butzers' plan to locate the names on the glass base ("primarily because we were interested in the illumination of the name at night from within the glass base," Hans Butzer noted) and wanted the names placed near the top of the chair backs to be more visible. To others, however, this also was too much like a tombstone, and the names remained on the base.

The Butzers had originally placed only the names of Murrah survivors in the existent Murrah wall in the side chapel; other survivors' names appeared near the Survivor Tree. This was changed, for the mission statement called for all survivor's names to be on the footprint. There was also sensitivity about how survivors' names were to be listed on the memorial wall. The Butzers originally envisioned listing by building, with the layout providing visitors a kind of map of the area that would orient them in this transformed memorial environment. There were objections that this was perhaps too graphic a depiction of the boundaries of survivor definition, and it was important for many that the Murrah Building be somehow designated as the target of the bomb. Consequently, four granite panels list the buildings and their survivors alphabetically, with the Alfred P. Murrah Building coming first.

Some family members were also concerned that too little of the fence would be incorporated into the memorial. In their original design, the Butzers envisioned three small sections of the fence coated in green plastic located near the children's area. They argued that it was not the fence that was important, but *what the fence allows to happen* (italics original). They believed that the design allowed for new sites for people to leave devotional items and noted that the fence and "its role in the history of the site will be fully explained and portrayed in the Memorial Center."[60]

As planning continued into 1998, however, family members were uneasy about "losing" a memorial site that had become so important to them. Several told me they would have been perfectly satisfied with just the fence as a permanent memorial. Only a few offered a minority view, that the fence was, in Toby Thompson's words, an "immature" form of memorial and should have given way entirely to the Butzer's design. In the fall of 1998, however, after several family members raised the issue with Robert Johnson, the Butzers were asked to incorporate more of the fence in their design. They recommended placing several hundred feet of the fence adjacent to the western gate marking "9:03," the "healing" side of the memorial. "We believe," they wrote, that this is "most appropriate, given the role the fence has already played for so many for so long." On October 26, 1998, the day after a public ground breaking ceremony at which Vice President Al Gore spoke, family members, survivors, and rescue workers gathered in a private ceremony to move several large sections of the fence to the new location.[61]

There was another sensitive issue that threatened to transform the site. Major disasters always produce what medical examiners refer to as "common tissue," unidentifiable human remains. At the time the bodies were released to their families, Ray Blakeney, chief of operations for the state medical examiner's office, informed them of the existence of common tissue. At some future date a decision regarding its disposition would have to be made.

(David Allen, Oklahoma City)

(David Allen, Oklahoma City)

The Oklahoma City National Memorial. (David Allen, Oklahoma City)

"My intent," Blakeney said, "was to resolve this in July of 1995, but Judge Matsch put a restraining order on it because defense attorneys wanted to use the common tissue to argue that this supposed 169th casualty was the bomber. The restraining order was not lifted until after the Nichols verdict."[62]

In early April 1998, Blakeney notified family members that "planning has now begun for this final interment" and asked them to indicate where they would like the tissue buried, in an area cemetery or at the bomb site. This issue had the potential to be extremely divisive. Many survivors were strongly opposed to transforming the site into a cemetery. There was disagreement among family members, and some thought only family members should decide the issue. Could the tissue be buried on the renovated GSA Plaza overlooking the site? Could it be buried at a church near the site? Would burial at the site exclude those who for religious reasons would not be able to go to the site if the tissue was buried there? The Butzers strongly opposed burial on the site. "Not only would it transform the site into a cemetery," Torrey Butzer said, "it would leave people with horrific images, rather than feelings of peace and hope."[63]

On October 4, 1999, the common tissue committee recommended that

The Memorial in winter. (David Allen, Oklahoma City)

A wintertime view of the Survivor Tree, now incorporated into the Memorial.
(David Allen, Oklahoma City)

the tissue be buried in the memorial grove of trees donated by the state of Iowa on the grounds of the state capitol, and on December 11, 1999, a short burial ceremony was held on the capitol grounds.

The Butzers had also envisioned climbing ivy covering the bleak and exposed wall that ran along the back of the Murrah footprint. But there was a strong feeling that ivy would "soften" the site, and consequently the decision was made to leave the wall exposed. The interesting issue of whether this memorial design created too soothing an environment by transforming a historic site into a memorial environment also troubled Jim Loftis, the architectural designer of the Murrah Building. He had entered the competition with a design that envisioned an abstract footprint of the Murrah Building and other surrounding damaged structures. He called these "damaged plazas," and he wanted a plaque marking where each person had been found. The design also included an elliptical pool with a black bottom on "ground zero," since this should be a spot, Loftis said, "that no one should touch." Loftis thought his design would "maintain the history of the site. I respect

On October 26, 1998, the day after groundbreaking for the memorial, a private fence moving ceremony for families, survivors, and rescue workers was held at 5:00 P.M. (Oklahoma City National Memorial Foundation)

the memorial plan they chose," he said, "but I think it is a site that now forgets the event that gave rise to it."

A few others raised similar issues. Cynthia Ferrell Ashwood, whose sister Susan was killed, thought that the plan to demolish the Athenian and Water Resources Buildings in the fall of 1997 was a "huge mistake." "One need only look at them and be able to imagine the power of the terrorist bomb," she said. "Particularly the Athenian wears the horror of terrorism. I do not think that a man-made exhibit in a museum can capture what is already exhibited at the Athenian Building." Referring to the sentence in the mission statement, "May all who leave here know the impact of violence," she wondered if visitors would see only "reflecting pools and trees, how will they ever know the impact of the violence that was inflicted?"[64]

Does the soothing, parklike atmosphere of this memorial help visitors appreciate the impact of violence? Since this is the site of the bombing, should more elements of the historic landscape (e.g., the shattered buildings) have been preserved? Or would the presence of such ruins focus too

Vice President Al Gore at the groundbreaking ceremonies, October 25, 1998. (David Allen, Oklahoma City)

much attention on the event and not enough on what was important to family members and survivors: the heartening response of so many, as well as their desire and need for the memorial to be a place in which individuals are remembered and their stories are told? The Butzers certainly thought that the impact of the event would be recalled through the empty chairs, the desolate walls, and a portion of the Journal Record Building that would be left in its damaged condition.

Many of those involved in the memorial process speak of the "journey" that they took together, about the "evolution" of so many individuals into a working bereaved community. Phillip Thompson believes that despite the arduous nature of the process, it was important. "In the beginning we helped keep the process focused. Much of our best work resulted from the review and comment of family members. If we hadn't been involved, or were only token representatives, it all would have been less cumbersome, but it wouldn't have had the passion that emerged from our pain and anger."

Some journalists interpreted this "pain and anger" (what they labeled "controversy") as meaning that something was "wrong," that, by implication, memorial processes are supposed to proceed smoothly, without rancor. What a strange assumption! Would we not find it a violation of the integrity of memory if, for example, Germany was able to decide easily on a Berlin Holocaust memorial? "Better a thousand years of Holocaust memorial competitions in Germany," writes James Young, "than any single 'final solution' to Germany's memorial problem."[65]

Oklahoma City is not Germany, but Young's argument—that it is through the process that people are most fully engaged with the searing issues they want to express in memorialization—is relevant. Any "easy" memorial solution to mass murder in Oklahoma City would have represented a strategy of avoidance, not one of agonizing engagement. Passionate arguments—over the closing of Fifth Street, about memorial hierarchies, about the design of a memorial, or the burial site of common tissue—are constitutive processes in the creation of public culture. A memorial process of integrity in Oklahoma City *had* to struggle with the sensibilities and convictions of so many different people with intimate connections to the bombing. It *had* to find a way to forthrightly acknowledge these clashing sensibilities and convictions and incorporate them in a larger vision of the purposes of memorialization. It is

a stunning achievement, in my opinion, that this process was able to enfran-
chise so many people, one reason that there were not warring memorial
camps emerging out of the process.

The Oklahoma City memorial process represented something quite significant in the history of public memorialization. Many memorials, of course,
exist to offer comfort, assuage grief, and inspire future generations to emulate
the virtues ostensibly enshrined in memorials. It would be hard to find a
memorial process, however, that included over three hundred people, many
of whom had just suffered traumatic loss. It would be hard to find a memorial
process consciously designed to be therapeutic, to help individuals become a
bereaved community and to engage mass murder through memorial planning. "So many people have been changed by the process," Phillip Thompson
observed. "We have moved from a desire to see our loved ones memorialized
in stone to a larger vision of what a memorial is and what it does. We moved
from unfocused emotion to reflections on what it means to us, and from
'what do I want' to 'what do we want to give as a gift to the world.'"

The memorial process served as an ingeniously designed model of com-

Robert Johnson, Chairman of the
Oklahoma City National Memorial
Trust Board of Directors and Karen
Luke, Chairperson of the Oklahoma
City National Memorial Foundation
Board of Directors. The trust over-
sees the activities of both the
National Park Service and and
Memorial Foundation. (David
Allen, Oklahoma City)

munity consensus building. It brought together a wide cross-section of the community. Some spoke in public for the first time, most learned the art of compromise, most learned how grief became manifest in so many different ways, most learned to listen and to be patient. Beth Shortt observed that the memorial process sparked increased civic engagement in the city. "I have seen people on boards and working with groups who never had done such work before." That people seared by immediate loss could practice the arts of democracy in the work of memorial making is a significant achievement.

Conclusion: Bonds of Affection

The bombing in Oklahoma City immediately became part of the nation's public culture. As we have seen, it threatened deeply rooted convictions of innocence, provoked and focused personal fears, vulnerabilities, and unresolved traumas, became a commodity to be used in ongoing cultural battles, sparked a tremendous variety of popular memorial expression, and led to the creation of a distinctive memorial process.

Memorials are, of course, expressions made by particular communities of memory, in this case a community made up of family members, survivors, rescue workers, and civic-minded individuals who were not so directly seared by loss. Through a painstaking process they learned to work together, crafting a mission statement that declared the memorial would be shaped primarily by the sensibilities of family members and survivors. It would not be done *for* them, but it would be done *by* them. Faith in the process and allegiance to the mission statement helped this large and diverse community of memory negotiate a host of difficult issues: the closing of Fifth Street, survivor definition, the role of professionals in memorial design evaluation and selection, the common tissue problem, and the location of the fence in the new memorial.

The massive number of people who continued to visit the site after the memorial's dedication on April 19, 2000—approximately 340,000 visitors by the end of September—brought yet another unexpected problem. Hans and

Torrey Butzer envisioned the sacred ground that contained the 168 memorial chairs as being open space in which people could walk among the chairs and perhaps leave memorial items. Some family members looked forward to sitting in the chairs, bringing friends and other relatives to them. The huge number of visitors, however, destroyed the grass around the chairs, and the area began to look shoddy and worn. For those tasked with the memorial's upkeep, this was more than an aesthetic problem. A worn physical memorial, especially around the chairs, could communicate indifference to the dead.

While the foundation struggled over how to satisfy both the desire for beauty and the desire for access—researching more resistant strains of grass, perhaps even the possibility of walkways—the area was cordoned off. Family members could be escorted to their loved one's chair, but the area was inaccessible to the general public. Some family members and survivors thought that a pristine memorial, especially the area around the chairs, was most important. Others argued that the memorial belonged to the nation and that access should be restored as soon as possible. Still others said that it was impossible to read their loved one's name on a chair in a back row without access.

On February 19, 2001, President George W. Bush joined in the dedication of the Oklahoma City National Memorial Center housed in the Journal Record Building and containing museum exhibition space, archival space, and office space for the Memorial Foundation and the Oklahoma City National Memorial Institute for the Prevention of Terrorism. The central attraction for the several thousand people who attended the outdoor dedication was the opportunity to engage the story of the bombing and its impact in the museum. Consciously modeled after the United States Holocaust Memorial Museum exhibition, the museum in Oklahoma City offers an intense narrative that opens by introducing visitors to a "day like any other." Moving into a fairly small room, groups of twenty-five to thirty visitors listen to an audiotape of a meeting that began in the Oklahoma Water Resources Board Building at 9:00 A.M. and contains the sound of the explosion.

Throughout the exhibition, there is an overwhelming presence of faces, names, and stories. There are the ordinary faces of early morning April 19, 1995, the last moments of ordinary time. There is the face of Judge Murrah, now forever associated with the bombing. When visitors hear the explosion on the audiotape, the room darkens and 168 faces shine brightly for a moment on a large screen and then fade away. There are the grief-stricken faces, names, and stories of family members, survivors, and rescuers in hundreds of photographs, in moving video presentations located throughout the exhibition, and in many stories visitors may access through computer. The 168 faces appear again in individual photographs in a memorial room, and there is a constantly moving vertical scroll of the 168 names and scenes of funerals, framed by constantly moving horizontal images of tombstones, memorial flowers, obituaries, churches, various religious symbols, all with the strains of "Amazing Grace," "Taps," and various hymns and organ music in the background. In the Memorial Center and at the outdoor memorial visitors meet the living faces and stories of family members and survivors who serve as docents.

With the opening of the Memorial Center, memorial expression was *anchored* in a specific site (clearly delineated sacred space), *embodied* by family member and survivor docents, *expressed* in the Memorial Center's exhibition, *preserved* in massive archival collections, and *disseminated* through the activities of the institute and the educational imperative of the foundation to engage in public education about the impact of violence, the human face of government, and the necessity of nonviolent means of social change as an integral element of civil society.[1]

The exhibition reinforced my sense that the memorial was in part a protest against the anonymity of mass death. *These* victims of violence would not be forgotten. Their deaths would be redeemed by becoming public. The specter of meaningless death would be contained through the physical presence of individual memorial chairs and through the civic rhetoric of "lessons" of the bombing. These dead, the memorial claims, are still among us, they still teach us, we redeem their deaths by our willingness to be touched and transformed by the public legacy of their deaths.

Visitors to the site also see the familiar uniforms of the National Park Service. The inclusion of the Oklahoma City National Memorial in the National Park Service's landscape of historic sites offers visitors a clue that this is not just a site deemed worthy of memorialization by a city, state, or private enterprise. It is part of the nation's official public memory.[2]

Will the prominence of the Oklahoma City bombing be ensured by its location in the nation's official memory? Will it become an enduring part of the national landscape, a site as important as Monticello, Gettysburg, or the Vietnam Veterans Memorial? Will a future terrorist act that inflicts even more death consign Oklahoma City to a less prestigious location on the landscape of violence? Or might such an act increase its prestige as the first event in a continuing body count of domestic terrorism? Already, its location among the pantheon of national historic sites has engendered what I think of as another insidious preferred narrative, one that situates the bombing within a comforting national narrative of patriotic sacrifice.

The transformation of mass murder into patriotic sacrifice began almost immediately. For example, the lyrics in Red River's country and western music video, "You Can't Break America's Heart," declared "freedom has a price," and "sometimes people have to give their lives to make sure the spirit of America survives." "Perhaps," one letter to Governor Keating surmised, "this is the sacrifice required to bring a semblance of order back to a world almost devoid of concern for a fellow human being." Occasionally newspapers used the rhetoric of sacrifice. The *Christian Science Monitor,* for example, informed its readers six days after the bombing that "all Americans have a responsibility to those killed and missing in Oklahoma to ensure their sacrifice was not in vain."[3]

The rhetoric of patriotic sacrifice figured prominently at the memorial's dedication ceremonies on the fifth anniversary of the bombing, April 19, 2000. Governor Keating told a crowd of approximately 25,000 that, like Gettysburg, the Oklahoma City memorial was "another American shrine, another patch of hallowed ground." Also speaking at the dedication was President Clinton, who said "there are places in our national landscape so scarred by freedom's sacrifice that they shape forever the soul of America— Valley Forge, Gettysburg, Selma. This place is such sacred ground."[4]

These words grated on me. However well-meaning, they seem profoundly misleading. These people's lives were not given in an act of conscious sacrifice for their nation; they were taken in an act of mass murder. The landscape to which Oklahoma City is connected is not Valley Forge, Gettysburg, and Selma, but sites of political terrorism and mass murder: the Sixteenth Street Baptist Church in Birmingham, Alabama, the McDonald's in San Diego, and Columbine High School.

Pam Whicher, wife of a secret service agent murdered in the bombing responded to my question about the president's words. "You are right that my husband was always prepared to give his life for others. He once told me that he believed he would die young, in the line of duty. I do not think this was in any way an honorable or constructive way to die, or what any law enforcement person would choose as a way to 'give' his life. Here's where my anger comes in. He was always prepared to defend the innocent, or put his life on the line to protect. He was given the opportunity to do neither in this situation. I believe we heal better when we accept the truth. This was nothing more than a damn waste of lives. All the more worthy of our heartbreak, and the families, all the more worthy of our sympathy." Her response is, I think, a magnificent example of the integrity of memory, of how someone seared with recent loss has the moral courage to resist the allure of preferred narratives.[5]

The title of this book indicates my conviction about the ongoing impact of the bombing. Despite my enduring suspicion about comforting stories that dilute the realities of violence, I learned that the stories of acts of kindness, the selfless work of rescue and recovery, and the pride in the Oklahoma Standard were not an evasion of the realities of the event but an important part of people's reaction to it.

Therefore, it seems appropriate to conclude with examples of the bonds of affection that exist alongside the toxic impact of the bombing. There were publicly invisible bonds, for example, between recovery personnel and family members of the loved ones whose bodies they had located or brought out of the building, as well as bonds between rescuers and survivors. There were also bonds of affection that brought together people from different cultures impacted by mass death, transnational links between bereaved communities. Concluding with these stories is not meant to create another preferred narrative—that "the good" always wins out in the end, providing a "happy ending" for so many people's enduring struggles. They do not in any way lessen the impact of the toxic narrative. They do, however, say something about human determination to offer acts of kindness and caring in the face of acts that threaten to obliterate our confidence in the power of the humane. "When people want to respond with kindness to victims in a tragedy," observed Rafael White, principal of Southeastern High School in Oklahoma

City, "all is not lost." Her words seem to me a humble and fragile truth in a dark time. These stories are her words in practice.[6]

I think, for example, of Priscilla Salyers, who worked in the federal customs office. The story of her dramatic rescue from the building was popularized in a *Lifetime* television movie, *Priscilla's Story*. She spoke at a special church service for paramedics who had worked at the site, remembering, she said, how "peace had come over me when a fireman held my hand when I was trapped in the rubble." (Numerous rescue personnel agonized over whether or not to leave those trapped with whom they may have had either physical or voice contact when a second bomb scare forced the evacuation of the building less than an hour and a half after the bombing. By approximately 11:30 A.M., rescue work continued, but by this time some people had died, and rescue workers often carried this burden.) Salyers offered them words of comfort, saying that even that last human touch could have been a moment of consolation for those who died. After her talk, a policewoman thanked her for lifting her burden. She had held an eight-month-old baby who died in her arms.[7]

I think of the rescue worker who found the body of Karen Gist Carr. He eventually located her family, offered them a piece of granite from the building, told them that he had gone to high school with Karen, and informed them that he had found her still seated in her office chair. "He told us she was easily recognizable," said Jeannine Gist, Karen's mother, "and it was important for us to know that."

I think of Michael Hanson, a New York City policeman who serves in the emergency service unit of the police department. His unit arrived in Oklahoma City on Thursday, April 20, and worked on the site for a week. They found the body of Carrie Lenz the first night. "We knew who she was because there was identification at her desk," he recalled. Along with rescue workers from around the nation, Hanson returned for the first anniversary. At a reception, he saw a man wearing a button with her photograph. "I didn't know if I should tell him I found his daughter," Hanson said, "but I thought of my three daughters, and if anything happened to them, I would want to know. I told him, 'I just want you to know that she was treated with the greatest respect.'"

Over the next few years, Hanson raised $97,000 in relief funds, and he returned to Oklahoma City for the dedication of the outdoor memorial on April 19, 2000. The day before, he found a photo of Carrie Lenz on the fence and hung a unit patch nearby. The next day, he met Lenz's mother, Doris Jones. "It was a privilege to be there for her," Hanson said. "We talked about her daughter, and I felt I knew her, she was not just a victim. I walked away knowing that my work was worth it."[8]

Bonds of affection also linked family members and survivors of the bombing with survivors of an earlier disaster in the West African nation of Cameroon. On August 21, 1986, while villagers slept, nearby Lake Nyos erupted and spread toxic gas over a ten-square-mile area, killing more than 1,700 people, as well as their precious cattle. Interfaith Disaster Recovery of Greater OKC joined with Heifer Project International—a development organization active among the rural poor—and local churches to sponsor an exchange program. Seventeen people, including family members and survivors from Oklahoma City, spent two weeks in the Cameroons in April 1997. Heifer International's Wendy Peskin wrote that "the whole group climbed for about an hour and a half to the Nyos Crater, to see and swim in the lake, and to hear stories the Nyos survivors told us as we sat on the rim of the crater."[9]

Eight Cameroonian survivors traveled to the United States in spring 1998, visiting various Heifer International projects, and spent a week in Oklahoma City during the third anniversary of the bombing. They toured the state capitol, received a salute from legislators, and met Governor Keating. On April 19, they placed a memorial from the Cameroons at the fence. Also on that day, Umaru Sule, who lost fifty family members when Lake Nyos erupted, received a scholarship on the Murrah site to attend Oklahoma State University.[10]

"Sule," as he is called, was the group's tour guide in the Cameroons. He had lived in one of the villages that was destroyed, surviving only because he had gone to market. As a young boy, he had run away from home to religious school, where he learned English. He was disowned by his father, who later relented and accepted him back. He studied animal science at the University of Massachusetts-Amherst for six months in 1989. Several members of the Oklahoma City group recalled as one of their "most moving memories" a climb to Lake Nyos, pausing as Sule told them "this is the heart of the disaster for me, where my family is buried." Ernestine Clark, a member of the survivor definition subcommittee who made the trip to the Cameroons, recalled "it was at this moment that the profound depth of connection between these people became apparent."[11]

Sule wished to study agriculture in the United States, and Clark was committed to helping him receive a scholarship for his work toward a master's degree. It was, she said, a "Herculean effort." Ernestine Clark and I visited Sule, his wife, and their young son in their small apartment in Stillwater, Oklahoma, in June 1999. He recalled for me the power of the meetings held in the Cameroons for the survivors of the two tragedies. For all of them, it seemed, "everything that happens, every other tragedy crashes against that wound we carry inside."

Like so many people in Oklahoma City, Sule has directed his energies to helping others, planning on returning to the Cameroons and applying the fruits of his education toward enriching its agricultural resources. Mutual recognition of the personal impact of loss and grief linked Sule with family members and survivors of the Oklahoma City bombing. He was able to study in this country through the caring and commitment of those touched by mass murder, and he wanted to repay that kindness by helping his people. How strangely hopeful, I thought, that my journey into the world of the bombing in Oklahoma City would lead me to the small apartment of a young Cameroonian survivor of a natural disaster. Perhaps Principal White had it right: All is not lost.

POSTSCRIPT

In a nationally televised speech on April 20, 1995, the day after the Oklahoma City bombing, President Bill Clinton assured the public that the perpetrators would be found, and that when they were, justice will be swift, certain and severe. These people are killers and they must be treated like killers.

The ensuing controversy over the fate of Timothy McVeigh—from his trial and death sentence in 1997 to his execution on June 11, 2001—showed, however, that there is no agreement on how to treat killers, or more specifically, mass murderers. Many of the impassioned arguments about the execution had to do with how McVeigh should be located in the human and national community. Is there a fundamental humanity in anyone, even the worst criminal, that the state cannot be justified in violating? Or are there acts so evil that their perpetrators forsake their claim to humanity? Would McVeigh's execution transform him into a martyr for other anti-government radicals? Would it be better to let him remain alive, imprisoned and isolated? "Executed now, he goes to his death young, vibrant, defiant—heroic to the twisted and angry," Paul Finkelman, a law professor at the University of Tulsa said in *USA Today*, "Left in his cell, he ages. The 'where are they now' pictures will show McVeigh wrinkled, raving and angry, frustrated to be alive."

Would allowing him to live make possible eventual repentance, perhaps even some form of forgiveness from those who suffered, allowing him to regain a penitent's place in the human community and a hope of spiritual redemption? Or was McVeigh's crime beyond redemption, making an irreversible sentence of death a just response? Family members and survivors in Oklahoma City were, of course, not of one mind on these issues, although it has been my impression that a significant majority supported the death penalty, at least in this instance. And while Bud Welch cautioned that "there is nothing good about watching a human take their last breath that is going to give you any peace," some clearly believed that the execution was a significant step in putting the event "behind them." The understanding that execution was a form of therapy, of "closure," was popular in the media, and played a role in the decision of Attorney General Ashcroft to allow family members and survivors to watch the execution on a closed-circuit broadcast in Oklahoma City. He hoped that it would "meet their needs to close this chapter in their lives."

Many family members and survivors understood that the execution and their right to view it might *not* be therapeutic, that it might in fact be traumatic. But at least it would remove the toxic presence of Timothy McVeigh from the national discourse and from their lives. Death would silence his voice: no longer would they have to endure the publicity from his letters to media, or highly-publicized interviews. There was some resistance to even a mention of the perpetrators in the Memorial Center. Planners eventually settled on small side rooms that told the story of the arrest and trial with minimal visual representation.

We have seen that fear of contamination from McVeigh haunted his home town and school in New York, and motels and small towns where he and Nichols stayed, and how even his corpse could not be allowed to contaminate the sacred ground where other military veterans rested. Already deprived of the right of military burial by 1997 legislation, McVeigh's body was cremated, and the ashes entrusted to one of his lawyers to scatter at an undisclosed location. Even this was too good for the editors of *National Review*, who declared that McVeigh should be dragged "through the desert behind horses until the bastard disappears."

The execution of Timothy McVeigh closes only another chapter in this ongoing story. (There is still the possibility of a state trial for Terry Nichols, who could yet be sentenced to death in Oklahoma.) The McVeigh execution will continue to fuel the intense debate over the death penalty on the meaning of justice, vengeance, forgiveness, reconciliation, repentance, redemption, and the sacredness of life. And it reveals an equally intense cultural experience of the symbolic power of a mass murderer and his threat to the purity of the body politic through his deeds, his continued life, and even the presence of his mortal remains in the soil of the nation.

As much as it is the final step of a legal process, the death penalty is a ritual of exclusion and cleansing, purging the alien bodies of domestic transgressors from the community. The execution of Timothy McVeigh will not put an end to the impassioned arguments about the death penalty, nor to the intense need for blood rituals of civic purification.

This postscript is adapted from an essay, "Purifying Ourselves of Timothy McVeigh," published in *Religion in the News*, volume 4 no. 2 (Summer 2001).

Notes

INTRODUCTION

1. The nine-story Alfred P. Murrah Federal Building was completed in April 1977. It was constructed of steel and concrete, its north face being mostly glass. It housed seventeen federal agencies and three nonfederal agencies, as well as the day care center. Four hundred fifty employees were housed in the Murrah Building. I thank Richard Williams for sending me "A Brief History of the Alfred P. Murrah Federal Building."

2. Harrison Rainie, "The Buried Sounds of Children Crying," *U.S. News and World Report*, May 1, 1995, p. 10.

3. Rochelle Gurstein, *The Repeal of Reticence: America's Cultural and Legal Struggles Over Free Speech, Obscenity, Sexual Liberation, and Modern Art* (New York: Hill and Wang, 1996), pp. 41-42.

4. Kenneth E. Foote, *Shadowed Ground: America's Landscapes of Violence and Tragedy* (Austin: University of Texas Press, 1997), pp. 179, 204. I have found one photographic collection of interesting landmarks on the nation's landscape of violence, Joel Sternfeld's *On This Site: Landscape in Memoriam* (San Francisco: Chronicle Books, 1996).

5. Michael Hedges, "April 19: The Day Americans Mark with Trepidation," *CJ Online National News* (Scripps News Service), April 19, 1998.

6. Quoted in Kenneth S. Stern, *A Force upon the Plain: The American Militia Movement and the Politics of Hate* (New York: Simon & Schuster, 1996), p. 57.

7. Timothy McVeigh, born in upstate New York in 1968, and Terry Nichols, born in rural Lapeer County, Michigan, in 1955, met when they both enlisted in the U.S. Army in 1988. McVeigh served in the Gulf War, receiving the Bronze Star. Each expressed intense hatred of the government for a variety of reasons. McVeigh, for

example, was a regular on the gun show circuit, was entranced with the apocalyptic novel *The Turner Diaries,* and was incensed by the government's actions at the Branch Davidian compound in Waco, Texas. There are many articles and books on McVeigh and Nichols. In addition to Stern's *A Force upon the Plain,* I found the following helpful: Richard Serrano, *One of Ours: Timothy McVeigh and the Oklahoma City Bombing* (New York: Norton, 1998); Mark S. Hamm, *Apocalypse in Oklahoma: Waco and Ruby Ridge Revenged* (Boston: Northeastern University Press, 1997); Phil Bacharach, "A Twisting, Turning Trail," *Oklahoma Gazette,* May 4, 1997, pp. 4-11; and "Citizen McVeigh," *Oklahoma Gazette,* November 21, 1996.

8. The City of Oklahoma City, *Alfred P. Murrah Federal Building Bombing, April 19, 1995 Final Report* (Stillwater, Okla: Fire Protection Publications, Oklahoma State University, 1996), pp. 10-12.

9. Ernestine Clark, personal account, Oklahoma City National Memorial Foundation archive (hereafter archives).

10. A study of injuries and illness in dogs working the Oklahoma City bombing reported that seventy-four dogs worked at the site for "patrol, explosive-detection, and search duties." See Roberta A. Duhaime, DVM; Dianne Norden, DVM; Barbara Corso; DVM, MS; Sue Mallonee, RN, MPH; M.D. Salman, BVMS, Ph.D., "Injuries and Illnesses in Working Dogs Used during the Disaster Response after the Bombing in Oklahoma City," *Journal of the American Veterinary Medical Association,* April 15, 1998, p. 1202. For reports on their emotional condition, see "Agony of Futile Searches Taking Its Toll on Rescue Dogs," *Daily Herald* (Algonquin, Ill.), April 24, 1995; *All Things Considered,* National Public Radio, March 17, 1996, transcript 2155-6.

11. Raymond Washburn, personal account, archive.

CHAPTER 1

1. *CBS This Morning,* April 20, 1995; juror appeared on *CNN Newsday,* June 14, 1997, transcript 97061402V11.

2. "Oklahoma City," *Life,* January 1996, pp. 42-46. See also Ben MacIntyre, "Exploding Our Invulnerability," *Los Angeles Times,* April 20, 1995; "Midwest Now Seems Vulnerable," *Des Moines Register,* April 20, 1995.

3. "Myth of Midwest Safety Shattered," *The Dispatch* (Moline, Ill.), April 21, 1995; Charlie Vincent, "After Bombing, We'll Never Feel the Same," *Detroit News,* April 22, 1995; Leonard Pitts, Jr., "American Innocence Buried in Oklahoma," *The News-Times* (Danbury, CT), April 23, 1995. Conservative Christian editorialist Cal Thomas expressed another dimension of innocence when he said, "Once God defined the norms of our society, but we decided we could do a better job." I wonder what year in our past offered evidence that God "defined" the norms of our society? And who, pray tell, decides how to interpret God's norms? About this, Thomas is, of course, silent. Better to be nostalgic for an America that never existed. Cal Thomas, "Bombing Proves Evil Exists," *Quad-City Times* (Davenport, Iowa), April 25, 1995.

4. R. W. B. Lewis, *The American Adam: Innocence, Tragedy, and Tradition in the Nineteenth Century* (Chicago: University of Chicago Press, 1955), p. 5.

5. Dickstein quoted in Walter H. Capps, *The Unfinished War: Vietnam and the American Conscience* (Boston: Beacon, 1982), p. 10.

6. David Nyhan, "Victim 1: Peace of Mind," *Boston Globe,* April 2, 1995.

7. Richard Goldstein, "We Have Met the Enemy," *Village Voice,* May 9, 1995. A lengthy list of anti-Muslim activities is found in "Rush to Judgment," a 1995 publication of the Council on American-Islamic Relations (CAIR). The *Boston Globe*'s Mike Barnicle believed that because the nation's "borders are open and our spine is nonexistent," foreign terrorists operated so freely in the United States. "U.S. All Heart, but No Spine," *Boston Globe,* April 20, 1995.

8. Webster remark in "Oklahoma Learns 'No Place Is Safe,' " *USA Today,* April 20, 1995; other quotes may be found in "Rush to Judgment," pp. 4-7. On April 20, Ted Koppel reported to his *Nightline* audience that "travelers fitting the general description of 'Middle Eastern,' whose journeys originated in or near Oklahoma City must have had some awkward moments yesterday." He raised the possibility, however, of other motives for the bombing. "There are some indications today that the bombing could have been the vengeful act of American drug dealers" (*Nightline,* April 20, 1995, transcript 3629). Agreeing with Steven Emerson was an editorial in the *Boston Herald,* "Send the Bombers to Hell," which declared, "Car bombs are not the American style in atrocity," and called for President Clinton to "launch a bombing campaign of such ferocity that the guilty country is rendered militarily helpless" (April 20, 1995). The *New York Times*'s A. M. Rosenthal lamented that "whatever we are doing to destroy Mideast terrorism . . . has not been working." See "Only Ending Era of Forgiveness Will Halt Terrorism," *San Gabriel Valley Tribune* (West Covina, Calif.), April 21, 1995. Syndicated columnist Georgie Anne Geyer, assuring her readers that she has "for 30 years covered terrorism in the world—and particularly in the Middle East," suggested that President Clinton might well have to declare an act of war against a "terrorist country." See "The U.S.A. Is the 'No Questions Asked' Country for Terrorists," *Denver Post,* April 21, 1995. Other columnists also called for war against whatever terrorist group was responsible. See George S. Smith, "A Declaration of War," *Northeast Arkansas Times,* April 21, 1995. See also the revealing interchange between Emerson, "Why Islamic Extremists Were the First Suspects," *Washington Times,* April 26, 1995, and the point-by-point refutation by CAIR's national communications director, Ibrahim Hooper, *Washington Times,* May 12, 1995.

9. CAIR, "Rush to Judgment," p. 6.

10. CAIR, "Rush to Judgment," p. 6.

11. CAIR, "Rush to Judgment," appendix.

12. Doyle quoted in "2 Sects, Ethnic Groups Face Media Accusations," *Sun-Sentinel* (Ft. Lauderdale, Fla.), April 20, 1995. See also "Branch Davidians Comment on Oklahoma City Bombing," *All Things Considered,* National Public Radio, June 20, 1995, transcript 1884-7; Dick Reavis, "Waco and the Militarists," *Baltimore Sun,* May 16, 1995. A memorial headstone for those killed in Oklahoma City was erected in 1997 amid memorials to Branch Davidians killed at Waco.

13. MacArthur quoted in "Jumping to Conclusions in Oklahoma City?" *American Journalism Review* 17 (June 1995): 12. A resident of St. Petersburg, Florida, objected to characterizing McVeigh as an "animal," arguing that it was an "insult to all animals. . . . especially offensive to the trained, brave dogs who valiantly entered the dangerous wreckage, helping their human rescuers find and save many lives, only to crawl out—many with injuries and bloodied paws—to be 'thanked' by being compared to the vicious humans who caused this terrible disaster." Letters to the editor, *St. Petersburg Times*, May 6, 1995, p. 17A. George Will, "Society's Paranoiacs Do Not Define Us," *Daily Oklahoman*, April 25, 1995; Lance Morrow, "The Bad Old Days," *Time*, May 8, 1995.

14. "Military Burial Ban OK'd Senate Unanimous, Swift in McVeigh Case," *Denver Post*, June 19, 1997; "McVeigh to Get Military Burial? Vets Outraged," *Tulsa World*, June 18, 1997; text from legislation quoted in *Commercial Appeal* (Memphis), November 22, 1997.

15. "The Soul and Character of America," *U.S. News and World Report*, May 8, 1995, pp. 10-11. Opening statement from Senator Hatch found in "Terrorism in the United States; The Nature and Extent of the Threat and Possible Legislative Responses," Committee on the Judiciary Hearings, United States Senate, 104th Cong., 1st sess., April 27, 1995, p. 2. The *Boston Globe's* Mike Barnicle also contrasted the perpetrators and the rescuers: "Savor the faces and voices of the anonymous heroes this weekend. They represent the wonderful mixed bloodline of America while this McVeigh, with the narrow, spiteful eyes of the bigot, represents only our darkest impulses, allowed to flourish in a land perilously close to suicide by silence." "Flag of Hope in Oklahoma," *Boston Sunday Globe*, April 23, 1995.

16. The term "heartland pathology" is found in the editorial "What Rough Beast?" *Nation*, May 15, 1995, p. 656. "An American Darkness," *New Republic*, May 15, 1995, p. 9. See also the insightful essay by Victoria E. Johnson, "Fertility among the Ruins: The 'Heartland,' Maternity, and the Oklahoma City Bombing," *Continuum: Journal of Media and Cultural Studies* 13, no. 1 (1999). In the *Oklahoma Gazette*, Phil Bacharach observed that Oklahoma was far from a peaceful place. Deaths from firearms were "13 percent higher than the U.S. death rate," and "about 500 Oklahomans each year die from guns." See "Packin' Heat: Oklahomans and Their Guns," October 5, 1995, p. 5. See also "Many Jarred at Finding Suspect Is an American," *Chicago Tribune*, April 23, 1995.

17. Catherine McNicol Stock, *Rural Radicals: From Bacon's Rebellion to the Oklahoma City Bombing* (New York: Penguin, 1997); "Violence No Longer a Stranger in Heartland—If It Ever Was," *Wall Street Journal*, April 21, 1995; Lawrence H. Hart, "Legacies of the Massacre and Battle at the Washita," *Oklahoma Today*, May-June 1999, pp. 59-63; and "Sand Creek and Oklahoma City: Constructing a Common Ground," *Mennonite Life*, December 1997, pp. 33-37.

18. Adam Gopnik, "Violence as Style," *New Yorker*, May 8, 1995, pp. 6-8; "McNair Example May Help Oklahoma," *Montgomery Advertiser*, April 26, 1995; William Pfaff, "Crackpots in an Old American Way," *Baltimore Sun*, May 4, 1995; "Driven by Fear, Right and Left Try Role Reversal," *Plain Dealer* (Cleveland), April 26, 1995; "Michigan Explosion Still Worst School Tragedy," *Detroit News*, April 22, 1999.

19. Tom Clancy, "We Must Not Lose Sight of Who We Are," *Los Angeles Times*, April 21, 1995; Daniel Schorr, "An American Way of Strife," *New Leader,* June 30, 1997, p. 3; Mohammad Bazzi, "The Arab Menace," *Progressive* 59, no. 8 (1995): p. 40; Dennis Byrne, "Oklahoma Fallout: Media Bigotry," *Chicago Sun-Times*, April 23, 1995; "Bomb Damage," *Sacramento Bee*, April 22, 1995. There were numerous sheepish apologies and strained justifications for suspicion of Muslims. See, for example, the show *Reliable Sources*, CNN, April 23, 1995, transcript 165; Richard Roeper, "Media Stumble Badly in Rush to Judgment," *Chicago Sun-Times*, April 24, 1995. There were also forthright defenses of suspicion of Muslims as "informed speculation." See "Tangled Up in Who," *Quill* 83, no. 6 (1995): 24; and Mona Charen, who said that it was "a reasonable deduction, not rank prejudice, that led to the suspicion of Arab terrorists," in "Liberals Too Quick to Place Blame," *St. Louis Post-Dispatch*, April 28, 1995.

20. "We Find the Enemy Within," *News Leader* (Springfield, Mo.), April 23, 1995; Richard B. Woodward, "White Mischief," *Village Voice*, May 2, 1995.

21. Stern's testimony found in U.S. Congress, Committee of the Judiciary, "Nature and Threat of Violent Anti-Government Groups in America," hearing before the Subcommittee on Crime, 104th Cong., 1st sess., November 2, 1995.

22. Nell Irvin Painter, "Hate Speech in Black and White," *Baltimore Sun,* May 8, 1995. Agreeing with Painter was Wilbert Tatum, editor of the *New York Amsterdam News,* who observed that O. J. Simpson engendered more hatred than did McVeigh and Nichols. "McVeigh is regarded with far more indifference by the public, civility by officialdom and restraint by the courts, the police and prosecutors than O. J. ever was . . . even though McVeigh was determined to overthrow our government." Similar comments were made by other African Americans. See "Claude Lewis Looking at America," *New York Amsterdam News*, May 31,1997. Some turned anti-Muslim rhetoric around and wondered if "all Christians will be held responsible, now that we know the Oklahoma City bombers come from a right wing Christian group." Lyn Cockburn, *Toronto Sun*, May 1, 1995.

23. *All Things Considered,* National Public Radio, March 31, 1997, transcript 97033114-212.

24. Carl Smith, "The Day After," *Chicago Tribune*, April 25, 1995; Katha Pollitt, "Subject to Debate, Bombing in Oklahoma City," *Nation,* June 5, 1995, p. 784.

25. Joyce Carol Oates, "American Gothic," *New Yorker*, May 8, 1995, p. 36; Michael Kazin, "McVeigh: An All-American Monster," *Los Angeles Times*, June 8, 1997. See also Robert D. McFadden, "Terror In Oklahoma: John Doe No. 1—A Special Report," *New York Times*, May 4, 1995.

26. See James William Gibson, *Warrior Dreams: Paramilitary Culture in Post-Vietnam America* (New York: Hill and Wang, 1994), and his discussion of the Oklahoma City bombing in "Is the Apocalypse Coming? Paramilitary Culture after the Cold War," in Charles B. Strozier and Michael Flynn, eds., *The Year 2000: Essays on the End* (New York: New York University Press, 1997), pp. 181-189. Quote on p. 181. Echoing Gibson's fears, Christopher Hitchens wrote in the *Nation* of the "residue of the parastate 'Special Forces' culture—just another installment of the endless revenge exacted on our society for its failed attempt to destroy the Vietnamese. In

a push-comes-to-shove period, the Gritzes and Metzgers and McVeighs would enlist in an authoritarian statist militia as an American Freikorps, fighting for race and nation." "Minority Report," May 22, 1995, p. 711.

27. The specter of "many thousands of armed and embittered citizens who are in a state of proto-rebellion" led England's *Guardian* to ask bluntly whether American culture was "just routinely sick in its obsessive pursuit of self-destruction, or is it now certifiably insane?" And the *Christian Science Monitor* informed its readers that the bombing had "revealed to Americans that the terrorist threat from within is just as dangerous as the threat from without." See "America's Angry White Males," *World Press Review*, July 1995, p. 28; "Oklahoma bombing exposes rise of antigovernment groups," *Christian Science Monitor*, April 24, 1995.

28. See three editorials in the *Omaha World Herald*, April 25, 26, 29, 1995; Julia Reed, "Behind the Bombing," *Vogue*, July 1995, p. 30.

29. "Militia Reference to Revolution 'an Insult,'" *Middlesex News*, April 23, 1995; Robert Friedman, "The Poison Tongue of 'Patriots,'" *St. Petersburg Times*, May 7, 1995; Thomas H. Kiske, "We Still Need Our Patriots," *Houston Chronicle*, April 30, 1995; David Greenberg, "Patriot Games," *New Republic*, July 17-24, 1995.

30. Trochmann quoted in "Militia Forum," *Nation*, July 10, 1995, p. 42; ABC News, *Nightline*, April 25, 1995, transcript 3632.

31. *Middlesex News*, April 23, 1995. Trochmann's links with neo-Nazi and Christian Identity groups are discussed in Morris Dees, *Gathering Storm: America's Militia Threat* (New York: HarperCollins, 1996); and Kenneth S. Stern, *A Force Upon the Plain: The American Militia Movement and the Politics of Hate* (New York: Simon & Schuster, 1996). Limbaugh quoted in Micah Sifry, "Anti-ditto," *Nation*, May 22, 1995, p. 708.

32. On the militia's use of Holocaust rhetoric, see Leslie Camhi, "Imaginary Jews: America Develops a Masada Complex," *Village Voice*, July 11, 1995.

33. Lou Prato, "Militias: Rushing to Judgment," *The World and I*, September 1995, p. 80; Paul Gastris, "Patriot Games: Legal Philosophy of Militia Movements," *Washington Monthly* 27, no. 6 (June 1995): 23; Barbara Dority, "Is the Extremist Right Entirely Wrong?" *Humanist*, November-December 1995, p. 13. See also, Alan W. Bock, "Weekend Warriors: Is the Militia Movement a Threat?" *National Review*, May 29, 1995; Phil Bacharach, "Loose Cannons: A Cross-Section of the Militia Movement," *Oklahoma Gazette*, May 9, 1996. There was marked interest in the militias among academics. See "Home-Grown Extremism: Scholars Are Not Surprised at What the Oklahoma City Bombing Has Revealed," *Chronicle of Higher Education*, May 12, 1995.

34. "Terror Jolts the Heartland, Leaving us Angry, Helpless," *News-Leader* (Springfield, Mo.), April 20, 1995. See also "Eight seconds to a New Beginning," *U.S. News and World Report*, June 5, 1995; Steve Otto, "Terrible Sight Spawns Feeling of Helplessness," *Tampa Tribune*, April 20, 1995; William Raspberry, "Randomness of Bombing Adds to Pain," *Tampa Tribune*, April 21, 1995.

35. David Broder, "Real-life Trouble Triggers Political Change," *Atlanta Journal and Constitution*, April 27, 1995; "After the Bombing," *Christian Science Monitor*, April 25, 1995; "What Rough Beast?" *Nation*, May 15, 1995, p. 655.

36. Walter Truett Anderson, "As World Is Coming Together, It Is Spinning Apart," *Star-Tribune* (Minneapolis), April 24, 1995; Jim Klobuchar, "Our Advances in Technology Make Targets of Us All," *Star-Tribune* (Minneapolis), April 20, 1995.

37. "Bombing May Alter Buying Habits," *Advertising Age*, May 1, 1995, p. 8; "Terrorism Challenges U.S. Political Culture," *Inside Politics*, CNN, July 29, 1996. *Harper's* editor, Lewis Lapham, thought public space essential for the practice of democracy, which "was made for open country and public spaces in which people spoke to each other face to face." Lewis H. Lapham, "Seen but Not Heard: The Message of the Oklahoma Bombing," *Harper's*, July 1995, n.p. For a gloomy description of an urban landscape profoundly altered by violence and fear of violence, see Mike Davis, *Ecology of Fear: Los Angeles and the Imagination of Disaster* (New York: Vintage, 1998).

38. "Before the Bomb Drops," *Management Review*, August 1995; "Life in Iowa May Forever Be Altered, Experts Say," *Des Moines Register*, April 21, 1995; "Bomb Forces Question: How Safe Are We?" *USA Today*, April 21, 1995.

39. Benjamin Forgey, "Does Safe Have to Mean Ugly? The Capital Balances Security with Design in the Face of Terrorism," *Washington Post*, September 5, 1998; "Regrettable Buffer of Fear," *Omaha World Herald*, May 16, 1995.

40. For specifics, see *World News Tonight with Peter Jennings*, April 19, 1999, transcript 99041906-j04. Also see Eve E. Hinman, "Lessons from Ground Zero," *Security Management*, October 1995, pp. 26-35; "Oklahoma Blast Forces Unsettling Design Questions," *ENR News*, May 1, 1995, pp. 10-16; "Weighing Future Safety of Federal Buildings," *ENR News*, May 8, 1995, pp. 8-10; Robert W. Marans, "Must We Work In Fortresses?" *Plain Dealer* (Cleveland), May 6, 1995; Eve E. Hinman and David J. Hammond, *Lessons from the Oklahoma City Bombing: Defensive Design Techniques* (New York: American Society of Civil Engineers, 1997); Allison Lucas, "When Disaster Strikes," *Sales and Marketing Management*, September 1995, p. 112; Tom Harpole, "What Would Be the Consequences If the Oklahoma City Bomb Went Off in New York, Houston, Minneapolis, or Los Angeles?" *Glass Digest*, February 15, 1998. The issue of safety glass arose in questions about the wisdom of President Clinton's 1996 directive for all federal facilities to require use of shatter-resistant film on windows. Some experts thought that in some cases, this could increase danger because such windows could break in larger and more deadly pieces in an explosion, and they could also trap gases in a building. See Douglas N. Mitten and Janet Gallant, "Are New Federal Security Standards Misguided?" *Security Management*, March 1996. On public architecture, see "Architects and Oklahoma City," *New Yorker*, May 29, 1995, pp. 32-33.

41. CBS *60 Minutes* interview of April 28, 1995, in *Weekly Compilation of Presidential Documents*, May 1, 1995, p. 690.

42. Anthony Lewis, "Abroad at Home: Faith in Reason," *New York Times*, April 21, 1995; Carl T. Rowan, "Add Freedom to Casualty List in Oklahoma City," *Chicago Sun-Times*, April 23, 1995.

43. "After the Heartbreak," *U.S. News and World Report*, May 8, 1995, p. 28. There were public discussions about how much freedom Americans were willing to give up within days after the bombing. See, for example, ABC News, *Nightline*, April 26,

1995, transcript 3633. A good history of the progress of the legislation is "Terrorism Bill Likely to Include Some Items Stripped by House," *Congressional Quarterly*, April 13, 1996, pp. 988-989. See also Harvey A. Silverglate, "Is It Paranoia or Fear?" *National Law Journal*, May 22, 1995, pp. A21, A23; and "Electronic Vigilantes Win Friends after Oklahoma Bombing," *New Scientist*, May 6, 1995, pp. 6-7. Before debate even began on antiterrorism legislation, Congress authorized $100 million to pay for hiring "25 intelligence analysts for a new FBI Counter terrorism center; 190 FBI surveillance specialists and 143 support personnel; 31 engineers and mathematicians to strengthen the FBI's expertise in intercepting digital communications; explosives experts to staff four ATF national response teams; and additional ATF intelligence analysts and explosives 'inspectors.'" See "Anti-Terror Efforts Meet with Wariness on Hill," *Washington Post*, May 30, 1995.

44. Clinton's remarks reported on CNN, April 24, 1996, transcript 772-2.

45. Susan Rosenfeld, a former official historian for the FBI, criticized the dominant view that "all governmental anti-subversive and antiterrorist activities have been both unwarranted and illegal. Neither assumption is totally correct. . . . Lost among the litany of compromised civil liberties are the actual threats to national security and the safety of Americans that Counter terrorism policies have addressed." Susan Rosenfeld, "The Delicate Balance Required to Cope with Terrorist Threats While Protecting Civil Liberties," *Chronicle of Higher Education*, July 7, 1997, p. B4. See also "Oklahoma City Bombing Three Years Ago Has Transformed the Federal Effort against Domestic Terrorism," *Kansas City Star*, April 18, 1998, for evidence of post-Oklahoma City bombing success in thwarting planned acts to "assassinate judges, poison water supplies, blow up a gas refinery and even bomb the FBI's national fingerprint identification center."

46. Eugene Methvin, "Anti-terrorism: How Far?" *National Review*, July 10, 1995, p. 32; Conor Cruise O'Brien, "Liberalism and Terror," *National Review*, April 22, 1996, p. 32.

47. Cynthia Tucker, "Terrorism Tests Our Principles," *San Francisco Chronicle*, April 21, 1995; "Oklahoma City Bombing," *Atlanta Journal Constitution*, April 21, 1995; "In the Name of Liberty," *Economist*, April 29, 1995.

48. Thomas L. Friedman, "Escaping Comparisons with Beirut," *Daily Oklahoman*, May 8, 1995.

49. "Don't Legislate in Haste," *New York Times*, April 25, 1995; David Broder, "Bombing Must Not Usher in Big Brother," *Houston Chronicle*, May 3, 1995. For specific critiques of various portions of antiterrorism legislation, see "The Schumer-Clinton Assault on the Constitution," *Village Voice*, May 9, 1995; "The Long Arm of the Law: Clinton's Anti-Terrorism Act Beefs Up Big Brother," *Village Voice*, May 21, 1996; and "Wrong Way to Recall the Bombing," *New York Times*, April 18, 1996.

50. "Bomb Forces Questions: How Safe Are We?" *USA Today*, April 4, 1996. A letter to the *San Francisco Chronicle* on April 25, 1995, argued that the planned antiterrorism bill "bears a striking resemblance to the dictatorial powers given Chancellor Adolf Hitler in the Enabling Acts, passed in July 1933."

51. "Radical Dangers: Political Reactions to the Bombing in Oklahoma City," *Nation*, June 5, 1995, p. 777; Barbara Dority, "Terrorism and Tyranny," *Humanist*, July 1995, pp. 39-40.

52. Richard J. Barnet, "The Terrorism Trap; Anti-Terrorism and the Reality of Civil Rights," *Nation,* December 2, 1996, p. 18. The *Nation's* David Cole agreed with Barnet's caution regarding the unprecedented nature of the terrorist threat, observing that the State Department's 1994 report on global terrorism indicated that terrorism "reached the lowest annual total in twenty-three years." "Terrorizing the Constitution: The Government's Anti-Terror Proposal Attacks Everyone's Fundamental Rights," *Nation,* March 25, 1996, p. 11.

53. Angelo Codevilla, "Anti-Terrorism or War?" *National Review,* July 10, 1995, pp. 35ff.; *Daily Oklahoman,* May 7, 1995. Agreeing with the *Daily Oklahoman* was Tom Bethell, Washington correspondent for the *American Spectator,* who observed that "repeatedly, conservatives have denounced the Oklahoma City bombing as a shocking and immoral act. What I have not seen is any acknowledgment by liberals that maybe the federal government has accumulated too much power, and needs to back off." Tom Bethell, "Turnabout Is Fair Play," *American Spectator,* July 1995, p. 17.

54. Letter to the editor, *Daily Oklahoman,* May 4, 1995. Liddy quoted in David Corn, "Playing with Fire," *Nation,* May 15, 1995, p. 657. The *Washington Post's* Richard Cohen observed that until pressure mounted on them to rescind his invitation, the Republican party was going to honor Liddy at a fund-raiser in 1995. See Richard Cohen, "The GOP and the Radical Fringe," *Sacramento Bee,* May 8, 1995.

55. The text of the president's speech on *CNN News,* April 23, 1995, transcript 1007-7.

56. After the bombing, the Federal Communications Commission began an investigation of shortwave radio programs that were thought to condone violence, and some stations dropped Liddy's program. The executive director of the National Sheriffs' Association began a letter-writing campaign designed to pressure Liddy to "tone down his anti-law enforcement rhetoric." See "Right-Wing Shortwave Comes under FCC Scrutiny," and "Oklahoma City Backlash Hits Airwaves; Talk Show Hosts Dispute Clinton's Criticism," *Broadcasting and Cable,* May 1, 1995, p. 6; "Removing Hate Talk From the Air Not a Curb on Free Speech Rights," *Omaha World Herald,* May 3, 1995; "Holding Fire," *Legal Times,* May 8, 1995.

57. Jonathan Alter, "Toxic Speech," *Newsweek,* May 8, 1995.

58. "Going too far; Fomenting hatred isn't simple dissent," *Star Tribune,* April 30, 1995; the *New York Times* editorial quoted in Bill Maxwell, "Silence Makes Liberals, intellectuals Guilty of Complicity," *St. Petersburg Times,* May 4, 1995.

59. Michael Lind, "Understanding Oklahoma," *Washington Post,* April 30, 1995; Frank Rich, "New World Terror," *New York Times,* April 27, 1995; Kevin Phillips, "The Fringe Factor," *Baltimore Sun,* May 11, 1995. An editorial in the United Kingdom's *Economist* observed that whereas in Europe, the far right have their own parties, "not so in the Republican Party, where the fringe is tolerated and wrapped into the grand coalition." "The Politics of Blame," *Economist,* April 29, 1995. Somewhat less elegantly, Richard Cohen argued that "the conspiracy that needs targeting is not the tenuous connections between hard-right politicians, moon-baying preachers and a collection of wackos-in-the-woods, but the GOP's amoral willingness to buss the buttocks of any jerk with a radio audience." Richard Cohen, "The GOP and the Radical Fringe," *Sacramento Bee,* May 8, 1995.

60. Adam Gopnik, "Violence as Style," *New Yorker*, May 8, 1995, p. 8.
61. Lorrie Goldstein, "Left, and Right, Should Be Ashamed," *Toronto Sun*, May 2, 1995; Jonathan Alter, "Toxic Speech"; "The Age of Rage," *Village Voice*, May 16, 1995; Robert Wright, senior editor of the *New Republic*, offered guidelines for responsible speech: "Does the power of your words depend on their appeal to the worst in human nature? Is what you're saying untrue? Does the nature of your particular audience make it plausible that your words will incite dangerous people?" "Newt Knows," *Pittsburgh Post-Gazette*, May 1, 1995. Several people argued that talk radio focused on the "pulse of the American public" and served as a safety valve for the "pent-up anger that seems to afflict so many Americans these days." Ellen Ratner, "After Oklahoma City: Talk Radio Responds," *Los Angeles Times*, April 27, 1995; "How Dangerous Are Our Airwaves?" *Atlanta Journal and Constitution*, May 5, 1995.
62. "Exploiting Oklahoma," *National Review*, May 29, 1995, pp. 15-16; William F. Buckley, Jr., "What Does Clinton Have in Mind?" *National Review*, May 29, 1995, p. 70. Charles W. Colson, "Stop Smearing the Religious Right," *Washington Post*, May 9, 1995; "Don't Link Delusional Nuts with Conservative Principles," *Seattle Times*, April 25, 1995. In his editorial Buckley sanitized G. Gordon Liddy's words cited earlier in the chapter into the following: "What he said—that if any official came to his house to requisition his pistol, he'd better shoot straight—was more rodomontade than a call to arms or hatred."
63. "Blame the Bombers—Only," *Newsweek*, May 8, 1995, p. 39. Others joined Limbaugh in arguing that deflecting blame to radio personalities revealed an "insidious national habit," one that unwittingly transformed perpetrators into victims. Writing in the *Montreal Gazette*, William Watson imagined McVeigh's lawyer arguing that his client was a "victim of a climate of hostility and hatred. This good but simple young man, who served his country honorably in the Gulf War, was driven to this most horrible act by venom-spewing, shock-radio hosts, by the excesses of the National Rifle "Association and by the mean-spirited rhetoric of 'the government-is-the-enemy, right-wing politicians!'" William Watson, "Right Wing Unfairly Blamed in Oklahoma Bombing," *Gazette* (Montreal), May 1, 1995. For its part, the National Rifle Association distanced itself from the bombing. See Tanya K. Metaksa, "Oklahoma City," *American Rifleman*, June 1995, p. 26; and in the same issue, Neal Knox, "Playing Politics with the Bombing," p. 14.
64. "For Starters, They're Americans," *Detroit News*, May 3, 1995; Jacob Weisberg and Jeffrey Goldberg, "Playing with fire," *New York*, May 8, 1995, pp. 30-35. Other editorials criticizing the President's attack as "tactical" include Fred Barnes, "Tactics, Tactics," *New Republic*, May 15, 1995, and John Ellis, "Clinton's Road to reelection Began in Oklahoma City," *Boston Globe*, November 2, 1996. Weisberg and Goldberg continue their criticism of the right's penchant for playing the "blame game" by noting recent examples: "Dan Quayle's criticism of Murphy Brown for contributing to the illegitimacy boom, Rush Limbaugh's blaming AIDs and homelessness on the 1960s, and the *Wall Street Journal*'s editorial page attacking 'magazines published by thirtysomething women in New York' for leading midwestern girls to become prostitutes on Eighth Avenue (in an editorial that prepos-

terously attributed blame for the 1993 slaying of abortion doctor David Gunn to the 1968 Democratic convention). Live by the sword, die by it, one is tempted to say...so to speak."

65. Robert S. McElvaine, "Perspectives on the Media," *Los Angeles Times,* April 28, 1995. See also William Raspberry, "Wretched Excess: Virulent rhetoric of Right and Left Poisons Us All," *Pittsburgh Post-Gazette,* May 4, 1995. Writing in the *Washington Post,* Jim Hoagland argued that a society in which electronic media has "joined or supplanted governing authorities and political leaders as authenticators of existence and recognition," must pay attention to the ways in which "stimulus and payoff ride the airwaves today in ways we still do not fully understand." "Demonizing Talk," *Washington Post,* April 30, 1995.

66. Jean Bethke Elshtain, "Civil Rites," *New Republic,* February 24, 1997, p. 23. The *Washington Post* also criticized the politics of blame, arguing that "There has been practically no point in the turbulent national life of this country during the past three decades in which any side in the argument—including this moment's accusers—could not itself have been accused, by the loose rules of this game, of having either incited someone to a heinous act or provided the philosophical justification for his committing it." "Who Did It?" *Washington Post,* April 23, 1995.

67. Otis H. Stephens, Jr., John M. Scheb II, *American Constitutional Law,* 2d. ed. (Belmont, Calif.: West/Wadsworth, 1999), p. 441.

68. Bork appears on *The Newshour with Jim Lehrer,* December 20, 1995, transcript 5423; Taylor's comments found in "After the Blast; Online Exchange," *Legal Times,* May 1, 1995.

69. Stuart Taylor, Jr., "On Lethal Speech and Attacking Miranda," *National Journal,* February 20, 1999, p. 450.

70. Stuart Taylor, Jr. "A Constitutional Suicide Pact?" *Legal Times,* August 5, 1996, p. 23. Taylor observes that the Supreme Court "already denies protection to other narrowly defined categories of speech that do great harm while adding little or nothing to the dissemination of truth. Libel and obscenity laws, for example, have not produced nightmares of censorship. And the evils against which they are aimed are surely no more grave than murder."

71. Pierce describes the fictitious attack: "The plate glass windows in the store beside us and dozens of others that we could see along the street were blown to splinters. A glittering and deadly rain of glass shards continued to fall into the street from the upper stories of nearby buildings for a few seconds, as a jet-black column of smoke shot straight up into the sky ahead of us.

All day yesterday and most of today we watched the TV coverage of the rescue crews bringing the dead and injured out of the building. It is a heavy burden of responsibility for us to bear, since most of the victims of our bomb were only pawns who were no more committed to the sick philosophy or the racially destructive goals of the System than we are.

But there is no way we can destroy the System without hurting many thousands of innocent people—no way. It is a cancer too deeply rooted in our flesh. And if we don't destroy the System before it destroys us—if we don't cut this cancer out of our living flesh—our whole race will die." Quoted in Phil Bacharach, "Loose

Cannons: A Cross-Section of the Militia Movement," *Oklahoma Gazette*, May 9, 1996, p. 6.

72. See, for example, the opening statement of Hartzler at McVeigh's trial. Stephen Jones, McVeigh's attorney, objected to focusing on *The Turner Diaries*, saying, "it is no more a blueprint, much less a reason, to blow up a federal building than … the "Day of the Jackal" is a blueprint to assassinate the president of France, or William Faulkner's novel *Sanctuary* is a graphic description of how men can rape women by instrumentation, or that *Lady Chatterly's Lover* can teach you how to make love." Both available at the Memorial Foundation's archive, "McVeigh Trial 4/24/97-5/13/97, transcripts Denver," or online at http://www.kwtv.com/news/ mcveigh/042497a.htm ; Robert Jay Lifton, *Destroying the World to Save It: Aum Shinrikyo, Apocalyptic Violence, and The New Global Terrorism* (New York: Metropolitan, 1999), chap 14, "American Apocalypse." For another interpretation on the religious dimension of the novel, see Brad Whitsel, "*The Turner Diaries* and Cosmotheism: William Pierce's Theology of Revolution," *Nova Religio* 1, no. 2 (1998), 183-197. See also Phil Bacharach, "Turner Diaries' Prepared for New Release by New York Publisher," *Oklahoma Gazette*, May 23, 1996, p. 17.

73. Michele L. Landis and Jane E. Larson, "The Killing Words; The First Amendment Shouldn't Shield the Author of the Oklahoma City Bombing," *Legal Times*, August 21, 1995, p. 23. In fact, some people scarred by violence were persuaded that "money often achieves what reason and moral force cannot," and turned to civil litigation against creators of violent films, computer games, and Web sites. Reese Cleghorn, dean of the college of journalism at the University of Maryland, opposed censoring violent speech but observed that the Southern Poverty Law Center had "flogged" the Ku Klux Klan "into oblivion with damage suits," and libel laws could make vulnerable radio stations that carry inflammatory talk show hosts. "Driving Up the Cost of Violence," *Toronto Star*, June 6, 1999; Reese Cleghorn, "Words and Violence: Drawing The Lines," *American Journalism Review*, June 1995, p. 4. The Southern Poverty Law Center also asked bookstore chains to "make an informed decision" about whether or not to sell the book. See Doreen Carvajal, "Group Tries to Halt Selling of Racist Novel," *New York Times*, April 20, 1996, p. 8.

CHAPTER 2

1. Charles H. Van Rysselberge, "The Oklahoma City Chamber of Commerce Response to April 19, 1995 Bombing of the Downtown Oklahoma City Federal Building."

2. Lawrence Langer tirelessly reminds his readers of the many ways in which the Holocaust is transformed into various narratives of evasion. See, for instance, *Admitting the Holocaust; Collected Essays* (New Haven: Yale University Press, 1995); and *Preempting the Holocaust* (New Haven: Yale University Press, 1998). I am not suggesting any kind of simplistic comparison between the Holocaust and the bombing in Oklahoma City. I do, however, think that modes of recollection in Oklahoma City reveal a similar search for comforting stories.

3. I have searched in vain for the source of Hannah Arendt's magnificent words, but I cannot find it. For another interpretation of the way different narratives were used, see James R. Allen, M.D., "After the Bombing: Public Scenarios and the Construction of Meaning," *Journal: Oklahoma State Medical Association*, April 1999, pp. 187-192. Pam Whicher, personal communication, September 13, 2000.

4. The first quotation is from a videotape interview with Dr. Blackburn done for the National Building Museum's exhibition *We Will Be Back: Oklahoma City Rebuilds*. Tape 1, *Boom or Bust*. The second quotation is from an interview with Blackburn, March 18, 1998.

5. Blackburn, interview, March 18, 1998. On events that have contributed to Oklahoma's identity, see Howard F. Stein and Robert F. Hill, eds., *The Culture of Oklahoma* (Norman: University of Oklahoma Press, 1993). See also Marsha L. Weisiger, "The Reception of the Grapes of Wrath in Oklahoma," *Chronicles of Oklahoma*, Winter 1992-1993, pp. 394-415. On the plight of Native Americans in Oklahoma, see Angie Debo, *And Still the Waters Run: The Betrayal of the Five Civilized Tribes* (Princeton: Princeton University Press, 1940). On the transformation of the term "Okie" after the bombing, see Taylor Holliday, "Sooner, Not Later, Okies Rebound Again," *Wall Street Journal*, January 4, 1996.

6. "Terror in Oklahoma," *New York Times*, May 7, 1995.

7. Carolyn D. Wall, ed., *Braced against the Wind* (Tulsa, Okla.: Council Oaks Books, 1995), p. 3. The poem is also reprinted in a special memorial issue of *Oklahoma Today*, "9:02 A.M. April 19, 1995. The Historical Record of the Oklahoma City Bombing," Winter 1996, p. 8. I thank Carol Hamilton for permission to use her poem.

8. Brokaw's tribute in Clive Irving, ed., *In Their Name* (New York: Random House, 1995), pp. 104-105. A quite similar progressive narrative emerged after the Chicago fire. Historian Carl Smith observed, for example, "fire literature repeatedly maintained that the main effect of the flames was to burn away vain inessentials to reveal the sound and solid integrity of the people, not so much reforming Chicago but . . . bringing the city's citizens back to their best selves." Carl Smith, *Urban Disorder and the Shape of Belief: The Great Chicago Fire, the Haymarket Bomb, and the Model Town of Pullman* (Chicago: University of Chicago Press, 1995), p. 39.

9. "Contribution to Oral History, Don H. Alexander, Senior Minister, First Christian Church of Oklahoma City," oral history collection, archives.

10. There are numerous magazine and newspaper articles about Rebecca Anderson. See, for example, " 'She Had a Gift to Give,'" *Journal of Practical Nursing*, June 1995, pp. 10-13, which reprinted a widely circulated newspaper article; "What We Ought to Remember about the Oklahoma Bombing Is the Heroism, Not the Terrorism," *Money*, June 1995, p. 13; "Notes from Interview with Debra Bailey and Bob Clift, 2/29/96," oral history collection, archive. The rescue and recovery operation was massive. Seventy-five fire departments, from as far away as Phoenix, Arizona, and San Diego, California, participated, and several firemen from other states came on their own as volunteers. The Oklahoma Emergency Medical Services Authority (EMSA) and American Medical Response Medics (AMR) were

joined by twenty-five EMS teams from Oklahoma, Texas, Colorado, Connecticut, and a Disaster Medical Assistance Team (DMAT) from Tulsa, Oklahoma. In addition, eleven urban search and rescue teams (USAR) from Virginia, California, Florida, Maryland, New York, Arizona, and Washington participated in rescue and recovery operations. This was all in addition to the many city and state agencies involved. The Department of Defense—offering the resources at Fort, Sill and Tinker Air Force Base—transported the USAR teams, gave assistance to the medical examiner's office, and provided notification teams for the military victims. This listing does not even begin to touch on the massive resources involved in crime investigation. The city's *Final Report* is an excellent resource for anyone wanting to appreciate the massive response to the bombing. See also a memo in the archives from Jane Thomas to Sydney Dobson, October 30, 1997, for a listing that gathers information from the *Final Report* and supplements it with information from some other sources.

11. Dr. Sullivan's story from the oral history collection, archive. Other quoted material is drawn from a variety of stories in *Caliber*, Spring 1996. This is an informative publication of the Junior League of Oklahoma City, reporting on various assistance efforts. Donations of time, money, and professional services of every conceivable kind were offered after the bombing. Professional journals proudly informed readers of their deeds. For example, a Minnesota company donated free hearing aids for those "with hearing loss resulting from the explosion." See "Micro-Tech Aids Victims of Oklahoma City Bombing," *Hearing Instruments*, August 1995, p. 3.

12. Many people affectionately remember how several artists who had come for the Arts Festival turned their talents to creating tape mural projects in the Myriad Convention Center. These artists went to several schools, creating murals based on themes of renewal and healing. Then they went to Oklahoma City Children's Hospital and then created the Hope mural for the rescuers. "Our offering would take the form of a living drawing, growing steadily amidst the constant toiling of the rescuers. A lot of talk centered on the angelic figures, flight and freedom, ascension of spirit, collaboration, heavenward flight, human/angel distinctions." Unpublished essay, "Hope in Oklahoma City," signed by the artists Michael Townsend, Erica Duthie, and Struan Ashby. Copy in author's files. See also "Artists' Angels Watch Over Workers," *Daily Oklahoman*, May 1, 1995.

13. City of Oklahoma City, *Final Report*, p. 66.

14. *Oklahoma Today*, p. 112.

15. *Daily Oklahoman*, May 12, 1995. Shortly after the bombing, the *Daily Oklahoman* began a column entitled "Acts of Kindness." See also Bob Herbert, "The Terrorists Failed," *New York Times*, April 22, 1995.

16. Keating quoted in "Rebuilding Blocks," *Washington Post*, May 15, 1995.

17. Norick quoted in "Bombing Puts a City Lacking Image on Hold"; DeRocker quoted in "Rebuilding Blocks." See also "Oklahoma Tends to Image," *Advertising Age*, May 1, 1995, p. 8. An Oklahoma real estate game modeled after the popular game Monopoly avoids all reference to the bombing. It is presented as a happy "game." See " 'Oklahoma City in a Box' captures city landmarks, icons in board

game," *Oklahoma Gazette*, October 27, 1999. The bombing also brought Governor Keating into the national spotlight. It is fascinating to listen to Oklahomans evaluate whether his national travels reflected a desire to spread the word about the virtues of the state and the good business opportunities awaiting, or whether it reflected inappropriate opportunism. See, for example, "In Wake of Disaster, Opportunity," *New York Times*, November 8, 1995; "Motive for Mourning Is Put to Political Test," *Washington Post*, November 26, 1995. There is still anger among some family members that the governor did not invite any of them to accompany him on a Thank You America tour of several cities.

18. I thank Charles H. Van Rysselberge for a copy of the chamber's brochure. Stoll quoted in "Terror in Oklahoma: Rebuilding; Wounded City Focuses on Redeveloping Its Core," *New York Times*, May 7, 1995.

19. See, for example, Ronaleen R. Roha, "Business among the Ruins," *Kiplinger's Personal Finance Magazine*, September 1995, pp. 154-155; "Businesses Gather to Resolve to Rebuild," *Boston Globe*, April 27, 1995; "Fiscal Fallout," *Dallas Morning News*, June 8, 1995; Phil Bacharach, "An Opportunity," *Oklahoma Gazette*, June 8, 1995.

20. See "Oklahoma City Memorial: An International Design Competition," p. 17; See "Murrah Federal Building Memorial Task Force: Oklahoma City Memorial Fifth Street Proposed Plan." See also "Memorial Foundation Works with Downtown Businesses to Create Neighborhood Network," *Daily Oklahoman*, November 18, 1996.

21. In an insightful essay, Mark Alden Branch observes that Oklahoma City's low population density make it unlikely that a "traditional dense urban character can ever be created within its 604-square miles. Instead, learning from theme parks, atmospheric ballparks, festival marketplaces, and other tourist lures, the new plan arranges attractions to create a pedestrian environment of a different kind—one based on special events rather than on daily routines." "After the Blast, Oklahoma City Builds," *P/A*, July 1995, pp. 45-46.

22. See Quraeshi's letter to Mayor Norick, April 28, 1995, mayor's files, archives; quote in "Vision for Renewal: A Design Workshop for Oklahoma City," p. 15. I thank Garner Stoll for sending me a copy of this document. As in the memorial process, the public was invited to participate, and the mayor's office received ideas "scrawled on paper napkins," while others were "intricately detailed." They included "the clumsy drawings of a child to interpretations of professional architects. They hold the key to redevelopment of a bomb-damaged city" (p. 13). In addition to NEA, the design workshop was sponsored by several Oklahoma City groups: the Arts Council and Second Century/Oklahoma City Urban Renewal, and of course, the city government itself. GSA, the U.S. Department of Housing and Urban Development, and the U.S. Department of Transportation also supported the project. Often proposals for urban revitalization—from the immediate needs of those whose business were damaged or destroyed to long-term plans for the city—were framed as a part of the response to the bombing. Recommendations from the Urban Land Institute, for example, which sent an advisory panel to Oklahoma City in early December 1995, declared in its report that the city could

"draw inspiration from its recent tragedy" by relocating federal offices to vacant downtown office space instead of considering construction of a federal "campus" north of the Murrah site. Scheduled for completion in 2003, the campus will house some of the agencies previously located in the Murrah Building. The city's "second opportunity arising from the bombing" lay in encouraging and assisting business owners to rebuild in the downtown area. See "Downtown Oklahoma City: An Evaluation of Development Potential and Real Estate Strategies for Rebuilding," An Advisory Services Panel Report (Washington, D.C.: ULI-The Urban Land Institute, 1996), pp. 47-48. For other examples of urban renewal proposals, see "A Proposed Mixed-Use Development for the Gianos Property," Stastny Brun Architects, 1997; "Downtown Oklahoma City Action Plan," RTKL Associates, Inc., and Keyser Marston Associates, Inc., March 24, 1997. These are in uncatalogued materials, archives.

23. Kenny Walker, interview, April 30, 1999. The exhibit's cocurator recalled a "huge opening" for the exhibition—approximately seven hundred people. Carolyn Goldstein telephone interview, February 4, 1999.

24. Sharon Blume, telephone interview, January 28, 1999. I thank Michael R. Harrison, associate curator at the National Building Museum, for sending me copies of the exhibition text, video presentations, and press clippings. For reviews of the exhibition see Benjamin Forgey, "Amid the Rubble, True Grit," *Washington Post*, November 18, 1995; "Exhibit on Oklahoma City Tells Tale of Survival," *Dallas Morning News*, March 22, 1996.

25. My thanks to Stephen G. Sisco of Oklahoma City for sending me a copy of his poem, "April 19, 1995, 9:02 A.M."

26. John Rusco, interview, June 9, 1999. All subsequent quotes from Dr. Rusco are taken from this interview.

27. Newton, interview, June 8, 1999. The activities of Interfaith Disaster Recovery can be followed in their newsletter, which first appeared in December 1995, with, for example, a description of a retreat for "seniors impacted by bombing." Dr. Jihad Ahmad, an Oklahoma City physician, and a member of Iqraa Amerika, an American Muslim group that emerged out of the Nation of Islam and now led by Warith Muhammad, son of Elijah Muhammad, was an active member of Interfaith. He offered yet another way to read the event religiously, inviting people "to reflect on the fact that in the Qur'an, God is merciful, and we have to consider the transcendent good that could come out of this. The world will, in the end, reflect the mercy of the creator." He also spoke of McVeigh as a product of "the well of hatred" in American culture, and he worried about "a lot of little McVeigh's brewing out there." Ahmad interview, June 6, 1999. See also Ahmad's sermon, "Who Is the Owner of the Heartland of America?" in Marsha Brock Bishop and David P. Polk, eds., *And the Angels Wept: From the Pulpits of Oklahoma City after the Bombing* (St. Louis, Mo.: Chalice, 1995), pp. 111-116.

28. David Packman interview, February 23, 1999. All subsequent quotes from Rabbi Packman are from this interview. Oklahoma City has 644 Protestant churches, 24 Catholic churches, 4 synagogues, and 1 mosque. The city is 75 perecnt white and 16 percent black, with fairly small Latino and Asian communities.

29. Harold Kushner, telephone interview, March 29, 1999.

30. "Blast Adds to Meaning of Holocaust Remembrance," *Daily Oklahoman*, April 29, 1995; "President Urges Stand Against Evil," *Daily Oklahoman*, May 1, 1995.

31. Phil Bacharach, "Squeezed by the Right: How Oklahoma Became a Sanctuary of Cultural Conservatism," *Oklahoma Gazette*, April 28, 1999, p. 18. For comment on some of the material resources contributed by religious communities, see "Groups Aid Blast Victims," *Christianity Today*, June 19, 1995, p. 45.

32. One book that addressed various theological questions directly is Al Truesdale, *If God Is God, Then Why? Letters from Oklahoma City* (Kansas City: Beacon Hill, 1997).

33. Alexander's sermon, "Words, Words, Words: An Enduring Gift," in *And the Angels Wept*, pp. 121-127. Quoted material from pp. 121, 124. Sometimes people used the word "miracle" in both ways, especially in talking about "miraculous" recovery of severely wounded children. See, for example, several articles about Brandon and Rebecca Denny, "Bomb Victim, 3, Home Again," *Daily Oklahoman*, July 27, 1995; "A Look Back: A City Restored," *Home Life: A Magazine for Today's Christian Family*, April 1996, n.p. See also Tamara Jones, "One Year Later: The Family That Triumphed Over Terrorism," *Good Housekeeping*, April 1996, pp. 83-85+.

34. Kennedy's sermon, "Easter's Been Disrupted," in *And the Angels Wept*, pp. 13-19. Quoted material, p. 15.

35. Long's sermon, "A Message of Hope," in *And the Angels Wept*, pp. 5-12. Quoted material, p. 9.

36. Jemison's sermon, "Triumph in the Midst of Trouble," in *And the Angels Wept*, pp. 99-104, quoted material, p. 104. Reverend Robert Allen, Oklahoma City Police Department chaplain Jack Poe, and state FBI chaplain Joe Williams were in charge of organizing the hundreds of ministers and professional chaplains who wished to serve at the site. Clergy who worked at the site were not required to have seminary degrees, but they did have to go through training from the National Organization for Victim Assistance. See "Chaplains Reunite, Reflect on Bombing," *Daily Oklahoman*, n.d.

37. Simms's sermon, "Reflections on a Nightmare," in *And the Angels Wept*, pp. 85-92. Quoted material, pp. 86-87.

38. Nick Harris, interview, November 12, 1998. Also see the interview with Harris in a videocassette produced by United Methodist Communications, "Why We Care: Oklahoma City," copy in author's files.

39. Meyers appeared on *Dateline NBC, One Year Later*, April 12, 1996. I thank Dr. Meyers for calling this to my attention.

40. *The Homeport Herald Weekly*, April 23, 1995, archives.

41. J. R. Church, "Tragedy Strikes Oklahoma City," *Prophecy in the News*, May 1995, pp. 4-6.

42. Joe Williams, interview, August 13, 1999; Graham's comments in *And the Angels Wept*, p. 54; Shevitz's comments in same source, p. 39.

43. Keating's comments in *And the Angels Wept*, p. 49.

44. "Lamentation Where We Live," delivered at the Mayflower Congregational Church, April 23, 1995. I thank Dr. Meyers for a copy of this sermon. Others

offered different readings of the doubting Thomas story in their search for the presence of God in the bombing, and in their attempt to provide a scriptural model for present doubt. Reverend Tish Malloy, pastor of Village United Methodist Church, also worked as a volunteer chaplain at the site. On April 23, she offered a sermon in which she spoke of how, like Thomas, so many people needed to reach out "to touch the woundedness." Like Thomas, "our vision is clouded by the smoke of the world's hate. . . . It is difficult to see the Lord and believe. . . . Jesus came to Thomas, in his unbelief. He did not punish him, and he will not punish you if you are doubting today." Malloy's sermon, "We Have Seen the Lord," in *And the Angels Wept*, pp. 67-72, quoted material, pp. 70-71.

45. Lee Benson, interview, August 12, 1999.

46. Joseph Ross, interview, August, 13, 1999.

47. Robin Jones, *Where Was God at 9:02 A.M.?* (Nashville: Thomas Nelson, 1995), pp. 33-34. Interestingly, while many conservative Christians would be loath to consider Christian Scientists their coreligionists, an editorial in the *Christian Science Monitor* also emphasized the need to discern the reality of the spiritual base of the universe in order to place the bombing in a proper context. "The forces that blow up and tear down and rip apart are found only within the material concept of the universe. And that, in turn, is found only within a material consciousness. But this material mentality and its view of a violent material universe is an impossible limit on God! He didn't make it, He didn't authorize it, He doesn't permit it. The shift in prayer—the shift away from a matter-based view of reality toward a God's-eye view—reveals a wholly different set of forces right where the destructive ones had previously appeared. And the forces that come from God are spiritual and good and harmonious." "For Oklahoma City and the World," *Christian Science Monitor* (reproduction in archives, undated).

48. See chapter 4, "The Miracle of the Supernatural," in *Where Was God at 9:02 A.M.?* pp. 65-78. Several of the clergy with whom I spoke had little patience with angel stories. One worried that people would think "God played favorites," and another said angrily, "If angels were at the building and were so involved in people's lives, why didn't they turn off the keys to the truck's ignition?"

49. Paul Fussell, *The Great War and Modern Memory* (London: Oxford University Press, 1975), chap. "Myth, Ritual, and Romance," pp. 114-154. Quoted material, pp. 115, 124. See also Fussell's *Wartime: Understanding and Behavior in the Second World War* (New York: Oxford University Press, 1989), pp. 48-51. I disagree with Fussell's claim that World War II was a "notoriously secular affair" (p. 51). For example, in addition to the crusading imagery that pervaded public rhetoric in several nations, there were numerous miracle stories about dead fliers returning their planes to home airfields, revealing the depth of their sense of duty.

50. Colleen McDannell, *Material Christianity: Religion and Popular Culture in America* (New Haven: Yale University Press, 1995), p. 1. See also "Faith Sustains Oklahoma City Bombing Rescue Workers," *Baptist Messenger*, May 18, 1995, pp. 3-4. The popularity of angels in American culture deserves much more attention that it has received. A good place to begin is Leonard Norman Primiano's "Angels and Americans," *America*, October 10, 1998, pp. 15-17; the videotape *Love, Somewhat*

Incarnate: Angels in Everyday Life (I thank Professor Primiano for bringing this to my attention), and the Soundprints cassette, *Angels and America*. I also benefited from grief counselor Jacquelyn Oliveira's seminar materials, "All about Angels." There are, as she pointed out, angel poetry cards, angel awareness seminars, angeloligists, books and audio cassettes offering instruction on how to contact angels through contemplative practices and guided meditation, new age channelers who will make contact with your guardian angel or the archangel Michael. There are angel clubs, angel magazines, angel boutiques, an angel watch journal, angel prayer groups, angel merchandise, and even, she noted, angel perfume at Saks Fifth Avenue. There college courses on angels and popular television shows, *Touched by an Angel,* for example. Primiano cited a Chrysler Corporation poll that discovered "75 percent of Americans believe in angels however they might define them, and 65 percent include in their homes some decoration featuring angel imagery" (p. 16).

51. Graham, *And the Angels Wept,* p. 57; Thomas Elliff, interview, September 23, 1999.

52. *Newshour with Jim Lehrer,* April 18, 1996, transcript 5509. Appearing on *CBS This Morning,* May 17, 1995, Oklahoma City Fire Department Lieutenant Mark Mollman said, "I had a relationship with God already, but I think a lot of people probably did find a new relationship or enhanced the one that . . . exists already."

53. "Interview with Dr. Robert Allen," Archives and Manuscript Division, Oral History Program, Oklahoma Historical Society, August 2, 1995; Jack Poe, chief of chaplains for the Oklahoma City Police Department, took credentials from some clergy who were paralyzed by the scene, and some self-styled lay clergy who picked up broken stained glass near the Methodist Church in order to make crosses to sell as fund-raisers. Poe, interview, November 11, 1998.

54. Garrison quoted in "Ministers Offer Prayers; Rely on God for Justice," *Daily Oklahoman,* April 24, 1995; Harris quoted in "A Shaken City, Ever Devout, Turns to God," *New York Times,* April 30, 1995.

55. Tish Malloy, interview, June 10, 1999. Ted Wilson, volunteer fire department chaplain, used the word "restored" instead of "recovery" when talking with workers at the site. "I wanted them to remember that they were restoring the bodies, restoring everything that could be given to a family." Wilson, interview, July 28, 1999.

56. Interestingly, a secular equivalent to this service also focused on the eyes. Rescue workers haunted by what they saw, smelled, and touched at the site sometimes turned to a form of therapy called EMDR, eye movement desensitization and reprocessing, in which horrific images are made visible in order to defuse their power. Judy Albert, a California therapist who trained numerous Oklahoma City therapists in EMDR, characterized it as "like an activated REM sleep, so the brain can make a normal adaptation." Albert, telephone interview, October 1, 1998. In another interesting ritual, Reverend Bruce Nieli, evangelism director for the U.S. Conference of Catholic Bishops, held a service at St. John the Baptist Catholic Church in Edmond, Oklahoma, in which "members wrote about their anger and burned the papers." *Daily Oklahoman,* May 1, 1995. The Healing of Memories service is described more fully in *Where Was God at 9:02 A.M.,* pp. 167-175.

57. Unless otherwise noted, all quotes from Bud Welch come from our interviews,

July 7, 1998, and March 23, 1999, and from several other informal conversations. See also "A Father's Urge to Forgive," *Time*, June 16, 1997; "Father of Blast Victim Reaches Out with Visit to Bill McVeigh," *Buffalo News*, October 2, 1998; Phil Bacharach, "A Lonely Message," *Oklahoma Gazette*, November 25, 1998; *Guide-Posts*, May 1999, pp. 3-6. Welch talked about his visit with Bill McVeigh on NBC's *Today*, October 16, 1998. I thank Bud Welch for sending me copies of his exchange with California's attorney general, Dan Lundgren, in the editorial pages of the *Sacramento Bee*, May 22, 1998, and June 20, 1998. Maria Ruiz Scaperlanda's *Their Faith Has Touched Us: The Legacies of Three Young Oklahoma City Bombing Victims* (Kansas City: Sheed & Ward, 1997) memorializes Julie Welch and two other young Catholics who were killed—Mark Bolte and Valerie Koelsch.

58. Except for the last sentence, the quoted material is from the text of Welch's speech to the National Association of Criminal Defense Lawyers, November 1, 1997, New York City.

59. Sister Helen Prejean, author of *Dead Man Walking*, popularized by Susan Sarandon and Sean Penn in a commercial movie, recalled visiting Oklahoma City to talk about the death penalty and the issue of forgiveness. "That trip," she said, "is permanently embedded in my mind." She spoke at Associated Catholic Charities to family members, survivors, and rescuers. "Many of these people knew their healing lay elsewhere" (than through vengeance). She understood, she told me, that "anger in the beginning may be important. It may sustain your life." Sister Helen spoke about how the term "reconcile" is often more appropriate than "forgiveness." "Reconciliation implies living in tension with one's anger, and offers the opportunity to be creative with it." She recalled one woman getting up at her talk and thanking Bud Welch for his public opposition to the death penalty. Helen Prejean, telephone interview, February 21, 2000.

60. See "Oklahoma Christians Rise Up," *Christianity Today*, June 19, 1995, p. 35; "3 Bombed Churches Celebrate Recovery," *Daily Oklahoman*, April 11, 1998.

61. George Back, interview, June 11, 1999. All quoted material is drawn from this interview unless otherwise noted. See also the interview with Back in a videocassette produced by United Methodist Communications, *Healing the Horror: Oklahoma City One Year Later*. Copy in author's files.

62. Quoted material on the memorial chains from "St. Paul's Cathedral Restoration Update," p. 15.

63. Susan Urbach, "Message Presented to St. Paul's Episcopal Cathedral, May 21, 1995." I thank Susan Urbach for sending this and other entries from her personal journals.

64. "Murrah Building Bombing Numbers," Governor Keating's office, undated archives. Copy in author's files. These same statistics for the children appear in "Effects of Oklahoma Bombing Persist," *Behavioral Health Treatment*, November 1997, p. 1. In their survey of Oklahoma City firefighters, for example, Dr. Robert Vincent and Sara Jo Nixon report that "82 percent of the firefighters reported contact with bodies or body parts and about 18 percent report a lot of such contact." "Predictors of Perceived Recovery among Oklahoma City Firefighters in the Aftermath of Their Participation at the Alfred P. Murrah Federal Building," pres-

entation at the fourth World Congress on Stress, Trauma, and Coping in the Emergency Services Professions: Research and Practice, 1997, Baltimore, Maryland. I thank Dr. Vincent for providing me a copy of this presentation.

65. David W. Smith, Ph.D., MPH, Elaine H. Christiansen, Ph.D., Robert Vincent, Ph.D., Neil E. Hann, MPH, "Population Effects of the Bombing of Oklahoma City," *Journal: Oklahoma State Medical Association*, April 1999, p. 193. See also Sue Mallonee, Sheryll Shariat, Gail Stennies, Rick Waxweiler, David Hogan, Fred Jordan, "Physical Injuries and Fatalities Resulting From the Oklahoma City Bombing," *Journal of the American Medical Association*, August 7, 1996, pp. 382-387. See also *Final Report*, American Psychological Association Task Force on the Mental Health Response to the Oklahoma City Bombing, July 1997. I thank Dr. Elinor Lottenville for giving me a copy of this report.

66. Newspapers and mass market magazines also focused attention on the toxic impact of the bomb, particularly around the anniversaries. See, for example, "Youngsters, Families Endured Unimaginable Pain," *USA Today*, April 15, 1996; "Living with the Nightmares," *Time*, April 15, 1996, pp. 61-64; "Walking Wounded," *People*, April 22, 1996, pp. 82-83; Rick Bragg, "Blast Toll Is No Longer in Deaths; but in Shattered Lives," *New York Times*, April 19, 1996; "The Orphans of Oklahoma City," *Newsweek*, April 22, 1996; "No End to the Pain," *People*, September 23, 1996, pp. 117-118; "Survivors' Songs," *Rocky Mountain News Online*, March 16, 1997; "A Tragedy That Won't Be Buried," msnbc.com/news/64773.asp, April 10, 1997; Rick Bragg, "In Oklahoma City, Recovery a House at a Time," *New York Times*, June 8, 1997; "A New Chapter," *Federal Times*, April 13, 1998; "A Wound That Never Heals: OKC Bomb Survivors Haunted 3 Years later," *Fort Worth Star-Telegram*, April 19, 1998; "Bombing's Scars: Survivor Flees Oklahoma for Cleveland, Hoping Distance Will Numb the Pain," *Plain Dealer* (Cleveland), October 25, 1998.

67. Jannie Coverdale, interview, March 18, 1999.

68. Laverna Williams, interview, July 27, 1999. See also " 'We're Not OK,' " *Federal Times*, April 22, 1996, pp. 1, 8, 10, 12-16.

69. Doris Jones, interview, November 10, 1998.

70. The issue of "medicalized grief" is treated at length in chapter 3. Quoted material in this and the two previous paragraphs from James R. Allen, M.D. FRCP (C), MPH; Suzanne Whittlesey, ACSW, Betty Pfefferbaum, M.D., J.D.; and Michele Ondersma, Ph.D., "Community and Coping of Mothers and Grandmothers of Children Killed in a Human-Caused Disaster," *Psychiatric Annals*, February 1999, pp. 86-88. This essay also notes that "most of the women we saw found some comfort from within their own group, although a few were overwhelmed and concluded that their grief was exacerbated by the tragedies of others" (p. 88).

71. James R. Allen and Barbara A. Allen, "Transactional Analysis from Oklahoma City: After the Bombing," *Transactional Analysis Journal*, July 1998, p. 206. See also Sandra F. Allen, Ph.D.; Eric L. Dlugokinski, Ph.D.: Laura A. Cohen, Ph.D.; and Jerry L. Walker, M.Ed.: "Assessing the Impact of a Traumatic Community Event on Children and Assisting with Their Healing," *Psychiatric Annals*, February 1999, pp. 93-98.

72. Dr. Robin Gurwitch, interview, October 28, 1999. See also "Minds of Young Are Left in Turmoil," *New York Times*, April 25, 1995.

73. Debra Hampton, interview, April 30, 1999.

74. On Robert O'Donnell, see Lisa Belkin, "Death on the CNN Curve," *New York Times Magazine*, July 23, 1995. Cindy Alexander, interview, August 13, 1999. Many of the different groups—fire, police, EMSA, for example—had their own system of disaster management. Alexander observed that a major problem was that some in the "helping professions" who were involved on-site and deeply affected by their work also tried to provide peer support. "We developed a risk scale, where you got so many points for what had happened to you while working at the building. So many points and you were judged to be too 'contaminated' to offer support." She also described an intricate system of techniques to help rescuers integrate their experiences: demobilization (techniques designed to relieve stress), defusing (15-20 minutes of personal interaction and stress management techniques), prebriefings (so that teams going to the building knew what to expect), and one-to-one meetings. Debriefings, she said, are best done sometime after participation in the event is over. "Rescuers were on twelve-, then ten-, then eight-hour shifts, and we made sure that the same person they talked with before they went on duty was there when they came off. We also made sure that there were always women on duty because men feel more comfortable crying with women," she observed, "and we provided chiropractors, massage therapists, so that we could take care of the whole person." See also Sara Jo Nixon, Ph.D., John Schorr, Ph.D., Angela Boudreaux, B.A., and Robert D. Vincent, Ph.D., "Perceived Sources of Support and Their Effectiveness for Oklahoma City Firefighters," *Psychiatric Annals*, February 1999, pp. 101-105; "After the Bomb: Oklahoma City Rescuers Talk about Their Experiences," *JEMS*, June 1995, pp. 40-41, 84-88. I thank Chaplain Joe Williams for providing me with copies of his papers, "Care for the Caregivers," and "The High Cost of Caring," author's files. See also "Williams Says Counseling Crucial to Rescue Teams," *Baptist Messenger* (Oklahoma), October 19, 1995, p. 5.

75. Phil Bacharach, "After the Fall: Rescue Workers Have Become the Latest Victims of the Federal Building Bombing," *Oklahoma Gazette*, January 13, 1999, pp. 26-30. Dr. John Tassey reported that "there have been 43 divorces among firefighters; and 53 divorces among police officers—well above what could be expected in two years" ("Effects of Oklahoma Bombing Persist"). See also, Heather Taylor, "Aftershocks: What I Saw, What I Did and Why I Tried to Kill Myself," *Mademoiselle*, April 1996, pp. 170-175; "Felled By The Aftershocks: The Toll from The Oklahoma Bombing Now Includes Hero Cop Terry Yeakey," *People*, May 27, 1996, pp. 121-122; "The Blast's Fallout," *USA Today*, August 4, 1998. See also the transcript of *Dateline-NBC*, April 19, 1999, "A Day Remembered," the grim story of a traumatized policeman who eventually did seek help. See also Richard A. Serrano, "Bombing-Related Suicides Reveal How Effects of Terror Still Live On," *Houston Chronicle*, April 28, 1999; "Struggling to Overcome Terror," *World News Tonight with Peter Jennings*, May 3, 1999, transcript 99050308j04. There were even stories of family suicide related to the bombing among employees at the hotel in which I usually stayed in Oklahoma City. Jason Bingenheimer told me about the suicide of his uncle, federal prosecutor Ted Richardson. He believed his uncle felt guilt because he was not chosen for the prosecution team and deeply affected by the loss of

friends in the Murrah Building. "In August 1997, he took his driver's license out of his wallet, took his jacket off, and shot himself while wearing an Oklahoma bombing memorial T-shirt. He had suffered some bouts of depression, but I think the bombing was the straw that broke the camel's back. He couldn't bear to be on the sidelines watching." Jason Bingenheimer, interview, October 29, 1999.

76. Quote on bomb threats from "Copycats Threat Scares Oakland," *San Francisco Examiner*, April 21, 1995. See also "Bomb Threats and Hoaxes Lead to Evacuations along West Coast," *Press-Telegram* (Long Beach), April 21, 1995. On scam artists, see "Scam-Artists Hard at Work," *Daily Oklahoman*, April 24, 1995; "Tips Given on Avoiding Scams," *Daily Oklahoman*, May 3, 1995.

77. Mas'ood Cajee, "Muslim Community Calls for Healing after KFOR TV 4's Hasty Accusations," *Oklahoma Gazette*, June 22, 1995, p. 9.

78. Council on American-Islamic Relations, "A Rush to Judgment: A Special Report on Anti-Muslim Stereotyping, Harassment, and Hate Crimes Following the Bombing of Oklahoma City's Murrah Federal Building, April 19, 1995," September 1995, pp. 9-11. See also Said Deep, "Rush to Judgment," *Quill*, July-August 1995, pp. 18-22; the bitter essay from Christopher Hitchens, "Minority Report," *Nation*, May 22, 1995, p. 711. Dr. Jihad Ahmad remembers how tense the immediate aftermath of the bombing was for members of any Muslim community. "We felt it, and whether one was black like me, or a Muslim from the Middle East, it was a difficult time. We felt tremendous relief when McVeigh was caught. It felt like a godsend." Ahmad, interview, June 6, 1999. The *Tulsa World* reported that when Abraham Ahmad returned to Oklahoma City after being detained, he attended the Sunday ceremony at the Oklahoma State Fairgrounds to show he was just a "normal Muslim." During the service, the newspaper reported, "many shook his hand. Some hugged him." "Jumping to Conclusions," April 25, 1995.

79. *All Things Considered*, National Public Radio, April 23, 1995, transcript 1826-1; "Muslims Continue to Feel Apprehensive," *New York Times*, April 24, 1995.

80. "Internet Seethes with Information about Explosion," *Daily Oklahoman*, April 23, 1995. See also "Far-Right Info Web: Rumors, Untruths," *Chicago Tribune*, April 26, 1995; "Barbed Wire Net," *Village Voice*, May 2, 1995; James Ridgeway, "A Conspiratorial Gathering: The McVeigh Trial Opens, with Theories and Strategy Aplenty," *Village Voice*, April 8, 1997; "Conspiracy Theories Flourish on Radical Shortwave Radio," *Daily Oklahoman*, April 24, 1995. An examination of conspiracy theory culture after the bombing would be a fascinating project in itself. The Memorial Foundation archives is a rich source of such material, including copies of the seemingly endless discussion on the Internet that continues to take place.

81. "Many Americans Think Conspiracy Involved in Oklahoma City Bombing," *Gallup Poll Monthly*, August 1995, p. 21. "Oklahoma Bombing Victims Sue Government, Day Care and Texas Chemical Company," Associated Press, April 19, 1997; copy in author's files. See also "An Unlikely Duo Makes Big Headlines in Oklahoma Blast," *Wall Street Journal*, March 25, 1997.

82. Key quoted in Mark Curriden, "Move Over, Oliver Stone," *ABA Journal*, September 1997, p. 34; "Oklahoma Grand Jury Dismisses Theories about Bombing," *Washington Post*, December 31, 1998. See also "OKC Bombing Case Overview," The

Oklahoma Bombing Investigation Committee (established by Charles Key). Glenn Wilburn died of cancer on July 15, 1997. Terry Nichols' brother James joined a host of others in publishing conspiracy literature. For a good example of the kind of arguments made by conspiracy theorists, see a "Special Oklahoma City Bombing Memorial Edition" of the *Spotlight* [which characterizes itself as "America's last real newspaper,"], October 11, 1999. The mainstream media was also fascinated with the unanswered questions about the bombing, particularly the possible existence of "John Doe 2." See, for example, Peter Carlson, "The Shadow: Did He Ever Really Exist?" *Washington Post Magazine*, March 23, 1997, pp. 11-15, 25-30; and ABC's *20/20* segment entitled "The Families Want to Know," which aired on January 17, 1997. It includes an interview with the Wilburns. See "OKC: More Truth Leaks Out," *New American*, February 17, 1997, pp. 15-17. Almost all of the family members and survivors whom I have spoken with strongly opposed the grand jury, believed that the trials had answered the most important questions about the bombing, and several worked actively and successfully to defeat Key in a recent election. Phil Bacharach wrote even-handed and thorough articles about nagging questions and conspiracy theories in the *Oklahoma Gazette*. See, for example, "Conspiracy! In the Throes of a Paranoid Nation," *Oklahoma Gazette*, June 22, 1995, pp. 5-7; "Casting Doubt: Were Others Involved in the Federal Building Bombing?" *Oklahoma Gazette*, February 13, 1997; "Unanswered Questions: The Federal Building Bombing and a Legacy of Conspiracy," *Oklahoma Gazette*, April 29, 1998.

83. Willa Johnson, interview, March 2, 1999; Angela Monson, interview, March 22, 1999; Kevin Cox, interview, June 10, 1999.

84. See "3 Join Lawsuit over Funds' Use," *Daily Oklahoman*, August 8, 1995; Cox and Monson quoted in "Bomb Relief Red Tape Puzzles Lawmakers," *Daily Oklahoman*, June 21, 1995; see also "Okla. City Aid Not Reaching Victims," *USA Today*, November 15, 1995; and a very important story, "Kindness of Strangers Forces Hard Decisions for Oklahoma Victims," *Wall Street Journal*, June 13, 1997. There may never be a full and final accounting of the millions of dollars that poured into Oklahoma City. Money came to family members and survivors directly— which often proved extremely awkward, to wake up and find an envelope of cash on your front door, for example—to various organizations, to churches, to the mayor and governor. On May 3, 1995, Governor Keating signed a bill establishing the Murrah Crime Victims Compensation Fund, to be administered by the Oklahoma Crime Victims Compensation Fund. Various funds were established to provide college scholarships to children "who either lost a parent or guardian...had a parent or guardian critically injured...or were injured in the building day care center." (See news release, "Year after Bombing, Scholarship Programs Report Results," *Oklahoma State Regents for Higher Education*, April 15, 1996). I thank Chancellor Hans Brisch for giving me a copy of this release. The Oklahoma City Community Foundation administered the Mayor's and Governor's Emergency Fund, and the Survivors' Fund Clearing House was set up to coordinate funds donated to various groups to address "unmet needs." This group was eventually named the Oklahoma City Resource Coordinating Committee, chaired by Daniel

Kurtenbach, the president of Oklahoma Goodwill Industries. "We served as a funnel for resources that had been donated, and we were a kind of 'last resort' before people fell through the cracks." As of July 1999, the committee had met 180 times and served 470 people, with a number of repeats. "We will exist as long as there are needs and resources," Kurtenbach said, "and we still distribute an average of $27,000 a month." Kurtenbach, interview, July 30, 1999. See also Grant Williams, "Oklahoma's Charities and the Bomb," *Chronicle of Philanthropy*, April 4, 1996, pp. 28-31, 34.

CHAPTER 3

1. Quoted in Paul Boyer, *By the Bomb's Early Light: American Thought and Culture at the Dawn of The Atomic Age* (Chapel Hill: University of North Carolina Press, 1994), p. 280.
2. Kai Erickson, *A New Species of Trouble: The Human Experience of Modern Disasters* (New York: Norton, 1994), pp. 229-230.
3. Erickson, *New Species*, pp. 232-233.
4. Ray Blakeney, interview, August 12, 1999; Thomas Demuth, interview, June 6, 1999; Alexander, interview, February 24, 1999. Unless otherwise noted, all quoted material comes from these interviews. I thank Reverend Donna Compton, resident chaplain at Presbyterian Hospital, for talking with me about her experiences working at the FAC and for graciously sharing some of her writing with me.
5. A color-coded name tag system identified staff and family members. "Each service or organization (e.g. clergy, mental health, medical, medical examiner, and media) was identified by a different color. Similarly, family members were designated with a blue dot for next-of-kin or a yellow dot for extended or immediate family members." Karen A. Sitterle and Robin H. Gurwitch, "The Terrorist Bombing in Oklahoma City," in Ellen S. Zinner, Psy.D., and Mary Beth Williams, Ph.D., eds., *When a Community Weeps; Case Studies in Group Survivorship* (Philadelphia: Brunner/Mazel, 1999), p. 169.
6. Milford Clay, who handled public relations at the Temple Funeral Home, remembered that members of the news media "wanted to cover services, and some even wanted to come into the embalming room which of course we did not allow. Some families did not object to cameras in the churches, some did." John Temple and Milford Clay, interview by author, March 22, 1999.
7. Elinor Lottinville, interview, July 29, 1999. Unless otherwise noted, all quoted materials come from this interview. John Temple and Milford Clay of Temple Funeral Home spoke about the unprecedented demands brought about by the bombing. "We had to forget about normal working hours, and our staff was able to handle the intensity of the work and the ghastly conditions of the bodies. We could only do one open casket service."
8. Kathleen Treanor, interview, March 20, 1998.
9. Demuth also spoke of those who, in the final days of the FAC, when the crowds had thinned, tried to claim they had loved ones in the building in order to find

relatives who did not want to be found by these people. "One person reported her sister and boyfriend and four children missing. We asked how they knew they were in the building, and they said they had dropped them off to go to Social Security. I knew something was wrong when the boyfriend pointed to a photograph of the Denny children in the newspaper and said 'that's them.' (Brandon and Rebecca Denny were severely wounded in the Murrah day care, but lived.) Detectives found that her four children had been taken from her by social services and placed in foster care, and they were using the bombing to try and find them. The police told them they had 15 minutes to leave the church." There are several similar stories.

10. David Hockensmith, Jr. interview, June 10, 1999. All subsequent quoted material comes from this interview unless otherwise noted.

11. Tassey, interview, August 10, 1999. All subsequent quoted material comes from this interview unless otherwise noted.

12. Dr. James Allen, interview, January 13, 1999. All subsequent quoted material comes from this interview unless otherwise noted.

13. Many of the people I spoke with used the terms "grief," "mourning," and "bereavement" interchangeably, and I have not tried to systematize their language. In my own usage of the terms, I have observed the very helpful distinction, provided by Peter Homans, that "grief is a painful emotion which is, so to speak, looking for a 'cure.'" Mourning is a ritual which, so to speak, 'heals' the pain of grief." See his introduction in Peter Homans, ed., *Symbolic Loss: The Ambiguity of Mourning and Memory at Century's End* (Charlottesville: The University Press of Virginia, 2000). I thank Peter Homans for sending me a prepublication copy of the introduction.

14. *Final Report,* American Psychological Association Task Force on the Mental Health Response to the Oklahoma City Bombing, July 1997, p. 36. Federal funding for Project Heartland began when the Oklahoma Department of Mental Health and Substance Abuse Services—named by Governor Keating as the "lead agency for the state in coordinating, organizing, and conducting mental health crisis response efforts"—obtained an immediate services grant of $754,053 from FEMA. Their funding ended on February 28, 1998, and the Department of Justice Victims of Crime Division supported Project Heartland through a grant of $264,000. "*A Report on Project Heartland,* Oklahoma's Crisis Counseling Services for Those Affected by the Murrah Federal Building Bombing on April 19, 1995," May 31, 1998, pp. 2-5.

15. See *Report on Project Heartland,* pp. 2-5.

16. *Report on Project Heartland,* p. 25.

17. See Robert Jay Lifton, *Home from the War: Vietnam Veterans—Neither Victims Nor Executioners* (New York: Simon & Schuster, 1973); and Wilbur J. Scott, "PTSD in DSM-III: A Case Study in the Politics of Diagnosis and Disease," *Social Problems,* August 1990, pp. 294-310. I also wish to thank Dr. Allan Young, professor of anthropology, in the departments of social studies of medicine, anthropology, and psychiatry at McGill University for his assistance. Both his book, *The Harmony of Illusions: Inventing Post-Traumatic Stress Disorder* (Princeton: Princeton

University Press, 1995), and our telephone conversations and personal meeting in Cambridge, Massachusetts, have greatly enriched my understanding of the origins, characteristics, and problematics of PTSD.

18. Judith Herman, M.D., *Trauma and Recovery* (Basic, 1997), p. 28.

19. Dr. Kay Goebel, interview, February 25, 1999. Dr. Goebel and I have had many subsequent conversations, each of which was most helpful in my thinking about this section of the chapter.

20. Arthur Kleinman, *Writing at the Margins: Discourse Between Anthropology and Medicine* (Berkeley: University of California Press, 1995), p. 181.

21. Kleinman, *Writing at the Margins*, p. 176. See also Arthur Kleinman and Joan Kleinman, "The Appeal of Experience; The Dismay of Images: Cultural Appropriations of Suffering in Our Times," *Daedalus*, Winter 1996, pp. 1-23.

22. Kleinman, *Writing at the Margins*, p. 187.

23. Henry Greenspan, "Lives as Texts: Symptoms as Modes of Recounting in the Life Histories of Holocaust Survivors," in George C. Rosenwald and Richard L. Ochberg, eds., *Storied Lives: The Cultural Politics of Self-Understanding* (New Haven: Yale University Press, 1992), p. 146.

24. Kleinman, *Writing at the Margins*, p. 180.

25. Eric Schlosser, "A Grief Like No Other," *Atlantic Monthly*, September 1997, p. 72.

26. Lawrence L. Langer, "The Alarmed Vision: Social Suffering and Holocaust Atrocity," *Daedalus*, Winter 1996, p. 58.

27. *USA Today*, May 22, 1995; "All Things Considered," May 23, 1995, transcript 1856-2; "The Face of Angst," *Demolition Age*, August 1995, p. 8; "Implosion lays Oklahoma City nightmare to rest," *Construction News*, July 3, 1995, p. 14; "The Alfred P. Murrah Federal Building in Oklahoma City, OK," *Engineering News-Record*, September 18, 1995, p. D-8.

28. *ABC World News Tonight*, July 4, 1995, transcript 5132; *CNN Prime News*, December 23, 1997, transcript 97122301V21. Soothing language of purifying the contamination of violence was also in evidence. For example, CNN reporter John Zarella reported on May 5, 1995, that a "cleansing rain fell in Oklahoma City." In my discussions with those involved in the recovery efforts, the rains that fell often made their jobs even more difficult; "cleansing" is not a word that they would use to characterize the rain. "Tribute Paid to Oklahoma City Victims," CNN, May 6, 1995, transcript 1094-4. See also "Grieving in Oklahoma," *Newshour with Jim Lehrer*, June 16, 1997, transcript 5851; Nadya Labi, "The Grief Brigade," *Time*, May 17, 1997, pp. 69-70.

29. Ellen Goodman, "Closure and the One-Minute Mourner," *Boston Globe*, n.d.; Errol Laborde, "Bringing Closure to a Word with a Pop Psychological Spin," *City Business New Orleans*, June 9, 1997.

30. Contrast this urge to establish term limits on grief with some survivors of the Nazi massacre of 642 people at the French village of Oradour-sur-Glane on June 10, 1944. Some survivors observed a "generation of mourning," and "a few old women . . . never abandoned their mourning." Sarah Farmer, *Martyred Village: Commemorating the 1944 Massacre at Oradour-sur-Glane* (Berkeley: University of California Press, 1999), p. 127. For insightful comments on the cultural function of

the idea of "healing" in connection with the Vietnam War, see Keith Beattie, *The Scar That Binds: American Culture and the Vietnam War* (New York: New York University Press, 1998).

31. Langer, "Alarmed Vision," p. 58; see also, Kleinman, *Writing at the Margins*, p. 180.

32. Jamie Kalven, *Working with Available Light: A Family's World After Violence* (New York: Norton, 1999), p. 292.

33. Survivor, interview, July 28, 1999; Dr. Brian Espe, interview, August 13, 1999.

34. I thank Pam Whicher for many telephone conversations, several e-mails, and several personal meetings in Maryland and, most recently, in Oklahoma City during the dedication of the memorial on the fifth anniversary.

35. Quoted material in this section comes from Florence Rogers, interview, July 6, 1998; Florence Rogers, "Mother Goose and the OKC Bombing," (draft of an essay Rogers wrote for a *Guideposts* writers workshop); Grayson Towler, "A Survivor's Tale: The Rebirth of the Federal Employees Credit Union in Oklahoma City," archives; and "In Wake of Oklahoma Explosion, Credit Union Rises From Rubble," *Wall Street Journal*, April 26, 1995.

36. Betty Price, interview, June 9, 1999; Jones, quoted in Phil Bacharach, "Art, but No Festival," *Oklahoma Gazette*, May 11, 1995, p. 25.

37. The Oklahoma Arts Institute has published a magnificent anthology of the creative work done at Quartz Mountain, *A Celebration of the Spirit*. James R. Allen, "After the Bombing: Public Scenarios and the Construction of Meaning," *Journal of the Oklahoma State Medical Association*, April 1999, p. 191. Mary Frates and Laura Anderson, eds., *A Celebration of the Spirit* (Oklahoma City: Oklahoma Arts Institute, 1997).

38. *Celebration of the Spirit*, p. 33. An exhibition of the artwork created at Quartz Mountain opened in the governor's gallery at the state capitol on December 6, 1995, and then traveled throughout the state through 1997. A number of Oklahoma artists recall that their work was affected by the bombing. One, for example, told me that her work had become "darker" after the bombing. She made porcelain animals and children with wired-on legs, and after the bombing she added a "swipe of black underglaze" to a ceramic baby and an unfinished bowl. Jan Eckardt Butler, letter and e-mail message to author, November 21, 1998, and January 1, 1999. Several expressed their disdain for other artists who focused on the bombing in their work. "I deliberately did not do any paintings about the bombing and was repulsed by artists that used the grief of others," a Tulsa artist wrote. "I felt the only people that had a right to express themselves artistically about the bombing were those that had been personally affected by a loss of a loved one. I did not think any artistic expression I could do concerning the bombing could possibly reflect the feelings of those that lost their present and their future. . . . I did not want to risk intruding upon the grief of the victims and their families and feared any artistic expression would be misunderstood or resented." Diane Salamon, letter to author, November 2, 1998.

39. Fred Anderson, interview, February 22, 1999.

40. Patti Hall, interview, June 7, 1999; Treanor interview, March 20, 1998.

41. Cheryl Scroggins, interview, October 22, 1998.

42. Coverdale, interview, March 18, 1999; Edye Smith Stowe, interview, July 27, 1999.
43. Marsht Kight, interview, October 21, 1998, and several other informal discussions. I thank Tom and Marsha Kight for sharing various video and text materials with me.
44. Dr. Paul Heath, interview, March 19, 1999, and several informal discussions. I thank members of the association for giving me permission to attend several meetings and to talk with them and get their reaction about my work on this project.
45. The phrase is from Ian Buruma, "The Joys and Perils of Victimhood," *New York Review of Books*, April 8, 1999, p. 4.
46. The Televised Proceedings for Crime Victims provision of antiterrorism legislation in 1996 required closed-circuit broadcast of a trial held more than 350 miles from the scene of the crime. For a careful account of these activities, see Jeffrey Toobin, "Victim Power," *New Yorker*, March 24, 1997, pp. 40-43.
47. Diane Leonard, interview, November 10, 1998; All subsequent quoted material comes from this interview. Cassell's testimony found in U.S. Congress, Senate, Committee on the Judiciary, Hearing, 105th Cong., 1st sess., April 16, 1997, *A Bill Proposing an Amendment to the Constitution of the United States to Protect the Rights of Crime Victims*, p. 109. Professor Cassell is a well-known advocate of victims' rights and a constitutional amendment. I thank him for sending me a number of his writings. See, for example, Paul G. Cassell, "Barbarians at the Gates? A Reply to the Critics of the Victims' Rights Amendment," 1999 *Utah Law Review*; Paul G. Cassell, "Make Amends to Crime Victims," *Wall Street Journal*, July 20, 1999; Laurence H. Tribe and Paul G. Cassell, "Embed the Rights of Victims in the Constitution," *Los Angeles Times*, July 6, 1998; Paul Cassell and Robert F. Hoyt, "The Tale of Victim's Rights," *Legal Times*, December 23, 30, 1996; Paul G. Cassell and Steven J. Twist, "A Bill of Rights for Crime Victims," *Wall Street Journal*, April 24, 1996.
48. Clinton quoted in Cassell, "Barbarians." The *Denver Post*'s Chuck Green argued for the importance of impact testimony after listening to the impassioned words of Kathleen Treanor in the Nichols trial. "After nearly a year of sterilized evidence, and complicated legal arguments, and soft tears, we were hearing the truth of what terrorism really causes—uncontrollable anger, inconceivable anguish, unhealing heartache." Observing that defense counsel Michael Tigar asked Judge Matsch to tell the jury to disregard her testimony because of its emotion, Green wrote, "inappropriate, my ass. Treanor is due all the anger she feels...and in full view of a jury of *her* peers. She deserves our admiration, not a wag of the judicial finger." "Mother Has Right to Rage," *Denver Post*, January 4, 1998.
49. Cassell, "Barbarians."
50. Cassell, "Barbarians," and "Make Amends to Crime Victims." The issue of a victims' rights amendment is a controversial one, with victim rights' groups lining up on both sides of the issue. Also somewhat controversial is the appropriateness of impact testimony, when those who have been affected by crime are allowed to testify in the sentencing phase. Some see this as an inappropriate intrusion into the judicial system, representing, in Wendy Kaminer's words, "the confusion of

justice and therapy," the idea—mistaken in her view—that the "criminal prosecutions should help crime victims heal." Wendy Kaminer, *Sleeping with Extra-Terrestrials: The Rise of Irrationalism and Perils of Piety* (New York: Pantheon, 1999), p. 202. Likewise, Michael Sandel, writing in the *New Republic*, argues that the therapeutic motive for testimony is "flawed," confusing "an effect of criminal punishment (that victims and their families take satisfaction in the outcome) with its primary justification—to give the perpetrator what he deserves." The compelling case for such testimony, he believes, is a "retributive one," to "provide the jury with a full account of the moral gravity of the crime." Such statements are made not for emotional reasons but to shape a just sentencing. Michael J. Sandel, "Crying for Justice," *New Republic*, July 7, 1997, p. 25. Certainly, there are many who would argue that such testimony serves a variety of functions, and the ability of a victim to stand and tell her or his story with the perpetrator present is part of the shaping of justice—let the punishment fit the crime—as well as an emotionally important act for the individual, an act of locating their loved one's importance in judicial memory.

51. Marsha Kight, comp., *Forever Changed: Remembering Oklahoma City, April 19, 1995* (Amherst, New York: Prometheus, 1998), p. 18.

52. Habeas corpus, "to have the body," refers to a "court's writ ordering a warden to release a person who has been incarcerated unlawfully." It came to be the means by which state prisoners appealed constitutional violations of their cases to federal courts. Quoted material from Peter Rubin, "Terror Struck: Gutting Habeus Corpus," *New Republic*, September 4, 1995, p. 17; CNN, April 20, 1995, transcript 50-10; Clinton quoted in "Habeas Bid Boosted by Bombing: GOP Ties Reform to Anti-Terrorism Bill," *Legal Times*, May 8, 1995, p. 1; Seidl quoted in Jonathan Nicholson, " 'I Feel We Did Make a Difference,' " *Oklahoma Gazette*, June 15, 1995, p. 13.

53. For arguments opposing habeas corpus reform, see Rubin, "Terror struck"; "Shell Game," *New Republic*, May 13, 1996, p. 6; David Cole, "Destruction of the Habeas Safety Net," *Legal Times*, June 19, 1995, p. 30.

54. Polly Nichols, interview, August 12, 1999. The 168 Pennies campaign was modeled after a program begun by Nancy Krodel, a Putnam City, Oklahoma, elementary school principal, who asked students to give nineteen pennies for each murdered child and consequently raised approximately $50,000. Polly Nichols would often accompany Clint Seidl, who was seven years old when his mother was killed in the bombing, and Miss America 1996, Shawntel Smith, on visits to schools. The campaign eventually reached thousands of schools in forty-four states and raised over $450,000.

CHAPTER 4

1. First poem found in governor's collection archives. I thank Reverend McAnally for her letter of January 4, 1999, and a copy of the *Oklahoma Peace Strategy*, June 1995, in which her poem appears on p. 10. "A Time for Healing" was the brainchild

of Oklahoma's first lady, Cathy Keating, who recalled "I had no official duties, but couldn't simply stand by, and I thought that this kind of service was something that would be helpful to family members and survivors, but also to the wider community." Keating, interview, June 15, 2000.

2. The president quoted in Ron Hutcheson, "The Way Oklahomans Are," *Plain Dealer* (Cleveland), May 11, 1995. See "An American Family," *U.S. News and World Report*, August 14, 1995.

3. See, for example, "Blast Opens Old Wounds For Veterans," *Daily Oklahoman*, May 29, 1995.

4. *Daily Oklahoman*, May 2, 1995.

5. Material in these two paragraphs from Mayor's Office—faxes, telephone log, gifts, and fundraiser info. 9663/756 archives. For local reaction to media scrutiny of the state and reaction to the trial and conviction of Nichols, see "Verdict Holds Few in Thumb," *Detroit Free Press*, May 31, 1997; "In Thumb, Anger Mixes with Relief, Sense of Peace," *Detroit Free Press*, June 14, 1997; "State Called a Far-Right Spawning Ground," *Detroit Free Press*, September 17, 1997; "Nichols Gets Little Slack in Michigan," *Detroit Free Press*, October 28, 1997; "Thumb Residents Hope Verdict Ends Scrutiny," *Detroit Free Press*, December 15, 1997; "In the Thumb, Some Upset over Lack of Closure," *Detroit Free Press*, December 24, 1997.

6. Brandon M. Stickney, *"All American Monster": The Unauthorized Biography of Timothy McVeigh* (Amherst, N.Y.: Prometheus, 1996), p. 283. The school's student council funded the erection of a small memorial plaque to those killed in the bombing.

7. On the motel room, see an Internet story, "Those with Coincidental Connections to Bombing are Uneasy with Fame" (originally appeared in the *Salina Journal*): http://archive.dailynews.net:8080/archi . . . na/1996/4/HNS-SJ=_bombing=_notoriety.html; Susan Mueller appears in a documentary, *Dateline Herington*, produced by KTWU, channel 11 in Topeka, Kansas, 1996. A copy of this is in the archives. See also a segment entitled "Small Town Reaction" on *The Newshour with Jim Lehrer*, May 19, 1995, transcript 5252. On the reaction of these small towns to the stereotyping that occurred, see "Work on Bomb Investigation Stings Personally at Fort Riley," *Kansas City Star Online*, May 2, 1995; "Town Back in Spotlight amid Bomb Probe," *Dallas Morning News*, May 21, 1995; "Town Feels Sullied by Notoriety of Case," *Topeka Capital-Journal*, March 30, 1997; L. M. Stein, "Small-Town Paper Defends Town's Image," *Editor and Publisher*, June 10, 1995, pp. 14-15. For a thoughtful examination of another Kansas community associated with the travels of McVeigh and Nichols, see Jo Thomas, "Behind a Seamless Facade, the Fractures of Discontent," *New York Times*, November 12, 1998.

8. Debi Martin, interview, April 28, 1999. For an interesting report on the task faced by postal workers, see "Piles of Letters Pulled Heartstrings in Postmaster's Office," *Saturday Oklahoma and Times*, July 8, 1995; and "Mail Pours in for Victims," *Tulsa World*, May 3, 1995.

9. For example, on June 24, 1995, players from the National Football League and the Hollywood All-Stars played a celebrity softball game—Hitting in the Heartland—in Oklahoma City, preceded by a "rescue worker appreciation day" ceremony. The

Korean Church Council of greater New York organized a bicycle marathon from Los Angeles to New York commemorating the fiftieth anniversary of Korean independence and the victims of the bombing. The team arrived in Oklahoma City on July 14, 1995, and participated in a special memorial service at the First Methodist Church. On June 25, 1995, gospel musicians from around the nation presented two concerts to raise money for the Oklahoma City Christian Relief Fund. The Memorial archives has dozens of audio cassette tapes of music sent to the city and the foundation. On June 7, 1998, New Jersey composer Dean Rishel's *Requiem for the Children* was performed at the First Presbyterian Church in Oklahoma City. Written in response to the bombing, the music "incorporates into its text poems and prose written by children from all over the world, set in part to the music of familiar children's songs and lullabies.... The various movements of the adults' Latin Requiem, convey pleas for mercy, the terror and confusion of a final judgment day, the holiness of heaven and earth, rage, peace, prayers for the children's eternal rest, and finally, an anthem of hope in a recognition of the children's eternal joy and innocence" (*Requiem for the Children*, media kit, copy in author's files). A doctor from Midwest City, Oklahoma, a suburb of Oklahoma City, wrote Mayor Norick on May 1, 1995 that he had received a call from Babatunde Olatunji, a "world class African Drummer," who wanted to do a "Healing Drumming" for the people of Oklahoma and was willing to come at his own expense. Stephen Stills, formerly of Buffalo Springfield and Crosby, Stills, Nash, and Young, held a benefit concert at the Oklahoma City Zoo Amphitheater in early May 1995 for children who had lost their parents in the bombing. "The thing I do best is sing," he said, "so for whatever insignificant help it would be, perhaps I can bring some comfort and continue with the healing process and try to keep the frayed nerves from becoming unglued as we ask the question: What cause is so urgent that it requires the slaughter of innocents?" (*Daily Oklahoman*, May 3, 1995). The Worthing Musical Comedy Society from England sent condolences. They were preparing to perform *Oklahoma* and "during this time we have learnt a good deal about the Oklahoma people.... Our thoughts are with you and will be all next week when we perform *Oklahoma*." The bombing was also a popular subject with country and western artists. There was scattered criticism of megastar Garth Brooks, who paid for a full-page advertisement in *Billboard* calling on radio stations and video stores to honor the first anniversary with a moment of silence and then by playing his song "The Change." "The world will not change me," he sings, and "love and mercy still exist." A video featuring the song included news footage of the aftermath of the bombing. Brooks responded to accusations that he was "cashing in" on tragedy by declaring that he didn't care what song was played; rather, "it just meant a lot to me as an Oklahoman to see the country music family salute its heartland on this day, in unity, by doing the same thing, whatever that may be." See Michael Zitz, "Garth Brooks Should Know Better," *Free Lance-Star*, April 18, 1996. The Memorial Foundation archive has numerous country and western recordings on audio- and videocassettes and compact discs.

10. One woman from Ohio wrote Mayor Norick on May 2, 1995, that she had "flipped my little desk calendar over and found this thought, and it seems so apropos for

the people of Oklahoma City." Her calendar note was Psalm 34:18, "The Lord is close to those brokenhearted and saves those who are crushed in spirit."

11. Not surprisingly, many family members grew angry and resentful at the commercialization of the bombing. For example, a 1996 Oklahoma Heroes Bachelor Calendar, featuring firefighters and sheriff's deputies who participated in rescue and recovery efforts, sparked anger because it planned to list the names of those killed. See Phil Bacharach, "Profiting from Tragedy," *Oklahoma Gazette,* December 28, 1995.

12. Information about the bench in *Official News Release,* Strategic Communications Wing ONE, Tinker Air Force Base, December 23, 1996; copy in author's files.

13. "Alive in the Midst of Destruction," *Progressive Florist,* August 1995, p. 29; another interesting form of memorial expression was the creation of five life-size plaster figures by art students at Oak Hills High School in Ohio: "a firefighter, representing rescue workers; a woman holding a teddy bear, representing children; a woman preparing to hoist an American flag; and a man and woman consoling each other." "Art Commemorates Blast's Heroes," *Cincinnati Enquirer,* n.d. These figures were eventually displayed at Enterprise Square in Oklahoma City. See "Cincinnati Statues Honor Oklahomans at Enterprise Square, USA," news release, February 15, 1996, archives.

14. "Quilts to Comfort Survivors," *Williamsport Sun-Gazette,* August 12, 1995; November 6, 1995.

15. I was able to see the quilt in the archives; quoted material is from letters from various artists about their work in a notebook on the quilt. These quilts are not public memorial acts in the same way that protest quilts such as the NAMES Project AIDS memorial quilt or peace quilts done in various countries, but it does share with them "the tactile, foldable quality of the cloth, the uniqueness of each panel, and the variation that speaks of the different hands that crafted it." For an insightful discussion of the AIDS quilt and the memorial function of quilting, see "Conversations with the Dead: Bearing Witness in the AIDS Memorial Quilt," in Marita Sturken, *Tangled Memories: The Vietnam War, The AIDS Epidemic, and the Politics of Remembering* (Berkeley: University of California Press, 1997), pp. 183-219. Quote is from p. 184.

16. Color images of these quilts appear in "Sewing Comfort out of Grief: The Oklahoma City Children's Memorial Quilt Exhibition," *Art Quilt Magazine* 8 (1997), pp. 16-23. Quote from p. 16. The archives contains approximately three dozen quilts that were sent to Oklahoma City.

17. The City of Oklahoma City, *Final Report: Alfred P. Murrah Federal Building Bombing, April 19, 1995* (Stillwater, Okla.: Fire Protection Publications, Oklahoma State University, 1996), p. 67; See also "Bomb Shrine Draws Visitors and Memorials," *Daily Oklahoman,* May 4, 1995; "Workers Pay Respects at Ruins," *Daily Oklahoman,* May 6, 1995; see also *Daily Oklahoman,* May 19, 1995, which reported that thirty to forty boxes of material had been stored by the city. On Friday, May 5, the memorial at 6th and Hudson was moved to the front of the Murrah remains, *Daily Oklahoman,* May 7, 1995.

18. Jon Hansen, *Oklahoma Rescue* (New York: Ballantine, 1995), pp. 53-54.

19. ABC News, *20/20*, "Terror in the Heartland," April 21, 1995, transcript 1516-2; *Daily Oklahoman*, April 25, 1995.

20. Calvin Moser, interview, March 20, 1999. His drawing appeared in the *Daily Oklahoman*.

21. Only several months before the memorial's dedication on the fifth anniversary of the bombing, I taught a special seminar at the University of Oklahoma. Someone who was still displeased with the memorial, believing his proposal the "right" one, sent me materials hoping that I would even at that late date lobby the foundation to change its plans!

22. The prospectus for this memorial included a number of commercial opportunities designed to benefit relief efforts. Maquettes of the statue could be sold to raise funds for the project, the prospectus announced, a jewelry line could be developed, and sales of posters and T-shirts could support charitable organizations.

23. Elizabeth A. Lawrence, "The Tamed Wild: Symbolic Bears in American Culture," in Ray B. Browne, Marshall W. Fishwick, and Kevin O. Browne, eds., *Dominant Symbols: Popular Culture* (Bowling Green, Ohio: Bowling Green State University Popular Press, 1990), pp. 143-144. Lawrence's fascinating essay briefly notes the special reverence that many cultures have had for bears, and she traces the origin of the teddy bear to a Brooklyn toy store owner, who created them for the Christmas season in 1902. His "inspiration" came from a *Washington Post* cartoonist's drawings of a bear hunt of Theodore Roosevelt, one of which depicted the bear as a frightened cub. Teddy bears, Lawrence speculates, "are idealized beings adapted solely to specific human needs. . . . With our teddy bears, whose sinlessness and solicitude sustains us, at least temporarily, we can make our world safer" (p. 151).

24. Fran Corey, interview, April 28, 1999. The owners of a small company, Treasured Teddy Bears, in Cherry Hill, New Jersey, offered to create teddy bears out of sentimental garments for children affected by the bombing.

25. "Stuffed Bear Takes Vacant Seat at UCO," *Daily Oklahoman*, April 28, 1995. The Teddy Bear Memorial Wall, created by Raymond Silvia, founder of the National Child Awareness Day Committee, was displayed in Oklahoma City in early June 1995. A wall with teddy bears dedicated to the children killed in the bombing joined other memorial teddy bear wall segments, and "any family member who has lost a young child is invited to bring an 8-inch teddy bear wearing a shirt with all the child's information printed on it." See "Teddy Bear Memorial to Honor 17 [*sic*] Children Who Died in Blast," *Daily Oklahoman*, June 2, 1995. The restored Center City Post Office, dedicated on March 13, 1998, was designated "Teddy Bear Station," and a teddy bear postal stamp was issued.

26. See, for example, "Memorial to Victims Has Local Support," *Edmond Sun*, August 25, 1995; "Bomb Memorial Nearly Ready," *Edmond Evening Sun*, March 7, 1997; "Ceremonies to Honor Victims," *Daily Oklahoman*, April 4, 1997; "Families Appreciate Park's Bomb Memorial," *Edmond Sun*, April 13,1997; "Memorial Brings Release For Families, Rescuers," *Edmond Sun*, April 15, 1997. The University of Central Oklahoma, located in Edmond, lost approximately thirty alumni and relatives in the bombing, and on the second anniversary the Heartland Plaza was dedicated on campus, designed to "provide lush vegetation, fountains, and seat-

ing for quiet reflection and meditation." See " 'A Place to Remember,' " *Edmond Evening Sun*, April 13, 1997.

27. A resident of Norman, Oklahoma, suggested a Smithsonian Museum of Native American History that would include a memorial to the bombing, a "lasting tribute to survivorship that should be a centerpiece of the...museum."

28. People suggested special flowers to remember the children, baby's breath and lilies of the valley, for example. Many family members and survivors created their own tree and garden memorials. See, for example, survivor Amy Petty's description of her memorial garden in "Remembering Oklahoma City," *Family Circle*, September 17, 1996, pp. 44-49. A Tulsa resident created a memorial garden in his front yard, in the shape of Oklahoma. See "Man Creates OKC Memorial out of Yard," *Tulsa World*, May 10, 1995. The Oklahoma Master Gardener Association remembered the murdered children through a wrought iron ball on a wrought iron pedestal filled with rose rocks. Some family members found it important to create their own memorial garden. Kathleen Treanor, for example, whose daughter Ashley was murdered in the bombing, said that "all the love and nurturing that I was no longer able to lavish on her was put into her garden." Kathleen Treanor, "Ashley's Story," unpublished manuscript, author's files.

29. "Memorial Planned in Holy Land for Bombing Victims," *Saturday Oklahoman and Times*, August 26, 1995; letter from Women's Zionist Organization in uncatalogued materials, archives.

30. In addition to creating elaborate memorial environments, the Internet has spawned cybermemorial shrines and services from simple single-page memorials with photographs to memorial scrapbooks "filled with photos, poems, images of angels with flapping wings, snippets of a voice from an answering machine, e-mailed messages from friends and strangers." See "Web Memorials Never Forget," *Edmonton Sun*, July 7, 1999.

31. There was very little correspondence or editorial discussion arguing that no memorial was needed. An eighth grader in Midwest City, Oklahoma, just a few miles from Oklahoma City, asked, "Why are you planning to spend millions on something to remember the past? Have you seen the outside of downtown lately? Homeless...Destitute...You are ignoring the lives being lived....Why not take the dollars you have raised and spend them on the living? (Dobson papers archives). A letter to the *Daily Oklahoman* noted that while there was little money for shelters for the impoverished, millions had been raised for the memorial. "Which is the more immediate problem? A roof over someone's head and a bath, and a meal? Or an inanimate symbol of respect and remembrance" (n.d.).

32. "Victim Search Could End Today," *Daily Oklahoman*, May 4, 1995; ABC News, *Good Morning America*, May 19, 1995, transcript 2331. A few days later, Keating characterized the building as a "monument to tragedy and horror, and it should come down as quickly as possible....It is an agonizing sight." *Daily Oklahoman*, May 23, 1995.

33. All quotes from Phillip Thompson in this and subsequent paragraphs come from interviews on January 28, 1998, and March 19, 1998. Whicher, personal communication with author.

34. Dot Hill, interview, March 23, 1999.

35. All quotes from Richard Williams in this and subsequent paragraphs come from interviews on March 16, 1998, and May 5, 1998, and from other informal conversations.

36. James Loftis, interview, April 28, 1999.

37. The Chicago architectural firm Ross, Barney & Jankowski had the task of designing a new federal campus, a two-block area just north of the Murrah site. See "A Safer Federal Building for Oklahoma City," *New York Times*, August 22, 1999.

38. Leo P. Whinery, "Who Was Alfred P. Murrah?" *Sooner Magazine*, Spring 1996, p. 3. Murrah graduated from the University of Oklahoma College of Law in 1928 and was in private practice until 1937, when he was appointed a U.S. district judge for Oklahoma. In 1940 he was appointed to the U.S. Court of Appeals for the Tenth Circuit, becoming its chief judge in 1959. In 1970, he was appointed director of the Federal Judicial Center. Judge Murrah died in 1975. Whinery characterized him as an "innovator in the fields of pre-trial procedure, complex and protracted litigation and sentencing" (p. 3). He also observed the "compelling irony" of the bombing, namely, "the lawless destruction of a building named in honor of a man who had devoted a lifetime to the rule of law and the administration of justice throughout the United States" (p. 3). The *United Methodist Review* offered readers Paul Murrah's reminiscences of his father. An attorney and resident of Oklahoma City, Paul Murrah said that had his father been alive when the building was bombed, "it wouldn't have made a bit of difference if it was named for him. He would have been in the churches with the families and he would have been with the workers in the rubble.... And it would have been with total conviction, sincerity, with nothing whatever to gain." And a 1996 biography of Judge Murrah observed that while the Judge would have been "saddened and angered by the senseless violence" ... he would also have been "incredibly proud of how Oklahomans responded to the tragedy," proud of the "sense of community which was so central to Murrah's being." John A. Lovelace, "A Son Remembers Alfred P. Murrah," *United Methodist Review*, June 16, 1995. See also Von Russell Creel, Bob Burke, and Kenny A. Franks, *American Jurist: The Life of Alfred P. Murrah* (Oklahoma Heritage Association: Western Heritage Books, 1996), pp. vii and viii.

39. "Demolition Set for Tuesday"; and "Building's Fall to Expose Public Feelings," *Daily Oklahoman*, May 18, 1995. The implosion so moved a seventy-three-year-old resident of Los Angeles that he designed a pyramid, with a "large acrylic tear drop, flooded with indirect lighting to create an everlasting memorial." Anna Sterling, a survivor who worked for the Oklahoma Department of Securities, observed that "the absence of the structure against the Oklahoma City skyline on Memorial Day echoes a silent memorial to all those affected on that day of days." See her personal account in the archives. Also concerned about the implosion was a nun who wrote Mayor Norick suggesting that the event be "ritualized." She included a possible memorial service, including a prayer that asked the deity to "make this a place of sacred remembrance. And, as we clear this sacred space, clear our hearts, comfort our people, continue your healing work among us now

and as we live into the future." She suggested the playing of "Taps," and the singing of the hymn "Holy Ground."

40. Garner Stoll, interview, January 30, 1998; Stephen Jones, interview, June 9, 1999. The Oklahoma Citizens Militia also objected to the implosion. One of their spokesmen said, "We're trying to find the truth, whatever that may be.... I think if we stop them from burying the evidence, it will stand out like a sore thumb." "Opposition May Delay Building's Demolition," *Daily Oklahoman*, May 16, 1995.

41. Jerry Ennis interview, February 26, 1999. The *Daily Oklahoman* of May 10, 1995, stated that "there was an early and overwhelming consensus not to save the structure. The remaining question was how to raze the structure quickly."

42. This in a file, "Poems forwarded to Kathleen Treanor, archives"

43. Carl Smith, *Urban Disorder*, p. 94.

44. "Some People Put Value on Objects Horrible to Others," *Sunday Oklahoman*, May 21, 1995.

45. "Crews Nearing End of Search," *Daily Oklahoman*, May 29, 1995; Kates, interview, February 26, 1999.

46. Heffner's comparison of Murrah rubble to pieces of the Berlin Wall was most appropriate. In *The Ghosts of Berlin: Confronting German History in the Urban Landscape* (Chicago: University of Chicago Press, 1997), Brian Ladd wrote of the "aura" of pieces of the wall, "that bespoke our deliverance from the Cold War" (p. 8). Like pieces of Murrah rubble, these "magical properties translated into its market value. The wall, symbol of the epic confrontation between capitalism and communism, became a capitalist commodity. Enterprising locals sold hacked-off pieces of concrete from tables set up at Checkpoint Charlie and the Brandenburg Gate. Others would rent you a hammer and chisel so that you could chop your own. Still other entrepreneurs, more ambitious and better capitalized, filled crates and trucks with this East German state property and supplied genuine Wall fragments to American department stores in time for the Christmas shopping season" (pp. 8-9). Heffner was not alone in thinking about the Berlin Wall. A former public school teacher in North Carolina wrote Governor Keating, urging him to "consider keeping part of the building as our 'Berlin Wall.'"

47. There are hundreds of federal memorials around the nation to the bombing, some of which use Murrah rubble.

48. See, for example, Denise Chong, *The Girl in the Picture: The Story of Kim Phuc, the Photograph, and the Vietnam War* (1999), and John Berger's "Photographs of Agony," in *About Looking* (New York: Pantheon, 1980).

49. Cindy Alexander, interview, August 13, 1999.

50. Ginny Moser, interview, March 20, 1999. Ginny Moser wrote an anguished three-page reflection entitled "A Letter to God's Angels," found among the many personal accounts housed in the archives.

51. John Avera, personal account in archives.

52. All quoted material in this and subsequent paragraph comes from Avera, interview, July 28, 1999.

53. All quoted material in this and subsequent paragraphs, unless otherwise noted, comes from Fields, interview, April 27, 1999. Baylee Almon's pediatrician, Dr. John

Beavers, received news that a "young female child was brought to Saint Anthony Hospital and was dead on arrival. I went to the morgue and viewed the body of a baby girl, lifeless and covered with dust, dirt and debris. The child's head was wrapped in a gauze bandage due most likely to a head injury. At first I did not recognize the child as being Baylee. Maybe it was due to the child's altered appearance because of the dust and dirt and bandages, or perhaps it was just my subconscious which would not allow me to see this child as the patient that I had known and cared for. I left the morgue and then returned with my office manager, and we both took a closer look at the innocent child who lay lifeless on the table. At that point we both knew this was Bayle and that she was gone. . . . In all my years of medicine, telling Aren Almon that Baylee was dead was the hardest and saddest thing I have ever had to do" (Beavers personal account in archives).

54. See "Gas Firm Wins Lawsuit Over Bombing Pictures," *Daily Oklahoman*, October 3, 1996, and "U.S. Judge Rules Photographer's Firing Was Legal," *Daily Oklahoman*, May 30, 1997. This ruling, in LaRue's second lawsuit in a year, stated that because Oklahoma Natural Gas "was exercising its legal rights as the owner of the photographs when it demanded that LaRue relinquish his claim to the photographs, ONG did not engage in extortion." See also "Photo Unites Pair as Fates Divide Them," *Dallas Morning News*, September 24, 1995.

55. All quoted material from Charles Porter in this and subsequent paragraphs comes from Porter, interview, January 13, 1999.

56. Some newspapers received angry calls from readers when the photograph appeared, and some printed justifications for using the photograph. When it appeared in the *San Diego Union-Tribune*, "80 readers called the newspaper to complain. Only seven commended the paper." See "Amateur's photo seen 'Round the World,'" *News Photographer*, July 25, 1995. See also Richard Cunningham, "Photographs (Again) Worth Several Words as Readers Complain," *Quill*, June 1995, pp. 16-17. Editorial staff at several newspapers held lengthy discussions about whether or not to use the photograph. The *Philadelphia Inquirer*'s national editor said "there wasn't a photo that better captured what happened there, so we decided to use it," but the *Sacramento Bee*'s assistant managing editor for news viewed it as "the picture of a corpse," and "we chose to go with a photo of a live child rather than a dead one." Both quoted in Joe Strupp, "The Photo Felt around the world," *Editor and Publisher*, May 13, 1995, pp. 12-13. See also "Reality Pushed to Edge," *Chicago Tribune*, April 23, 1995. Steve Benson, a Pulitzer Prize winning editorial cartoonist for the *Arizona Republic* was strongly criticized by Governor Keating, Aren Almon-Kok, Chris Fields, and the International Association of Fire Fighters for a cartoon depicting Fields labeled as a "death penalty fanatic," holding Baylee Almon, and saying, "Oh, stop your whining," as Baylee says, "Please, no more killing." Benson, who serves as a volunteer police officer, said, "It was a metaphor. The child represents the good in society, purity, trust. A baby doesn't come into the world with blood lust. In this cartoon, the firefighter represents and is labeled 'death penalty fanatics,' wedded to the notion that society must exact revenge in the form of human blood. I'm saying listen to the children, 'No more killing'" (Benson quoted in the *Arizona Republic*, June 20, 1997. See also, "Fire-

fighters Seek 'Republic' Cartoonist's Apology," *Arizona Republic*, June 19, 1997; "Tot's Image Stabs at Hearts Again," *USA Today*, June 20, 1997); "A Letter to Our Readers," *Arizona Republic*, June 21, 1997; "National Furor over Editorial Cartoon," *Editor and Publisher*, July 5, 1997.

57. Brooks Douglass, interview, July 30, 1999. I thank him for letting me read the transcripts of the proceedings.

58. During Almon-Kok's attempt to stop the unauthorized use of the image, Lester LaRue's attorney asked her about this licensing agreement. She responded, "I want the use of the picture to be under control... my daughter's dead, but she's still my daughter and I still want to protect her." Under questioning from her own attorney, Brooks Douglass, she said that she understood that the statue would be sold as a commemorative item to cities and fire stations, for example. See the deposition of Aren Almon, July 29, 1996, U.S. District Court, West District, Oklahoma, case CIV-95-1557-C.

59. A reproduction of the card and the advertising is in an uncatalogued box of materials in the archives and in author's files.

60. Roger P. Baresel, president, Advantage Marketing Systems, Inc., to Chris Fields, October 23, 1995, Douglass papers.

61. All quotes by Aren Almon-Kok in this and subsequent paragraphs, unless otherwise noted, come from interviews on July 10, 1998, and November 10, 1998. Appearing on ABC's *Nightline* on April 5, 1996, with Aren Almon-Kok and John Avera, Chris Fields remarked, "When they talked about other victims, they showed... a studio portrait, or a family picture that they had.... When they talked about Baylee, they always showed the photo, and I think Aren wants Baylee to be remembered as Baylee Almon with a smile across her face, not—not Baylee Almon, the baby in the fireman's arms" (Transcript 3880).

62. See "Two Years after Losing Her Baby in the Oklahoma Bombing, Aren Almon Finds a Moment of Bliss," *People Weekly*, April 21, 1997 pp. 155-156. See also, Aren Almon, "A Mother's Long Goodbye," *Newsweek*, April 14, 1997, p. 40; "Baylee's Mom Remembers Daughter's Birthday Party," *Daily Oklahoman*, April 18, 1996; "Victim's Mother, Airman to Wed," *Daily Oklahoman*, September 15, 1996.

63. Aren Almon-Kok was not the only recipient of offers to use vacation facilities from members of the public. One letter informed Mayor Norick, "We are extending to any person or persons you feel need a very private retreat from the terror and heartache you have all gone through and are going through, several of our homes tucked away in Spirit Lake, Idaho." Another offered a two bedroom condominium in St. Croix, Virgin Islands. "I don't want any publicity for this," the mayor was told, "just to reach out and help."

64. I am very grateful to Aren Almon-Kok for letting me read through materials in her home. I do not recall how I came upon the Web site.

65. Several undated newspaper articles from the *Dothan Eagle* may be found in uncatalogued materials in the archive.

66. Many family members, particularly those whose young children had been murdered and who became identifiable through the media, received numerous memorial items, as well as some bizarre offers. Edye Smith Stowe, for example,

whose two boys Chase and Colton were killed, received a letter from a man offering her his nephew as a replacement for the boys. She also received football helmets, Bibles, statues, embroidery, candles, announcements that fifteen boys were named after them, and jewelry. Local fireman gave her the corner of the blanket that they used to carry the boys out of the building. "I received thousands of letters and sent everyone a thank you card with the boys' image on it," she said. "I still keep in touch with approximately fifty people. I got marriage requests, letters from prisoners, the mentally ill, school classes, and poems from people around the world" (Stowe, interview, July 27, 1999).

67. See "Artwork Unveiled at St. Anthony," *Daily Oklahoman*, June 2, 1995; "Picture of Healing," *Dallas Morning News*, April 26, 1997. One woman was moved by the Holy Spirit, she wrote, to paint a vision that appeared to her husband and also to a friend, a vision filled with angels covering the Murrah Building. "An angel is taking an animated Baylee from the arms of the fireman, and the child is pointing in joy as she recognizes Jesus." This from a four-page document, "Angels All Around," in uncatalogued materials, archives, and a copy in author's files. I thought of this document when I visited the Nicoma Park First Baptist Church, in a small rural community a short drive from Oklahoma City. This church lost five members, ranging in age from five to twenty-four. In the sanctuary, there are three stained glass windows dedicated to victims. One was dedicated to Anthony Christopher Cooper II. It depicts Jesus standing in a burgundy robe, holding a child. It is a gentle and nurturing image. It is unlike the fireman and the baby, in that this child has not been killed, but it is like the image in the tenderness of the embrace. I also saw several images of firemen and children that depicted the fireman in the role of a rescuer, not a recoverer of bodies. In the reception area of the offices of Midwest Wrecking, for example, there is a large desktop sculpture from the Oklahoma State Firefighting Association dedicated to Midwest Wrecking for their work during recovery efforts. There is a seated fireman, perhaps in a window ledge, legs outside as if trying to maintain his balance, holding an infant as flames lick the edge of the window.

68. See the *Daily Oklahoman*, May 5-6, 1995, for Keating's comments.

69. A telephone interview with author, August 26, 1999. I also thank Sam Butcher for a telephone interview, December 6, 2000.

70. After expert sleuth work, the Memorial Foundation's Jane Thomas found this forgotten statue after I told her that Aren Almon-Kok thought that it had been stored by the city. We found it in an Oklahoma City wastewater building. It was made of black scrap metal, nine feet across at the base, and over eleven feet in height, weighing fifteen hundred pounds. The statue was shipped by truck from Virginia, was never on public display, but was for some months kept behind a curtain in the Myriad Convention Center. It is now the property of the Oklahoma City National Memorial Foundation.

71. Karl Watkins, interview, March 17, 1998. See "Oklahoma City Memorial: An International Design Competition," p. 7, in uncatalogued materials, archives. Copy in author's files.

72. Press packet, "Protecting People First Foundation," copy in author's files.

73. See, for example, Thomas Allen, *Offerings at the Wall: Artifacts from the Vietnam Veterans Memorial Collection* (Atlanta: Turner, 1995); Kristin Ann Hass, *Carried to the Wall: American Memory and the Vietnam Veterans Memorial* (Berkeley: University of California Press, 1998). There is also a collection of material from a fence erected near Columbine High School in Clement Park to memorialize those murdered in the shootings April 20, 1999. See "Park Officials Cope with Mountain of Grief in Colo.," *USA Today*, March 23, 2000.

74. Martha Cooper and Joseph Sciorra, *R.I.P.: Memorial Wall Art* (New York: Henry Holt, 1994), p. 10; second quote from, "Old Tradition of Roadside Crosses Is Renewed: Accident Victim Memorials Grow in Popularity," *Salt Lake Tribune*, May 18, 1996. Informative newspaper accounts of various spontaneous memorials include: "A Shrine for Palatine?; Victim's Dad Wants to Raze Brown's, Memorialize 7 Slain," *Chicago Sun-Times*, February 24, 1993; "On Walls, Memories of the Slain Are Kept," *New York Times*, January 28, 1994; "Shrine to Colosio a pilgrimage for mourning in Mexico," *San Diego Union-Tribune*, April 15, 1994; "Where a Tragedy Occurred, A Coming Together," *New York Times*, January 22, 1995; "S. C. Lake Becomes Shrine for Smith Boys," *Des Moines Register*, January 22, 1995; "Mourners Move Cemetery to the Street With Spontaneous Shrines," *Los Angeles Times*, February 5, 1995; "When Grief Becomes A Roadside Attraction," *Chicago Sun-Times*, November 14, 1995; "Memorial Dedicated for Teens Shot in a Field Six Months Ago," *Jupiter Courier* (Jupiter, Fla.), September 25, 1996; "Sympathy of Strangers," *Omaha World-Herald*, January 26, 1997; "The Blooming of Public Shrines," *Vancouver Sun*, November 7, 1997; "Monuments to the Dead Take On Decisive Hues," *Vancouver Sun*, December 6, 1997; "Memorial to Child Victims," *Sacramento Bee*, May 21, 1999; "Roadside Remembrances," *Bangor Daily News* (Bangor, Me.), April 25, 1998. There is an occasional "letter to the editor" complaining about such spontaneous memorials. A March 19, 1999, letter to the *St. Louis Post-Dispatch*, for example, complained about the "depressing effect of passing these [roadside memorials] on vacations, traveling to and from birthdays, weddings and holidays with friends and family." This Missouri resident wondered if it wouldn't be more appropriate to "grieve at the burial place? Isn't it more respectful to the dead to be remembered with dignity instead of left for gawkers to ogle the unsightly reminders from the road?"

75. This ongoing stream of small crosses replaced large wooden crosses placed near the Survivor Tree in the Easter season just before the first anniversary. GSA removed them, and Memorial Foundation curator Jane Thomas remembered, "I was haunted by them. It looked like a graveyard from the Civil War."

76. Cooper and Sciorra, *R.I.P. Memorial Wall Art,* p. 14; see also C. Allen Haney, Christina Leimer, and Juliann Lowery, "Spontaneous Memorialization: Violent Death and Emerging Mourning Ritual," *Omega: The Journal of Death and Dying* 35, no. 2 (1997): 159-171.

77. Jane Thomas notes that the Memorial Foundation's archives contains "26,768 cataloged artifacts . . . 1296-cubic-feet of unsorted documents and artifacts, contents conservatively estimated at over 300,000 pieces." The collection contains much more than just material from the fence, of course. There are "150.5 linear feet of sorted documents, 729 individual documents and 38 oversized boxes of documents.

...20,289 photographs...9 linear feet of vertical files and 12 linear feet of books." Communication with author, February 7, 2001. I have spent innumerable hours with Jane Thomas working in the archives, and often I just wrote notes to myself about our conversations. On several occasions we did have "formal" interviews, usually consisting of our walking together through the collection and having her talk about particular categories or even individual items. These I can date, but other conversations I cannot. One of our "walk-throughs" took place on September 14, 1998.

Collection of materials began shortly after the bombing, when Bob Blackburn, then deputy director of the Oklahoma Historical Society and William Welge, director of archives and manuscript division provided space in the Historical Society's building to house collections. The Murrah Federal Building Task Force, convened by Mayor Norick in July 1995, appointed an archives subcommittee to "identify and preserve documents and bombing artifacts for historic research, future exhibits, and a possible museum." Eventually, a GSA warehouse used by federal agencies for storage of investigative materials housed the archives. Quoted material comes from Carol Brown, " 'Out of the Rubble': Building a Contemporary History Archive. The Oklahoma City National Memorial Archives," *Perspectives* [newsletter of the American Historical Association], October 1999, pp. 28-32. See also "Overview of Oklahoma City Memorial Foundation (OCMF) Collections," July 22, 1996, and "Holding on to History," *Dallas Morning News*, April 16, 1996. There are innumerable newspaper articles about the fence. A representative example is "Perimeter of Pain," *Washington Post*, January 25, 1996.

78. A photographic exhibition sponsored by the Oklahoma Arts Council, Heritage Education Resources and the Oklahoma City National Memorial Foundation spoke directly to the public significance of the fence. In May 1998, a call for entries went to Oklahoma photographers for submissions. Eventually twenty-nine photographs were chosen for an exhibition entitled *As We See It: The Murrah Memorial Fence.* The exhibition, viewers were informed, "honors the victims and survivors of the bombing... affirms the persistence of the human spirit and capacity for compassion... explores how Oklahomans have captured this chain link memorial on film." Accompanying the photographs were remarks from the photographers. Norman, Oklahoma, artist Jamie Haxtou said, "I was amazed to see all the images. At first it was local, you know. They were very personal. The things that were being placed on the Fence were very personal. Notes, and little items, and a lot of ribbons and flowers. And as time went on, it amazed me how our little circle got bigger. I remember going down there and people from Ireland had put things down... how people from all over the world; our little circle turned into the entire world." The exhibition was held in the East Gallery at the state capitol from April 13 to May 29, 1999. There was also discussion at the Arts Council of a touring exhibition. I thank Betty Price, executive director of the Oklahoma Arts Council, and Debby Williams, the council's visual arts director, for sharing exhibition materials with me.

79. Williamson quoted in *USA Today*, August 29, 1996. Promotional material notes that the Greene family "has been visited by angels and asked to help redefine what it means to be a good neighbor and recapture the American dream. So Russell, his

wife, Claire, their son Joshua, daughter, Dinah, and Russell's mother Hattie, and nephew Nathaniel, have packed their belongings into a trailer and hit the road, breathing in all the sights and sounds of the U.S." (Ferguson uncatalogued materials, archives).

80. The two-part segment, "A Hand Up Is Never A Hand Out," appeared in May 1998. The text of the second segment is in the Ferguson uncatalogued materials, archives.

81. The archives subcommittee of the Memorial Foundation has written guidelines for items on the fence in addition to materials relating to victims. Fragile items (e.g., paper) are removed within thirty days, "durable" items (e.g., teddy bears) are left until an area needs to be thinned. For the entire policy, see the Memorial Foundation's news release, *Thousands of Items Left on Fence in One Year Represent Thousands of Lives Touched by Event.*

82. On Christmas Eve 1995, an Associated Press report declared that "a few Christmas decorations, withered flowers and faded ribbons still hang on the fence surrounding the empty site of the bombed federal building." *The Dallas Morning News* of December 24, 1995, titled this report, "Memorials Dwindle at Site of Bombing." Contrary to this report, memorial energies have remained remarkably constant at the fence, increasing at holidays and the anniversary of the bombing.

83. Memo, July 8, 1997, Dobson papers, archives. Poems about the Survivor Tree appear on the fence. For example, "The Old Survivor Tree" has the tree talking about its purpose to visitors:

> I too bare the bomber's scars
> For all the world to see
> Now I know my purpose
> As the Old Survivor tree
> I have lived one-hundred years
> As I stand here leafy green today
> A symbol of living hope
> To all who pass this way.

84. Welch, interview, July 7, 1998. See also "Task Force Wants Elm Tree to Be Part of Bomb Memorial," *Journal-Record*, March 1, 1996; "Tree Becomes Living Symbol," *Dallas Morning News*, April 19, 1997; "Survivor Tree Gets a Little TLC," *Daily Oklahoman,* February 25, 1998.

85. Mark Bays, telephone interview, September 20, 1999.

86. Oklahoma Urban and Community Forestry 1998 grant application, "Life of the Oklahoma City Survivor Tree," Survivor Tree materials, archives. Seedlings were first distributed at the second anniversary. The Oklahoma Forestry Services provided survivors and family members an instruction sheet on how to plant and care for the seedlings. It told them that the seeds were "the first generation produced by the Survivor Tree following the tragedy of April 19, 1995. The provided mulch packet comes from Survivor Tree branches pruned last year." See "Survivor Elm Tree Seedling," Survivor Tree materials, archives.

87. "Remarks by the President at Ceremony on Behalf of the Oklahoma City Memorial Foundation," August 13, 1997. Survivor Tree materials, archives. During con-

struction of the memorial, activity near the tree was closely monitored to minimize impact to its root system. Memorial design will ensure that the tree is well
protected. An elevated walkway around the tree allows air movement, and the tree
has its own irrigation system.

88. Heath, interview, March 19, 1999.

CHAPTER 5

1. Jones, interview, September 18, 1998; John and Sandy Cole, interview, February
   26, 1999. Treanor, interview, January 30, 1998. I also thank Kathleen Treanor, who
   let me read some of her own writing, "Ashley's Story."
2. Robert Johnson, interview, January 28, 1998. All quotes from Robert Johnson in
   this and subsequent paragraphs from this interview and from meetings on September 15, 1998, September 23, 1999, and various other informal discussions.
   Mayor Norick announced the Leadership of the Task Force on June 13, 1995.
3. Jimmy Goodman, interview, April 27, 1999.
4. A brief history of the task force is found in the Oklahoma City Memorial Foundation Memorial Mission Statement, adopted March 26, 1996. Quoted material,
   p. 2.
5. Denman, interview, January 29, 1998. All quotes from Rowland Denman in this
   and subsequent paragraphs come from this interview unless otherwise noted.
6. Phyllis Stough, interview, September 14, 1998.
7. According to the task force document presented at the Murrah Federal Building
   Memorial Task Force Orientation Meeting, St. Luke's Methodist Church, July 26,
   1995. The purpose of this subcommittee is "to carefully focus on the feelings and
   opinions of those most directly affected by the bombing. All members of Victims'
   Families and Survivors Liaison Subcommittee are invited to participate not only
   on this subcommittee, but also on the other subcommittees if they so desire."
   Other committees were as follows: administration, archives, budget, design solicitation, government liaison, memorial ideas input, public fund-raising and public
   and private grants, public relations.
8. After learning that his mother's remains could not be recovered until after the
   implosion—indeed, might never be recovered—his family had held a memorial
   service in her hometown of El Reno, with many firemen who had been active in
   the rescue and recovery efforts in attendance. "The church was packed," he recalls,
   "and I remember thinking 'no way would there be so many people here had she
   died some other way.' It was at that moment I realized that this was way beyond
   me and my family."
9. Hill, interview, March 23, 1999. The *Memorial News*, a newsletter for families and
   other "constituents" reported in its September 1995 issue that at this meeting
   "Mayor Norick was asked if there were other committees which were developing
   a plan for the downtown area. He stated, 'As far as I am concerned, there is no
   other committee. This is the one that will be heard and this is the one who will say
   what is to happen.' He went on to say that both he and the City Council realize

that to not listen to the families would be political suicide and that no one wants that. He also said that the majority of the people assisting the families were an incredible resource and were all dedicated to the cause and truly wanted to help."

10. LeAnn Jenkins, interview, June 7, 1999.

11. Amy Petty, interview, October 22, 1998.

12. Nichols, interview, August 12, 1999.

13. See design solicitation committee reports, September 11, 1995 and September 14, 1995, in uncatalogued design competition materials, archives.

14. See "Memorial Ideas Input Subcommittee, Memorial Constituents Subgroup Final Report, February 27, 1996," uncatalogued memorial process materials in archive. Those identified as constituents in the final report included churches, neighbors in surrounding areas, Regency Tower dwellers, clergy, federal and state agencies and employees housed in the area, students and teachers, medical and hospital staff, mental health professionals, rescue workers, volunteers, the arts community, business and property owners in surrounding area, nonprofit and agency staff, media, visitors at the site, and mail correspondents. According to the report, 127 agencies were contacted.

15. Quoted material from appendix B of the mission statement, the final report of the memorial ideas input subcommittee, "Summary of Public Input," pp. 10-11.

16. All the surveys are included in the archives.

17. Quoted material from the preface to the mission statement, and from the report of the design solicitation committee to Murrah Memorial Committee, September 19, 1995, uncatalogued design competition materials, archives.

18. Beth Shortt, interview, July 6, 1998. I am extremely grateful to Beth Shortt for sending me files on her work with the mission statement and with the survivor definition committee. Quoted material is from either our interview or this material.

19. Quoted material in this and the previous paragraph comes from the "Operational Plan," p. 9.

20. Paul Spreiregen, "Oklahoma Memorial—A Path Fraught With Pitfalls?" *Competitions*, Spring 1996, p. 2. For another criticism of the process, see Saunders Schultz and Theodore Wofford, "Oklahoma City Memorial—A Dissenting Opinion," *Competitions*, Summer 1997, p. 3.

21. Beth Tolbert, interview, September 18, 1998.

22. Donald Stastny, telephone interview, September 6, 2000. All subsequent quoted material comes from this interview.

23. Eventually, the organization became the Oklahoma City National Memorial Foundation.

24. These issues were raised in meetings of the task force on June 19, 1996 and July 18, 1996. Minutes available in Dobson papers, archives.

25. Unless otherwise noted, material used in this section is from the Oklahoma City Planning Commission file. I am very grateful to Garner Stoll, Oklahoma City's planning director, for providing me with this file, including a videotape of the planning commission meeting of September 12, 1996, and for his helpful interview on January 29, 1998, and further telephone conversation on September 15, 1999.

26. The president of the Portland, Oregon, investment corporation that owned the Regency Towers wrote Robert Johnson, "We had high hopes that the leadership we showed would be followed by other city efforts to quickly rebuild in the area. To date, nothing has occurred in the area that surrounds the Regency Tower. It's not easy to sell apartment living in an area that has become a wasteland."

27. Watkins, interview, March 17, 1998; task force letter to Paul Brum, director, Public Works, August 12, 1996.

28. Steven Parish defines hierarchy as "any practice or meaning system through which inequality or dominance is culturally organized, conceptualized, and valued." See Parish, *Hierarchy and Its Discontents* (Philadelphia: University of Pennsylvania Press, 1996), p. 70.

29. The site, administered by the National Park Service, is called the Washita Battlefield National Historic Site. Interpretive materials talk clearly about the controversy, however.

30. For such a call to action, see "A Safer World for Children," *Press-Telegram* (Long Beach, Calif.), April 20, 1995.

31. Marian Wright Edelman, "Saving the Children; Taking a Stand," *Emerge*, June 1996, pp. 58+; some editorials focused on gun violence, noting that "the insanity that ignites the fuse to a weapon of mass murder is the same insanity that pulls the trigger of the handguns that senselessly kill shopkeepers, police officers, schoolchildren, neighbors." "Who Mourns For Gun Victims," *Des Moines Register*, May 12, 1995; Bill Linn, "Hurt in Their Own Homes; Disaster Strikes Our Children Every Day," *Phoenix Gazette*, May 13, 1995. Also see "The Hidden Epidemic of Fatal Child Abuse," *San Francisco Chronicle*, April 30, 1995.

32. Dave Shiflett, "Just Put Yourself in Militias' Boots for a Little While," *Denver Rocky Mountain Post*, May 7, 1995. Alexander Cockburn also calls attention to the forgotten dead of Waco in "Beat The Devil," *Nation*, May 15, 1995, pp. 659-660. Still another group of "forgotten" victims was acknowledged in the wake of the bombing in a letter to the *Buffalo News*, May 5, 1995. "The death toll in Oklahoma City is not expected to exceed 200," the letter noted. "When compared with the 390,000 Americans who die each year from smoking-related causes, the Oklahoma figure pales considerably."

33. In addition to the two killed in the Water Resources Building, there were two other fatalities outside the Murrah Building: one in the Athenian restaurant next to Water Resources, and one in the parking lot across the street from the Murrah Building. Hierarchies of suffering were also present among Holocaust survivors. William Helmreich quotes novelist Sonia Pilcer, "Treblinka survivors feel superior to the ones who were in Terezin—summer camp in comparison—who are above those in labor camps, who supersede the escapees to Sweden, Russia, and South America. The key question is, where did you spend the war? The more dire the circumstances, the more family murdered, the greater the starvation and disease, the higher the rung in this social register." *Against All Odds: Holocaust Survivors and the Successful Lives They Made in America* (New York: Simon & Schuster, 1992), pp. 173-174.

34. Jeannine Gist, interview, March 21, 1999.

35. Memo from Ernestine Clark to Advisory Committee, November 4, 1996, uncatalogued survivor definition committee materials, archives. The memo asked committee members to respond to the working definition of survivor.

36. Ernestine Clark to author, September 15, 1999.

37. The committee was selected for "diversity of opinion, ages, occupations, 'where they were [at] 9:02,' and for diversity of personal interpretation of the term 'survivor.'" Members included survivors from various buildings, family members, interested citizens from nearby downtown sites that were also affected, and a liaison from the Design Solicitation Committee.

38. See a very important document, "Survivor Definition for Purposes of Fulfilling the Memorial Mission Statement Only" (undated), uncatalogued survivor definition materials, archives.

39. Thomas T. Uhl, "Bystander Emotional Distress: Missing an Opportunity to Strengthen the Ties That Bind," *Brooklyn Law Review*, Winter 1995, pp. 3-4. I thank Professor Sanford Levinson of the University of Texas Law School for introducing me to this material in the field of law.

40. Uhl, "Bystander," p. 6.

41. Quoted material in this and previous paragraph from 48 Cal.3d 644, 771 P.2d 814, 257 Cal. Rptr.865.

42. Williams, interview, September 22, 1999.

43. The state of Oklahoma did use a zone of danger in their regulations governing who could purchase Oklahoma City bombing survivor license plates. (There were also bombing victim license plates available to family members.) Survivors had to be "physically present in the Bombing's primary destruction zone at 9:02 A.M. on Wednesday, April 19, 1995." This area included "the site of the Alfred P. Murrah Federal Building, the Oklahoma Water Resources Board Building, the Athenian Restaurant Building, the Journal Record Building, the Downtown YMCA Building, the Regency Tower Apartments and other such landmarks destroyed or heavily damaged by the bombing." Memo from LeAnn Jenkins to federal agencies, January 9, 1996, uncatalogued materials, archives.

44. Quoted material from a revealing committee document, " 'Who is a survivor?' Descriptions from July 24 meeting." Shortt material.

45. "Oklahoma City National Memorial Foundation Definition of Survivor."

46. Letter to committee, November 7, 1996, uncatalogued materials, archives.

47. Susan Urbach was injured in her office in the Water Resources Building. On April 3, 1997, she wrote the committee in the hopes that they would take extensive damage to business in the area seriously. "As one who has consulted small business owners going on a decade, I can tell you that to be a business owner means that your business is an absolute personal extension of yourself.... It may be 'just a' fill in the blank business to you, but it is life and identity to that business owner." Quoted material from board of directors meeting, minutes, September 24, 1997, archives; "Oklahoma City Memorial Foundation Survivor Definition for Purposes of Fulfilling the Memorial Mission Statement Only," p. 4, uncatalogued materials, archives. Although the survivor definition subcommittee did not continue to meet after fall 1997, alteration of the inner boundary continued into 1998.

On June 22, the board of directors noted that a decision was reached "to modify the survivor definition by changing the boundaries to include the southwest corner of 6th and Harvey and the southeast corner of 6th and Robinson," thus "squaring" off the primary zone of danger. Board of directors meeting, minutes, June 24, 1998.

48. On Sunni Mercer's art, see Elizabeth Lowry, "Something to Hold On To," *Oklahoma Gazette*, November 11, 1998, pp. 18-22. A number of people were actively involved in bringing the garage exhibition to fruition. Survivor Richard Williams recommended the space, provided by GSA, and a number of people from the foundation participated in gathering the artifacts, cleaning the space, and working out the design.

49. Sunni Mercer and Thomas Toperzer interview, September 14, 1998. See "A Sense of Serenity," *Dallas Morning News*, January 5, 1997; "Inspiration Sought in Horror," *Los Angeles Times*, January 7, 1997; "Exhibit Conveys Oklahoma City Tragedy to Memorial Designers," *Houston Chronicle*, February 7, 1997.

50. Peter Wyden, *Day One: Before Hiroshima and After* (New York: Simon & Schuster, 1984), pp. 338-339; text from exhibit.

51. Joanne Riley, interview, March 19, 1999.

52. See a memo entitled "Evaluation Panel and Selection Committee Criteria," September 20, 1996, for information on the selection process and the design selection process "methodology." Design solicitation materials, archives. The nine members of the evaluation panel were family member Toby Thompson; survivors Richard Williams and Polly Nichols; Robert Campbell, architecture critic for the *Boston Globe*, who received the 1996 Pulitzer Prize for distinguished criticism; Richard Haag, who founded the department of landscape architecture at the University of Washington, and twice received the American Society of Landscape Architects President's Award for Design Excellence; Bill Moggridge, senior fellow of the Royal College of Art and trustee of the Design Museum in London; Michaele Pride-Wells, assistant research professor in urban design at the University of Kentucky; Adele Naude Santos, founding dean of the School of Architecture at the University of California-San Diego, and a practicing architect and urban designer; Jaune Quick-To-See Smith, painter and printmaker of Native American art exhibited internationally.

53. Minutes, Design Solicitation Committee, June 17, 1996, archives.

54. The Selection Committee consisted of Laurie Beckelman, vice president of the World Monuments Fund; landscape architect Ignacio Bunster-Ossa; family member John Cole; Luke Corbett, chairman and CEO of the Kerr-McGee Corporation; GSA survivor Tom Hall; Dr. Paul Heath, a survivor from the Veterans Affairs Office; San Francisco artist Douglas Hollis; family member Jeannine Gist; Lars Lerup, dean of the Rice University School of Architecture; David Lopez, president of Oklahoma Southwestern Bell; survivor Calvin Moser; Oklahoma City mayor Ronald Norick; family member Cheryl Scroggins; family member Philip Thompson; and family member Bud Welch.

55. Quoted material is from comments of the design evaluation panel to the Selection Committee, June 20, 1997, and "Report of Selection Committee," Oklahoma

City Memorial Design Competition, and from family/survivor comment cards. All this material is in design competition material, archives.

56. Unless otherwise noted, quoted material from the Butzers is from interviews with Hans and Torrey Butzer, October 22, 1998, and September 23, 1999, numerous informal conversations, and from the text of their design presentation to family members and survivors on August 11, 1997, found in design competition materials, archives. See also Kathryn Jenson White, "To Touch the Human Spirit," *Sooner Magazine*, Fall 2000, pp. 5-9.

57. The Butzers proposed apple and pear trees, but fruit-bearing trees do not flourish in Oklahoma's harsh climate. Hans Butzer notes that on November 22, 1997, "Torrey and I presented four tree types for the site: three on the north side and one for the south. Only one was truly fruit-bearing in the edible sense: the Mexican plum. This tree does well in the heat.... Second is the Chinese pistache [which] offers lots of shade, heat resistance, a non-edible bluish-green olive-like fruit in the late summer/fall, and a magnificent red fall color. Lastly on the north side, we have the Oklahoma redbud [which] blooms in April, and has beautiful waxy leaves.... On the Murrah footprint ... only cone-bearing loblolly pine trees are found. The Murrah footprint is surrounded with coniferous trees while the other deciduous trees on the northern portion of the site lose their leaves in the fall, the Murrah site always has life at its perimeter." Hans Butzer, personal communication to author, November 14, 1999.

58. Butzer presentation text, August 11, 1997, design competition materials archives, copy in author's files.

59. See "Pre-Bid Conference, Oklahoma City National Memorial Foundation," August 13, 1998, design competition materials, archives. Hans Butzer's comments in Butzer presentation text, August 11, 1997. *Time*'s Roger Rosenblatt, visiting Oklahoma City on Memorial Day, 2000, thought the chairs raised these questions: "Is one supposed to sit in them? If so, does one sit to be close to the dead, to be in their place and assume their perspective? Does one sit in judgment, vigilance, serenity, longing? Does one sit in protest, as at a sit-in, against acts of terrorism and anarchy? Does one sit with America? ... Do they represent the normal and unthinkable at once—people at work, going through their routines, sitting at their desks, in chairs?" Roger Rosenblatt, "How We Remember," *Time*, May 29, 2000, p. 26.

60. See "Memorial Design Recommendation Report," Oklahoma City National Memorial Foundation, n.d., design competition materials, archives.

61. See letter from Hans and Torrey Butzer to family members and survivors, October 13, 1998, design competition materials, archives.

62. Blakeney, interview, August 12, 1999. The common tissue also included an unidentified leg. After the bombing, there were eight severed legs to be identified. Blakeney recalls the tremendous efforts made to identify this leg. The military boot on the leg was even sent to the FBI laboratory in Washington, D.C. By early 1996, he said, "we were at a loss." Finally, he looked again at the file of Lakesha Levy, an airman at Tinker Air Force Base who had been in the Social Security Office when the bomb exploded. He grew suspicious that she had been buried with the wrong leg.

They took the mystery leg to New Orleans, exhumed her body, and found that she had indeed been buried with the wrong leg. "I can't tell you how many thousands of hours we have spent since trying to identify the leg we brought back. I don't think we'll ever know. It has been embalmed so thoroughly that we can't get results from DNA testing. We will probably bury it with the common tissue." See "Mother Fears Son May Be 169th Victim of Murrah Explosion," *Sunday Oklahoman*, August 20, 1995; Phil Bacharach, "No. 169: Discovery of Severed Leg Latest Mystery to Arise from Federal Building Blast," *Oklahoma Gazette*, August 24, 1995; Jo Thomas, "Officials Discount Lead on Leg Found in the Bombing Rubble," *New York Times*, August 24, 1995; "169th Victim Near 'Epicenter' of Blast, Expert Says," *Daily Oklahoman*, September 1, 1995; "2 of 5 Missing City People Found in Bid to Identify Leg," *Daily Oklahoman*, September 7, 1995; "Families to Decide Fate of Bomb Victim's Leg," *Daily Oklahoman*, April 11, 1998; "Oklahoma Bomb Victims' Families Asked about Remains' Fate," *Dallas Morning News*, April 11, 1998. Blakeney is convinced that the extra leg does not belong to a 169th victim, but to someone already accounted for.

63. Letter from Blakeney to family members, April 6, 1998, uncatalogued materials, archives, copy in author's files. I had the opportunity to attend a meeting about the common tissue problem on July 7, 1998.

64. Ashwood to Memorial Foundation, June 21, 1997. Demolition of both the Water Resources and Athenian Buildings was completed in October 1997. Deb Ferrell-Lynn, Susan Ferrell's cousin, also wrote suggesting that both buildings remain in their damaged state and that they become a "permanent part of the memorial, much liked bombed buildings...in Europe." Although they "may cause some to be disturbed and distressed," she said, "they are still real reminders of how horrible this crime is." Letter to Robert Johnson, June 9, 1997. Both letters in Family and Survivor Notes on Memorial Ideas, archives. For a good description of the area a year after the bombing, see "Slow to Heal," *Dallas Morning News*, March 31, 1996.

65. James E. Young, *At Memory's Edge: After-Images of the Holocaust in Contemporary Art and Architecture* (New Haven: Yale University Press, 2000), p. 92.

CONCLUSION

1. The institute began its public work with two conferences. The first, "How Terrorism Affects Our Freedom" coincided with ground breaking for the memorial, on October 25, 1998, and the second, "Exploring the Modern Terrorist Mindset" was held the day before the memorial's dedication on April 18, 2000. The Memorial Center uses the federal government's definition of terrorism: "premeditated, politically motivated violence perpetrated against non-combatant targets by subnational groups or clandestine agents, usually intended to convince an audience." Noting, however, that between 1985 and 1995 "only one visible incident of terrorism" occurred in the United States, exhibition text informs visitors that there were in fact many others, "aimed at intimidating groups of people with ideological,

racial, ethnic or religious differences." It will be interesting to see if the institute adopts a wide-ranging working definition of terrorism to include, for example, ecological terrorism and the bombing of abortion clinics.

2. The relationship between the Memorial Trust and the National Park Service is unique. The congressional legislation crafted in 1997 to create a "national" memorial envisioned a memorial environment under local control but allied with the National Park Service. Control over interpretation and preservation was housed in the Oklahoma City National Memorial Trust, most of whom were from Oklahoma, sensitive to local concerns. It is responsible to Congress, and it owns the memorial. It also received $5 million dollars appropriated by Congress to defray the cost of building the memorial. The foundation is responsible for the membership program, fund-raising, recruitment of volunteers, and the docent training program, and is a liaison to the community. Robert Johnson emphasized that the memorial unlike any other National Park Service site, does not receive any ongoing congressional appropriation to defray operating expenses. The trust pays Park Service employees from the ongoing membership program, an admission fee to the Memorial Center, revenue from the Memorial Center store, interest from an endowment, and revenue from special events, such as the Memorial Marathon, held on April 29, 2001.

3. Copy of "You Can't Break America's Heart" in author's files. Letter found in governor's collection, archives. "After the Bombing," *Christian Science Monitor,* April 25, 1995.

4. "Remarks of Governor Frank Keating, Oklahoma City National Memorial Dedication, April 19, 2000"; "Remarks by the President at the Oklahoma City National Memorial Dedication," April 19, 2000. Copies in author's files.

5. Whicher, personal communication with author. Nurse Rebecca Anderson, who died in rescue efforts, can be said to have given her life. An editorial in *Money* magazine recognized this: "We all wanted to help. Rebecca Anderson happened to die doing it. One can only add that in a democracy like ours, you can't give your life for any higher cause." Frank Lalli, "What we ought to remember about the Oklahoma bombing is the heroism, not the terrorism" *Money,* June 1995, p. 13.

6. Rafael White, interview, July 30, 1999.

7. Priscilla Salyers, interview, May 1, 1999.

8. I met Michael Hanson during the dedication events, and I thank him for a telephone interview, November 17, 2000.

9. "Summary Assessment by Wendy Peskin," copy in author's files. I thank Wendy Peskin for providing me with this copy and for consenting to a telephone interview, October 6, 1999.

10. Family members and survivors have also been linked with Kenyans who lost loved ones in the bombing of the U.S. embassy in Nairobi in 1998. I thank Susan Urbach for telling me about a July 2000 trip to Kenya.

11. Clark, interview, June 10, 1999. I am very grateful to Ernestine Clark for driving me to Stillwater, Oklahoma, and introducing me to Sule and his family.

INDEX